P9-BZN-344

How to Live a
Life of Adventure

The Art of Exploring the World

Frosty Wooldridge

authorHOUSE®

AuthorHouse™
1663 Liberty Drive
Bloomington, IN 47403
www.authorhouse.com
Phone: 1-800-839-8640

© 2011 Frosty Wooldridge. All rights reserved.

No part of this book may be reproduced, stored in a retrieval system, or
transmitted by any means without the written permission of the author.

First published by AuthorHouse 11/8/2011

ISBN: 978-1-4634-2028-4 (sc)
ISBN: 978-1-4634-2029-1 (e)

Printed in the United States of America

Any people depicted in stock imagery provided by Thinkstock are models,
and such images are being used for illustrative purposes only.
Certain stock imagery © Thinkstock.

This book is printed on acid-free paper.

Because of the dynamic nature of the Internet, any web addresses or links contained in
this book may have changed since publication and may no longer be valid. The views
expressed in this work are solely those of the author and do not necessarily reflect the
views of the publisher, and the publisher hereby disclaims any responsibility for them.

Dedicated to:
Dr. Roger Teel
For his sagacious humor, his profound spiritual instruction and his
ability to inspire people to live successful lives.
He teaches dynamic mental processes
and principles that shift
illusory dreams
to realities.

What is adventure?

Adventure offers every human being the ability to live "the" moment of his or her most passionate idea, fantasy or pursuit. It may take form in the arts, sports, acting, travel or other creative endeavors. Once engaged, a person enjoys "satori" or the "perfect moment." That instant may last seconds or a lifetime. The key to adventure whether it is painting, dancing, sports or travel is to throw yourself into your quests with rambunctious enthusiasm and zealous energy. Your exploits will lead you toward an uncommon passion for living. By following that path, you will attract an amazing life that will imbue your spirit and fulfill your destiny as defined by you alone. Along the way, you will savor the sweet taste of life pursuing goals that make you happy, rewarded and fulfilled. As a bonus, you may share your experiences with other intrepid human beings who laugh at life, compare themselves with no one and enjoy a fabulous ride.

Frosty Wooldridge

CONTENTS

*F*OREWORD

In search of adventure, Marco Polo traversed Asia for 24 years. Captain James Cook sailed around the world. Amelia Earhart flew across the Atlantic Ocean. Ernest Shackleton walked toward the South Pole under bitter conditions. Junko Tabei became the first woman to summit Mount Everest. Captain Nemo submerged to 20,000 leagues under the sea. Louise Boyd explored the Arctic as well as the Antarctic and became the first woman to fly over the North Pole. Indiana Jones carried a whip while pursuing the "Raiders of the Lost Ark."

Reinhold Messner climbed the highest peaks on seven continents. Eric Weihenmayer became the first sightless person to climb Mount Everest. In 1899, Nelly Bly raced around the world in 72 days. Bob Wieland traveled 3,400 miles across America on his hands. Ultimately, Captains James T. Kirk and Jean-Luc Picard raced at warp speed to "Go where no one has gone before."

Each of those characters, either real or fictional, defined or defines humanity's longing to explore the far reaches of this planet and beyond. Each of those personalities possesses a certain excitement or true-grit to struggle toward some ultimate reward or prize.

"What reward?" you might ask. That can only be defined by the persons questing for it and only they can answer the pursuit for themselves. In the end, it's the living of adventure that expands anyone's world and brings a sense of triumph to whatever degree the difficulty of the quest he or she chooses.

Let us add this reality check: adventure doesn't have to be wild, crazy or dangerous. It can be as sublime as constructing a bird house, painting a picture, sitting by a pond, writing poetry or sharing a walk with a friend down a leaf-strewn path through magnificent autumn colors. You define your own adventure style and you pursue it at your chosen speed throughout your life.

An item that I am thankful for in my youth stemmed from how my parents raised me. My mom encouraged my siblings in a variety of activities. My dad introduced us to multiple sports. He instilled in us a never-give-up attitude.

If I faced a difficult task academically or athletically, or even a problem that arrived on my doorstep whether I expected it or not—liked it or not—my father put his arm around my shoulder and said, "Son, you can do that."

That truth locked into my mind and gave me a foundation of confidence and fortitude that carried me through many challenging adventures. For those that choose vigorous exploration, remember this: adventure may not always be comfortable, but it is always adventure.

As a high school teenager, I noticed a picture of the Great Wall of China in my 10th grade world history book. I mentioned to my teacher Mrs. Rainwater, "I'm going to walk on the Great Wall of China some day."

She answered rather sternly, "You can't climb the Great Wall because China is closed to all travelers."

"My dad said that things always change," I replied. "If I am persistent, I can do anything I set my mind to do."

"Harrumph," she muttered.

Years later, China opened up.

I purchased a one-year plane ticket around the world. Along the way, I stepped off the plane in Hong Kong. I traveled by bicycle, boat and train into Beijing. I pedaled up to the Ming Dynasty tombs. A day later, I pedaled up to the Great Wall of China. I jumped off my bike to the enthusiastic attention of Chinese kids selling "Great Wall" T-shirts. I bought one and still wear it on special occasions.

Moments later, I climbed the steps and walked on the Great Wall of China. Of all the mementos on my memory-shelf in the front room and on my photographic adventure wall, I treasure the shot of me standing in the foreground and the Great Wall of China curling over the mountains in the background. Naturally, I sent a picture to Mrs. Rainwater.

Years later, on one of my transcontinental bicycle rides, I pedaled through the city where I graduated from high school. A film crew met my brother Howard and me at the edge of town. They filmed us and asked a battery of questions. A newspaper man interviewed us, too.

That night, they splashed us all over the local news. Next day, the newspaper arrived with a half-page filled with our pictures and the interview. Our mom beamed all over the place. Later, the phone rang.

"Hello," I answered.

"Is this Frosty?" the lady asked.

"Yes ma'am," I said.

"This is Barbara Rainwater," she said. "I saw you on TV last night and in the papers today. I am very proud of you. I never thought that you would amount to much, but when I received that picture of you on the Wall of China, a big smile came over my face that one of my students did well in this world. Your mother must be very proud. I am amazed at all the world travel you have done. It sounds like you are living an interesting life."

"Thank you," I said. "Thanks for being a great teacher. Unknowingly, you set a sense of determination in my mind to walk on the Great Wall of China."

"I remember telling you that you would never walk on that wall," she said, "but you proved me wrong and I am glad you did. It just goes to show what a little resolve will do for you."

You are invited to incorporate this understanding into the core of your being: the resolve within your mind makes everything in your life possible.

Along my life path, some folks have said, "You're one lucky dude." Others thought somebody helped me out financially. If the truth be told, I worked for every mile I ever traveled across this planet. While luck may carry anyone into positive life experiences, the smarter and harder one works, the luckier one becomes. You design your life. You make your own luck. You create synchronicities in your life via your mental, emotional and physical forward movement. As you live your life, you dream, you choose and you actualize your adventures. Your choices propel you toward a rewarding life. For those who make poor choices, they live a life with little to cheer about when they face their last moments.

One writer said, "By passionately believing in what doesn't exist; you create it."

Hopefully, along the way, you inculcate and incorporate expanded ideas and understandings that add to your wealth of confidence and resolve to live your dreams. At first, you may feel some trepidation. That's normal. Try out little adventures until you work up to the big ones.

In this book, you will read various adventures to whet your appetite. Each story shares an important lesson. You may enjoy instructional sections alternating with adventure chapters that may inspire you toward your own pursuits. Please appreciate that your passions may turn to painting, poetry or sculpting. I have painted, sculpted and written poetry. As to an artist's touch, I get a kick out of the dozen paintings I have created in my life. It all gets down to creative expression physically, mentally and emotionally. With unlimited choices, each of us may choose various creative outlets over our lifetimes.

Additionally, you will learn the techniques and mental understandings that will propel you into a life of adventure as you define it. For that matter, you may use these tenets to live a successful life and enjoy fantastic connections with friends who share your zest for living.

You might note the dramatic cover shot for this book comes from a moment with my friends Doug Armstrong and Bryan Halleck on their way to the Matterhorn in the Swiss Alps. Doug has traveled across all seven continents via bicycle, backpack, train and bus. He came from an average family. Bryan has traveled worldwide, too. Since they lived their dreams, you enjoy the same opportunities.

Additionally, Bob Johannes, Jayne Sutton, Linda Humphrey and Sandi Lynn added their excellent editing and critiques to make this book its very best. I thank each one of them for their guidance. A special thanks goes to bestselling author Dan Millman who provided me with key ideas that transformed this book into its final rendition. I am deeply thankful to each one of you on a personal level. You gave a lot of time and interest in this project.

Thanks goes to my parents Vivien and Howard Wooldridge for their steadfast support and loving care over the years. Thanks to my brothers Rex, Howard, John and my sister Linda for their support and sharing of these adventures. A huge thanks goes to my lady Sandi for her enthusiasm, creative efforts and endless support during this undertaking. Thanks to Adeline Helma for her delightful enthusiasm that touches my life daily. Thank you Gary and Marty North for making a positive impact on my early years. Thank you Don Collins and Sally Epstein for your work for all of humanity. Thank you Denis LeMay, Gary Hall, Jeff Blackburn, Paul Austin, John Brown, Steve Boyka, Doug Armstrong, Bryan Delay, Uwe Rothe, Sandy Colhoun, Diane Fisher, Lance Hill, Mike Machuga, Dan and Trevor Lynn, Gerd Bollig, Rick Chiesa, Reg Gupton, Joe Comer, Ann Maines, Mary Gruda, Elaine and Larry Gingrich, Lance Hill, Pam

Gilbert, Rick Hoying, Ken Hoying, Tim Costello, Scott Poindexter, Jan and Anneke Westra, Herb and Carma Johnson, Keith, Luke, Hannah and Linda Whited, Hans and Erika Matzke, Manny and Sue Varriel, Deb and David Martin, John and Marylou Tanton, Paul and Kathleen Corrigan, Bob and Marie Johannes, Reinhold and Monika Spindler and many other friends that have made a special impact on my life. Finally, thank you Al Wilson for your friendship and sharing many of these adventures.

To you the reader, at the end of your life, much like a baseball game, you will have enjoyed great times, dangerous times, heroic times and mundane times. As you round third base heading into home, you will be scratched and bruised. You may have endured a few broken bones and scared yourself half to death several times. More importantly, you will have lived any number of amazing adventures.

As you slide into home, you will be worn out and used up. You will have left your guts on the field. Without a doubt, as you stick out your foot to tag home plate on your final breath, you will show everyone a mile-wide grin as you chuckle to yourself, "Wow! My life has been one heck of a fantastic ride!"

Frosty Wooldridge

SECTION I – PREPARATION FOR ADVENTURE

This section provides you with information on how to get your feet wet. It also offers you stories from others that charged into their own adventures without hesitation. This section shows men and women from all walks of life how to engage themselves and their talents. It also offers you ideas on how to make money before an adventure or while you are living the adventure. The alternative chapters present you with those who have explored this planet in various ways.

Chapter 1—How and where to start your adventures

"I would rather be ashes than dust. I would rather my spark burn out in a brilliant blaze than be stifled by dry rot. I would rather be a superb meteor, every atom in magnificent glow—than a sleepy comfortable planet. The proper function of man is to live, not merely exist. I shall use my time." Jack London

At eighteen, few of us possess any idea as to what we want to do with our lives. A third of American teenagers drop out of high school. Only 25 percent head into college and even less graduate. Most teens and post-twenty adults take the first job available without knowing what they want or what they like. Many teens and young adults in their twenties marry quickly and find themselves with a family. That choice disciplines their focus for the next 20 years. It narrows options for world travel and/or pursuing jobs that interest them.

Looking back, one of my high school friends married, became a father and took a job selling cars. He settled into an average life of watching football, weekends at the backyard barbecue and two week vacations annually.

When I spoke with him at the ten year reunion, he said, "Man, I wish I had gone to college. I wish I could have become an architect. Sure wish that I would have had a chance to travel before I settled down with a family."

At the 20th reunion he said, "Man, I hate my job. I have high blood pressure. My kids are lazy."

I didn't have the heart to tell him that I had cycled all over Europe, visited 50 countries, biked to Alaska for a summer, ran 30 triathlons, spent two winters ski-bumming in deep powder and planned on a third bicycle ride across America a week after the reunion.

Additionally, do you ask friends about their year? How many times have you heard, "Same ole same ole."

Henry David Thoreau said, "Most men live lives of quiet desperation."

THOREAU SAID SOMETHING ELSE EVEN MORE PROFOUND

Thoreau also said, "If you advance confidently in the direction of your dreams, and endeavor to live the life which you have imagined, you will meet with success unexpected in common hours. You will pass through an invisible boundary; new universal and liberal laws will begin to establish themselves; and you will live with a license of a higher order of beings."

Anyone who reads Thoreau might find his sage advice a beacon for living a fulfilling life. The key is to leave your life open to opportunities, ideas and change—offered by education, travel, reading books and joining clubs. When you do, you will meet others who love to explore their spirits, minds and potential talents. Once you mingle with those people, their ideas cascade onto and into you.

For example: I moved to Colorado during my early twenties. I loved to go skiing on weekends. While riding ski lifts, I met people from every walk of life. Almost without exception, we engaged in conversation. By listening, I always received their advice on life or what excited them. At other times, I heard about someone they admired.

In the summer, I pedaled my bicycle along the foothills from Boulder to Lyons, Colorado, a distance of 16 miles. I met hundreds of interesting men and women. One of them, Ward, invited me to go bicycle touring. A year later and totally unsure of myself, I pedaled coast to coast across America. I loved it.

Back in Boulder, I met a man named Paul on the tennis court who liked to climb mountains. We began our climbing quest for all 14,000-foot peaks in Colorado and beyond. Not only did I climb in Colorado, but in Alaska, the Patagonia, Andes, Himalayas, Alps, Antarctica and the Pyrenees.

While on a ski trip, I met another man named Gary who invited me to go rafting with him. Over the years, I rafted the Green, Yampa, Colorado, Arkansas, Shotover, Rangitikei and dozens of other rivers on different continents.

Please note the common thread of these opportunities. You have the choice of getting into the game of life at whatever point you desire. Once you move into that arena of people, fortunate human interconnections arise and new opportunities open up to you.

MOVE INTO PLACES WHERE ADVENTURE SEEKERS PLAY

Even if you don't quite know what you like, you can find out by trying different sports through clubs, events and activities. If you're a water person, you might like to move to the ocean. If you want to try your hand at sailing, move to Miami, Florida or San Diego, California or Bar Harbor, Maine. You can obtain a job as a cook on a sailing ship or move to Alaska and procure a job on a crab boat. If you like to try your hand at rafting, you can move to Colorado, West Virginia or Oregon where you can secure a job as a rafting guide or outfitter. You might take a side job and do grunt work the first year, but with time and new friends, you will become a qualified rafting guide.

Do you like to ski or do you want to learn how to ski? Move to a ski resort. You might become a lift operator. Later, you may become a ski instructor. I became an ID checker at the door of a tavern until they needed me to become a bartender. I earned a lot of money slinging drinks from 4:00 p.m. to midnight. I skied all day. By the way, waiting tables and bartending at night pay the most money and allow day skiing. Get used to gliding in the trackless deep powder at 12,000 feet. Yahoo!

KEY POINTS FROM THIS CHAPTER

1. Find out what interests you by trying everything deliberately.
2. Advance toward your life with dreams and imagination.
3. Join clubs with people who share your interests.
4. Move to regions that may give you greater opportunities.

*C*hapter 2—*Walking across America on his hands*

"Remember the high board at the swimming pool? After days of looking up at it you finally climbed the wet steps to the platform. From there, it was higher than ever. There were only two ways down: the steps to defeat or the dive to victory. You stood on the edge, shivering in the hot sun, deathly afraid. At last you leaned too far forward. It was too late for retreat, and you dived. The high board was conquered, and you spent the rest of the day diving. Climbing a thousand high boards, we demolish fear, and turn into human beings." Richard Bach

On this bicycle ride across America, by sheer chance, I ran into the most amazing man I have ever met in my life. He enthralled, captivated and completely reduced me to tears. At the same time, he has inspired me every day of my life. His courage has become my courage. His integrity has become my life goal. I hope he inspires you as much as he has inspired me.

Do you become depressed? Feel sorry for yourself? Not tall enough? Not thin enough? Not smart enough? Not rich enough?

After meeting this man, you will never complain a second for the rest of your life. Beyond that, try to grasp each ounce of appreciation for the little things—being able to walk, talk, speak, hear, touch, feel and laugh. Take nothing for granted, especially your health.

"Courage is one thing. A sense of purpose another. When you

put them together in one human being, the world can be changed."
John Brown, world traveler

On that summer bicycle tour across America, I pedaled through heavy traffic as the Pacific Ocean faded in my rear view mirror. The Los Angeles smog choked me for 50 miles into the Mojave Desert. After crossing the Colorado River, I breathed easier when the air pollution flowed south toward Phoenix. I pedaled into the mountains. Climbing steep grades took hours. I sweated, struggled and grumbled. At the same time, I learned patience. Finally, I learned to love the long climbs. Why? I gathered their beauty into my spirit. As my legs grew stronger, the pedaling became incidental. I listened to the birds. I saw coyotes cross the road in front of me. Above, hawks soared in circles on their lunch patrols. At the top, I gulped water from my bottle and felt a sense of accomplishment for having succeeded. Soon, my spirit soared as I glided down from great heights like an eagle.

In New Mexico, I crossed the Continental Divide and descended into the desert on Route 380. With a blazing sun overhead, I glided along the two-lane pavement. Sweat dripped from my face and arms. Cactus grew on both sides of the road. A hazy mist swept through the valley in front with mountains to the north of me. Every breath crowded my mouth as if someone stuck a hairdryer in front of my face and turned it on full blast. Heat waves rippled over the pavement as I descended further into the barren landscape. The thermometer hit 103 degrees by the time I pedaled south of Roswell, New Mexico.

Ahead, I noticed a lone figure walking along the left side of the road. I found it difficult to imagine anyone walking down the highway in that torrid temperature.

"I wonder what that guy's doing walking in this heat?" I muttered to myself. "Looks like he's got a dog with him, too."

Seconds later, "That's not a dog!"

I gasped, doubting my eyes. I strained harder to discern what I saw.

I squinted at a man walking on his hands. Within a few seconds, I discovered why. His legs were missing.

Less than forty yards away, I saw the lone figure reading a book while walking beside another man walking on his hands. A camper van was parked on the shoulder a half mile ahead. I rode up even with them. Something inside made me stop. I lowered my bike onto the gravel on the right side of the road.

I couldn't help crossing the highway. No matter who this man was, he possessed inconceivable courage. What was he doing walking on his hands in the desert? He saw me and stopped. He lowered his body down to the ground. He rested it on a leather pad that covered his two severed legs just below the groin. His Paul Bunyan upper arms led down to his hands, which grasped two rubber pads. Sweat soaked his T-shirt. His light hair framed a tanned face punctuated by a pair of clear eyes. He flashed a beautiful smile.

"Hi, how are you doing?" I said while approaching with my hand extended. "My name is Frosty."

"Glad to meet you," he said as he shook my hand. "I'm Bob Wieland and this is my friend Arnie."

"Pleasure to meet you guys," I said. "Bob, I'm more than a bit curious seeing you out here in the desert."

"The same could be said about you," he said. "What are you doing out here?"

"I'm bicycling across America."

"That makes two of us," Bob added. "I'm walking across. I'd bike but my legs are too short for the pedals."

I laughed. His humor caught me by surprise. We bantered a few minutes about the weather. Bob gave me a short history of his journey. He started in Los Angeles and climbed through the mountains. He crossed over several 9,000-foot passes. His friend fixed meals, but often people asked them into their homes for the night. If no one offered a night's lodging, both men slept in the back of the camper pickup. His friend drove the vehicle ahead and came back to walk with him. His companion read a book while guiding Bob down the left side of the highway. Bob lost his legs in combat in Vietnam. I asked him when he had started.

"I've been out 19 months and have completed 980 miles," he said. "At my speed, I can finish this adventure in two more years, maybe less."

"Why are you doing it?" I asked.

"There's a lot of adventure out here on the road," said Bob. "I suppose I could sit back and get fat watching TV for the next fifty years, but I want to do something with my life. I want to make a difference. I have to make do with what I have left. You know the saying, you only go around once."

"You have my greatest admiration," I said, shaking his hand again.

It was one of those moments when you don't quite know what to do or say. I just met the most incredibly courageous man in my whole life and he was looking up at me from the pavement. No legs! He stood only three feet tall. His hands had become his feet. That gray leather pad was belted to his bottom like a baby diaper. Those rubber pads on his hands became his wheel tread on his arduous journey. I gasped inwardly at the enormity of his quest.

"Guess I better get moving," I said, reluctantly.

"Take care," Bob said. "Have a good ride. I'll get there one of these days."

"There's no doubt that you will reach the Atlantic Ocean," I said.

As I turned away from that amazing human being, tears filled my eyes. I started crying half-way across the road. His quest staggered my imagination. My friends thought I was nuts taking a transcontinental bicycle trip, but they had no understanding of how easy I had it compared to Bob Wieland. Miles and years down the road that moment colors my mind as vividly as the day it happened.

Most human beings suffer handicaps in one way or the other—physical, mental or emotional. What is the important point? It's how they handle their limitations. Bob concentrated on what he could do, not on what he couldn't do. Instead of giving up, he pushed forward into the unknown not only determined to succeed, but expecting to succeed.

George Bernard Shaw celebrated people like Wieland when he wrote, "This is the true joy of living, spending your years for a purpose recognized by yourself as a right one. To be used up when they throw you on the scrap heap of life. To have been a force of nature instead of a selfish little clod of ailments and grievances complaining that the world will not devote itself to making you happy."

Bob Wieland pushed himself through 3,400 miles of hardship that few people could comprehend. He gutted his way up mountains, sweated his way across deserts and fought through raging rain storms. Every labored breath drew him closer to his destination.

Two years later, I listened to National Public Radio while eating breakfast one morning. Bob Wieland reached the Atlantic Ocean thus succeeding in his quest to walk on his hands across America. He journeyed for 3,400 miles. It took him three years, eight months and six days.

I sat at the breakfast table crying like a baby because that man had given me courage to face my own struggles in that one meeting in the New Mexico desert. I'm sure he touched thousands more on his remarkable journey across America. Here's to you, Bob Wieland, to your courage, your humor, your passion and your life.

KEY POINTS FROM THIS CHAPTER

1. Whatever life throws at you, it's your choice on how to handle it.
2. Attitude and options become more powerful than negative occurrences in your life.
3. Engage friends who share your passions to further your own quests.
4. Maintain your resolve and expect to succeed in your adventures.

*C*hapter 3—*Discovering what makes you tick*

"All men and women are born, live, suffer and die; what distinguishes us one from another is our dreams, whether they are dreams about worldly or unworldly things, and what we do to make them come about. We do not choose to be born. We do not choose our parents. We do not choose our historical epoch, the country of our birth or the immediate circumstances of our upbringing. We do not, most of us, choose to die; nor do we choose the time and conditions of our death. But within this realm of 'choicelessness', we do choose how we live." Joseph Epstein

You may find that any of the quotes at the head of each chapter may touch you, ring your bell or mesh with your vibrations. If so, savor some of the books by such authors. Does a life of adventure depend on whether you are an extrovert or introvert? How about smart or otherwise? Does it matter whether you are rich or poor? How about confused or highly articulate? Does it depend on whether you are a male or female? What if you are black, white, brown or yellow?

Thankfully, every human being in a free country enjoys the right to "Life, liberty and the pursuit of happiness."

Therefore, what are you doing with your gifts? How are you expressing your life? What makes you excited? In which direction will you travel? What dream has your name on it?

BOOKS CAN LEAD THE WAY TOWARD A SUCCESSFUL START IN LIFE

At first, I read books required in high school for course work. In college, I read the compulsory manuals for tests. Luckily, in a Creative Writing 201 class, the professor asked us to read some far-reaching books beyond mainstream thought.

I picked up Aldous Huxley's **Brave New World.** In that book, I read about a perfect civilization where every human began life in a test tube with perfect temperatures and nutrients until he or she reached his or her birth moment. They lived in a perfect climate, enjoyed their perfect food, all the recreation they wanted and worked at the perfect job for their brain power. If they suffered depression, they popped a pill to make them happy.

By chance, one of the technicians bumped one guy's test tube and caused him to be born with a glitch. As he grew older, he began to think outside his programming. He didn't like his perfect world at all. He talked his girlfriend into consciousnesses. They escaped the bubble city and fled into the wilderness.

They experienced hunger, thirst, cold and suffered mosquitoes biting them as well as a few animals that gave chase. At the same time, they found themselves alive and alert to the pulsing vibrations of life. You may have seen that kind of existence by the Na'vi on the planet Pandora in the movie "Avatar."

They never returned to the perfection of the bubble city.

Once I read that book, I told myself that I would not live in an air-conditioned house to drive in an air-conditioned car to work in a climate-controlled cubicle to return to the air-conditioned car to go to the air-conditioned grocery store and back to my air-conditioned house. Special note: if you press me for the truth, okay, I'm a wimp as I enjoy an air-conditioned house on hot days.

While I do enjoy the comforts of home, a shower and hot food, I love my time in the wilderness. My mouth waters when I'm sitting around campfires with steaming food on the embers. I throw another log on the fire while the smoke curls into the night sky. A million stars twinkle overhead and the scent of the wilderness mingles with every cell in my body. I relish sitting around that fire with friends:

Have you ever sat by the campfire?
When the wood has fallen low;
And the embers start to whiten,
Around the campfire's crimson glow.

With the night sounds all around you,
Making silence doubly sweet;
And a full moon high above you,
That makes the spell complete.

Tell me were you ever nearer,
To the land of heart's desire;
Than when you sat there thinking,
With your face toward the fire.

Huxley shaped my life with his book. He could shape yours, too. Some other writer could do the same with a subject that enthralls your spirit. (See Chapters 42 and 43 for writers that may inspire you.)

By the way, Bob Wieland is the only double amputee to run the Hawaii Ironman Triathlon and finish the marathon without the use of a wheel chair. He finished four days later, but, he finished. While we are talking about him, here are some more triumphs by Bob Wieland. After walking across America on his hands, when the first hand-cycles arrived years later, he hand-pedaled his bicycle across America, first east to west, and then, west to east.

Is he wild or what? Look him up on the Internet. He's set world records in the bench press and he's run the New York Marathon and several others. I can't keep up with the man and I own two perfectly good legs. He has inspired millions.

"A large volume of adventures may be grasped within this little span of life, by him or her who interests his or her heart in everything." Laurence Sterne

KEY POINTS FROM THIS CHAPTER

1. Books can offer avenues for your own creative process.
2. You may enjoy advice in the form of life stories.
3. Check out Chapters 42 and 43 for top authors that may inspire you.
4. You may become inspired by another person's quests.

Chapter 4—Arrested for having too much fun

"Plunge boldly into the thick of life, and seize it where you will, it is always interesting." Johann Wolfgang Von Goethe

No matter where you travel on an adventure, you leave your normal daily orbit and fly into other cultures, languages and conditions. It matters little which state or which country or which continent. You will find yourself in the thick of life and you will always, as Goethe said, "...find it interesting." Sometimes, great anger may consume you, but then, wild laughter at the folly and capriciousness of humanity may follow. This tale offers a range of emotional reactions.

Outside Vicksburg, Mississippi on Route 80, my brother Howard and I cranked east through the midday heat.

Heat waves rippled off the summer pavement while the blazing sun baked the land. Trees lined the highway with crows and sparrows flying in all directions. One crow was having a difficult time as four sparrows darted in on him, pecking at his feathers. Each time they attacked, he dove away from them.

"Those guys are giving that big bird a hard time," said Howard.

"I have never figured out why they attack a crow like that," I said.

"Maybe it gets down to territorial turf," said Howard. "Hey, we should make Vicksburg pretty soon. You want to stop at a salad bar place and clean them out?"

"Good idea."

Riding in the south during the summer cooked bicyclists with heat and humidity. It was so hot we looked like one of those commercials where they fry an egg on the hood of a car. We were the eggs. Howard and I left a trail of splashes from our sweat-soaked bodies.

Nonetheless, we looked forward to the Civil War monuments in Vicksburg. We smiled and waved at passing cars. The people in the Deep South moved at a snail's pace. Folks seemed to get a kick out of our riding cross-country through their state. They took pictures of us along with their families crowding around our bikes.

With so much attention, we had a lot to talk about after leaving a photo session. People said the darnedest things about touring riders. They kept us laughing because they thought we were either courageous or crazy.

As we chatted back and forth, a police cruiser passed us traveling west. We waved at him. He waved back but had a stern look on his face.

I watched him go by in my rear view mirror. Seconds later, he turned the car around and flipped on his flashing red lights.

"That cop turned around," Howard said.

"Must be he got a call for an emergency back down the road," I said.

I expected the cruiser to fly past us. But it didn't. The police officer pulled in behind us.

"That cop is pulling us over," I said.

"Probably for speeding," Howard joked. "Maybe he's going to give us a ticket for going too slow. Now wouldn't that be a good one? No, he's going to give us tickets for not having a license to drive a bicycle."

We pulled our bikes to a stop. A rotund, middle-aged officer in a blue uniform got out of his cruiser. We stood astride our bikes looking back at him. We weren't sure why he had stopped us.

"Afternoon boys," he said, walking up to me.

"How are you, sir?" I said.

"I'm fine," he said. "When I passed you boys, I noticed you were smiling and laughing."

"Yes, sir," Howard said. "We're having a great day. We just love it here in Louisiana. In fact, we're hoping to meet Huckleberry Finn when we cross the Mississippi."

"How far ya'll going?" the officer asked in a brusque voice.

"We're cycling across America," I said. "Pacific to the Atlantic."

"You boys ever had your heads examined for mental righteousness?"

"Our mom told us we were crazy to ride our bikes across America," Howard said. "But, so far, the craziness hasn't killed us."

15

The officer looked over our packs as if he might be looking for something.

Right then, I didn't like this guy's demeanor. My dad always told us to be polite and keep smiling at a policeman. This was one of those times to be extra polite.

"Have you had a good time in Louisiana?" he asked in a stern voice.

"Yes, sir," I said. "We've had a real fine time and we're looking forward to Mississippi."

"Right now, you're in my jurisdiction," he said. "When I drove by you, it looked like you were having a lot of fun."

"Yes, sir, you could say that," Howard said.

"Would you say you're having too much fun?" the man asked, straight faced.

"Too much fun?" I said, quizzically. "Well, er, yes sir, we're probably having too much fun. Right, Howard?"

"Yes sir, that's right, we're having too much fun."

The officer stepped closer. He looked serious. Maybe I had seen too many movies with redneck cops hassling people. Nonetheless, I was concerned. He looked the part. He sported a thick neck, crew cut, short fat fingers, belly hanging over his belt and boots that hadn't been polished in several months.

"I hate to say this, boys, but there's an ordinance in this county against having too much fun. People have gotten out of hand in the past from partying too much. Because I'm an officer of the law, I'm sworn to uphold that ordinance. I have to write ya'll a citation. May I see some form of identification?"

"Sure, officer," we replied, giving him our driver's licenses.

"A law against having too much fun?" Howard said.

"That's right, boys," he said. "You wait here while I write you up. I see you're brothers."

"Yes, sir," I said.

"I'll be right back in a few minutes," he said, walking away.

"This is crazy," Howard said. "This guy is out to lunch. He's only got one oar in the water. He's 51 cards short of a full deck."

"He's got a badge and gun," I muttered.

"He can't give us a ticket for having too much fun," Howard said. "That does it! I'm going right into the county courthouse and demand a jury trial on this one. I mean, this is nuts. We can't take this lying down.

We'll take this one all the way to the Supreme Court. Too much fun, right!"

"I thought he was kidding," I said. "But he's not kidding."

While we waited, I drank a quart of water and switched my bottles on the down tube to have a full one ready. It was warm water, but quenched my thirst. Darned if I could figure out what we had done to get this cop upset. But I had learned never to argue with a police officer. They enjoy absolute authority. Minutes later, he walked up to us with two tickets in hand.

"I know ya'll think this is out of line," he said. "But I don't make the laws. I just enforce them. By the way, I like riding bicycles, too. How come you boys are riding mountain bikes with drop bars?"

"They're more durable and we don't get many flat tires," I said. "They ride smoother. Plus, we have three positions for our hands with drop bars. Straight bars fatigue our hands by keeping them in one position."

"I'll have to remember that," he said. "By the way, I live in Vicksburg. Are you boys hungry?"

"Yes, sir," we replied, not understanding why he was so friendly when he had given us a ticket.

"There's a nice restaurant called Aunt Dorothy's right after you cross the Mississippi," he said, after giving us our tickets and walking away.

He drove toward Vicksburg. I stood astride my bike looking at Howard who was just as incredulous as I was.

"What in the heck just happened to us?" I asked.

Howard looked down at his ticket and started laughing.

"What's so funny?" I asked.

"Read it," Howard said, laughing and slapping his thigh.

On the ticket in long hand it read, "This is a citation to the Wooldridge brothers for having too much fun on their bicycle trip across America. You can either pay a large fine down at the county courthouse or you can come over to my house (directions below) and take showers, plus eat my wife's great cooking. You're welcome to stay overnight. My kids would love to hear about some of your experiences. It would be an honor and a pleasure to have you visit us."

"I'll be danged," I said.

After riding into town that evening, we followed Officer Buford Jackson's directions to his house. We leaned our fully loaded touring bikes against the white railing on the front porch of an old southern home where a couple of rockers awaited for the evening sunset and friendly conversation.

We knocked on the front door.

When the door opened, I had never seen a wider smile, a bigger grin, a larger heart or a face so full of mirth and mischief as I saw on Buford Jackson at that moment. Behind him, two little girls and a boy must have been told that their favorite movie star and his brother were coming to dinner. Their faces reflected youthful expectation of something special about to happen in their lives.

That evening, we ate a dinner set for a king. Adeline Jackson was the perfect hostess. We answered dozens of questions from the children named Shirley, Paula and Zach. It was truly an evening of having too much fun.

The next morning we pedaled onto the highway. I was reminded again as I had been hundreds of times in the past, that people are beautiful. Never assume you know what or who they are. No matter what their color, religion, job, or location---people are unique, and mostly, they are doing the best they can with their lives.

Even with all the challenges going on in this society, it's basically a generous, caring, respectful and decent nation. I know we focus on the news every night because bad news travels fast. But when you think of every little child who smiles at you, your life is blessed. When you greet someone and pay them a compliment, you change the world. When it's returned to you, it changes your world.

In the case of Buford and Adeline, our world became richer because we were smiling and having too much fun. Howard and I thanked them for their generosity, humor and their children with bright eyes filled with expectation. Most of the world is filled with people like Buford and Adeline.

I hope to get arrested many more times for having too much fun.

KEY POINTS FROM THIS CHAPTER

1. Anything good can happen at any time on an adventure.
2. Look for the good in everyone you meet.
3. Share with everyone a smile and a good story.
4. Pay compliments to strangers that will return a hundred fold.

Chapter 5—Men and women living their adventures

"The most beautiful people we have known are those who have known defeat, known suffering, known struggle, known loss, and have found their way out of the depths. These persons have an appreciation, sensitivity and an understanding of life that fills them with compassion, gentleness and a deep loving concern. Beautiful people do not just happen." Elisabeth Kubler-Ross

You might think that all those people out there living all those adventures enjoyed some kind of special wealth or privilege. In nine out of ten cases, most of them arrive at their destinations from ordinary means—hard work, savings, patience and determination.

I came from a farm background. I picked cucumbers as a kid. I milked cows with my grandpa. I planted corn, mowed hay and cut silage. Later in my teen years, I held four jobs in the summer: paperboy seven days a week, pool cleaner, lifeguard and dishwasher. I worked all through college as well as summers.

The following individuals lived their adventure dreams. They came from backgrounds similar to mine, and more than likely, yours.

Harriet Anderson, 72 years old, has completed 17 Ironman Triathlons in Kona, Hawaii. It's the biggest and toughest triathlon race in the world. She must swim 2.4 miles in the ocean, then bicycle 112 miles over hot terrain, and finally, run a 26.2 mile marathon over blisteringly hot lava fields. Nonetheless, for the past 17 seasons, this woman has competed and won in her age class every year. What drives her to run a race that most 20-year-olds won't attempt? That's the glory of this lifetime. As Yogi Berra, the baseball great said, "It ain't over till it's over."

Bob Wieland walked across America on his hands. Why? Because he suffered a double amputation in the Vietnam War. Did he let his personal condition stop him? Did he whine, complain and get drunk like Lt. Dan in the movie "Forrest Gump"? Did he drink beer and eat junk food so he could exit the planet early? No! He accumulated more world records than most people with two legs. How did he do that? Answer: attitude, passion and purpose. If he can do what he has done, you can do anything you desire.

Howard Woodridge became the first man in the 21st century to ride his horse across the United States. He rode self-contained. Wooldridge strategized along the route to provide food and water for his horse. He's the first man and only man in history to ride back across the United States. You might say, "Sure, but the horse did all the work." Howard walked every third mile to save his horse Misty from breaking down on those 3,500-mile adventures. www.thelongridersguild.com

Steve Stevens owns the world record of 29 days for riding a Penny Farthing high wheeler across America. He earned a spot in the Guinness Book of World Records. Additionally, he has ridden on six continents with his Penny Farthing. You can see his stunning collection of high wheelers at his museum in Golden, Colorado. He features a superb collection of bicycles, books and other cycling paraphernalia from hundreds of years ago. www.goldenoldy.org

Verlen Krueger and Steve Landick paddled their canoes 28,000 miles around North America for three years. They started on the Grand River in Grand Rapids, Michigan. They paddled up to Lake Superior, then, out the St. Lawrence Seaway, down the Atlantic coast to the tip of Florida and then into the Gulf of Mexico and up the Mississippi River to more rivers in Canada all the way to the Arctic Ocean. From there, they paddled down the Yukon River to the Pacific Ocean and on down the west coast of North America to the Baja Peninsula in Mexico. Then, up the Colorado River into the middle of the Arkansas and they portaged by hand and by themselves to other rivers until they returned to Lake Michigan. Their feat stands today as one of the greatest canoe adventures on record.

Verlen and his wife then set out several years later to canoe from the Arctic Ocean to the Mississippi River and down into the Gulf of Mexico. They crossed over the Gulf of Mexico and entered the river systems of South America and canoed the central part of the continent, crossed over the Amazon and finished up at the bottom of the world in Tierra del Fuego to Ushuaia at the tip of South America.

Before he died in 2004, he had paddled canoes and sea kayaks over 500,000 miles and raced in countless events. www.28thousandmilecano echallenge.com

Nancy and John Vogel, along with their twins Daryl and Davy, ages nine at the beginning of the ride, pedaled their bikes from the Arctic Ocean in Alaska to the bottom of South America, some 18,000 miles in three years. The boys became the two youngest children to succeed in such a feat in the Guinness Book of World Records. www.familyonbikes.org

A Swedish man named Goran Kropp bicycled 12,500 kilometers from Stockholm, Sweden to Kathmandu, Nepal. He carried 170 pounds of mountaineering gear. From there, he climbed Mount Everest solo without oxygen and back down. Returning, he carried all his gear 12,500 kilometers back to Sweden. In a freak climbing accident, Kropp died in 2004. His girlfriend took up where he left off. He intended a circumnavigation of America by hiking and kayak. His girlfriend, Renata, finished it for him. You may read about her adventures. www.RenataChlumska.com

Heinz Stucke rules the bicycle touring world. He has bicycled around the planet to over 150 countries in the past 48 years. You can visit his website for a glimpse into his endless bicycle tour. www.heinzstucke.com

Amelia Earhart became the first female to fly solo across the Atlantic. Later, she died attempting a circumnavigation of the planet. If you're looking for inspiration, read her story and see the movie. She shows that any woman can do anything at any time in history.

Eric Weihenmayer, totally blind, has climbed all of the highest peaks on seven continents. He lives down the road from me in Golden, Colorado.

He's a father, husband, local hero and an inspiration to millions of disabled persons around the world. www.touchthetop.com

My friend Pasquale Scaturro of Denver, Colorado climbed Mount Everest two times and ensured that Eric Weihenmayer successfully reached the summit of Everest as the expedition leader. Scaturro hiked across Africa and became the first man to raft down the Blue Nile. I remember sitting around at his 50th birthday party. He had already written out a list of 100 more adventures he wanted to complete in his second 50 years.

In 1999, on a ride from Canada to Mexico, I met a New Zealander woman named Jane who pedaled her bicycle, solo, around the world for three years. As we sat on the rails at the top of Logan's Pass in Glacier National Park in Montana, I couldn't help feeling awed by her courage, stamina, resolve and personable demeanor. Yet she proved to be very quiet and unable to present a dynamic personality. It goes to show you that you can be an extrovert, introvert, shy, outspoken, quiet, loud and a number of other personality traits and still pursue your dreams.

In 2011, John and Kate Suscovich set out from New York on a 24,000 mile bicycle tour around the world. They expect to see as many countries as possible on their sojourn around the planet. You may contact them and follow their journey at www.foodcyclist.com

Doug Armstrong cycled six continents and explored Antarctica. He's visited over 130 countries. He's hiked the Pacific Coast Trail, Appalachian Trail and scuba dived in all the oceans. He teaches math classes in Alaska, but once the summer arrives, he's off into the wild blue yonder. I met him in a hostel in Wellington, New Zealand 25 years ago. Today, I am continually astounded at his quest to visit all 193 countries before he leaves the planet.

Basha Fromky rode her horse Pompey from St. Petersburg, Russia to London, England. She's funny, outgoing and tiny of stature, but she can ride that monster of a horse named Pompey. She is in the planning stages of riding him five years around the world. www.thelongridersguild.com

Five years ago, I began my canoe trip down the Mississippi River to paddle 2,552 miles from Lake Itasca, Minnesota to New Orleans in the

Gulf of Mexico. On the tenth night, I camped with two brothers canoeing down the Mississippi to fulfill a lifelong dream. At the ages of 72 and 74, those two men made a pact to canoe the river when they were young. But life and families caught them up in regular living. That summer, they made their dream come true.

Around the campfire the first night, one of the brothers named Elmer, recited the entire poem of Robert Service's "Cremation of Sam McGee." It took 10 minutes to recite. He didn't miss a word.

Brenda Joyce, a friend that I met in Antarctica, 68, enjoys a trait she calls "Dromomania." It is an inordinate desire to travel. She has traveled from the Arctic to Antarctica and 170 countries. When I contacted her for ideas for adventure travel, she answered from her job in Thailand.

Did you feel the message of this chapter? It matters little what your age, your sex, your past or your circumstances—you can live one or one-hundred adventures in your life.

"When you walk to the edge of the light you have, and you take the first step into the darkness of the unknown, you must believe that one of two things will happen: there will be something solid for you to stand upon or you will be taught to fly." Patrick Overton

KEY POINTS FROM THIS CHAPTER

1. Average people can become great by self-determination, guts and gumption.
2. Anyone at any age can achieve incredible feats on every level.
3. You can start out young or old to live your dreams; it's up to you.
4. You can use your age to your advantage when you are younger and stronger.

*C*hapter 6—The life and times of the Coffin Man

"This being human is a guest house. Every morning a new arrival; a joy, a depression, a meanness, some momentary awareness comes as an unexpected visitor. Welcome and attend them all! Even if they're a crowd of sorrows who violently sweep your house empty of its furniture. Still, treat each guest honorably. He may be clearing you out for some new delight. The dark thought, the shame, the malice; meet them at the door laughing, and invite them in. Be grateful for whoever comes, because each guest has been sent as a guide from beyond." Malal al-Din Rumi

The people along the journey make any adventure special. They approach me at every stop. Curious and full of questions, they make my day with their homespun hospitality. They advise me about local events and interesting places to visit. I'm invited into their homes for a hot shower and dinner. But it's those eccentric characters that cross my path that intrigue my imagination. They express infinite possibilities for the human spirit.

Most of us enjoy a chance to fill up our lives with seventy to eighty years of living. We can use them as we see fit. Some of us do it in highly imaginative ways. For a few, travel is the ultimate freedom of expression. It brings the unknown into focus.

Traveling east toward Vermont on Route 373, I stood on the dock waiting for the ferry to take me across Lake Champlain. Spring colors decorated upstate New York. The boat wasn't due for another hour. I pedaled around the parking lot until I found a spot to write in my journal.

I'm usually the center of attention with flags flying and a dozen bananas hanging off my rear packs. Not that day! Another traveler commanded my attention.

In the corner of the parking lot, a buckboard wagon right out of a John Wayne movie stood silently in the shade. It featured a shortened harness on the front along with a blue and white cotton surrey top. Pots and pans hung from the sides along with a fold-out table and bench. It featured four large wagon wheels. A series of laminated news clips were tacked to the sides of the frame. The most curious aspect of this contraption wasn't evident until I rode closer. A gold-trimmed black coffin comprised the main compartment of the wagon. The news clips featured a dozen languages.

A man who looked in his late fifties stood off to the side. Long silver hair flowed from under his cap and he sported a goatee. His eyes matched the sky. He bantered with some Aussie tourists about some experiences in Australia.

I looked at the news clips until I found one in English from the London Ti nes. This guy had traveled through 85 countries on five continents. They ca ed him The Coffin Man.

Backing up, I aimed my camera for a shot.

"Hold it, sonny," he said. "Please read my sign before you take a picture."

"What sign?" I asked.

"Right here," he said, pointing.

I moved closer to the rear of the wagon. It read, "If you are going to take a photograph, I ask that you donate $1.00 and I will stand in the picture with you. This is the way I make a living for my travels."

"Sounds fair enough to me," I said, handing him a buck.

After the shot, I asked him how long and why he had been traveling with his buckboard.

"It's been twenty years this coming May," he said, stroking his goatee. "It dawned on me when I was forty that my life was passing me by. My kids were grown and my wife died of breast cancer. I was broke, but in good health. I worked a year to save up money to travel around the world. Within ten months, I was broke again. But by that time, I had the travel bug. I figured I wanted to see every place on this planet. I hungered to get back on the road. That's when I thought up this idea to make money while I traveled. It's the cheapest way to go and I make a decent buck along the way."

"Where's the horse?" I asked.

"You're looking at him," he said, slapping his sinewy thighs.

"You pull that wagon?" I gasped. "How do you get it up the mountains?"

"I've cut out any extra weight, so it's pretty light," he said. "Here, you can pick up a corner to see how light it is. You'll be surprised."

I laid my bike down and picked up a corner of the wagon. It weighed about 200 pounds, maybe more, but I could see that a strong person could pull it up a mountain grade.

"So where do you sleep?" I asked.

"Sonny, it doesn't take an Einstein to figure that one out," he said.

I looked up at the wagon.

"No," I said.

"Yes," he said.

"Hey, you guys! My wife and I would like to take a picture of you two crazy people," a man said. "After that, we'd like to take you out to lunch, if you don't mind."

"You don't have any idea how much I eat," I told him.

"No, you won't believe how much I eat," said the Coffin Man.

The couple snapped our pictures before taking us to lunch. They asked more questions than a reporter. They were fascinated by our different modes of travel. Late into the afternoon, we finished a long discussion of world politics, people and countries around the world. I had missed the ferry, but could catch it in the morning.

I asked the Coffin Man what was one of his favorite adventures in his travels.

"It's hard to pick out one favorite moment out of hundreds," he said. "But once, I was caught in a monsoon rain on a muddy road in India. I had given up hope of getting out of there for the rest of the day. As luck would have it, three guys rode by on their own modes of transportation."

"What was that?" I asked.

"Elephants," he said. "They hitched up one of those beasts with a rope to my wagon and motioned me to hop on board with them. I didn't know how to get up on one of those things, so they motioned me to the front of the beast. I stood there when the elephant got up close to me and rolled out its tusk in front of my foot. I stepped into his curled snout and that elephant hoisted me up to his back. It was the most exciting elevator ride to the second floor of any building I've ever taken."

We camped together that night. We both agreed that we had an incurable love for travel. I crawled into my tent and looked out the netting to see the Coffin Man climbing into his bed. I don't mind saying that it was a strange feeling watching this man who was so much alive and who was living such an incredible life, casually climb into his coffin and close the lid behind him.

Our discussions that day excited my passions for travel and reminded me of a piece written by John Steinbeck in his book *Travels with Charley*.

"When I was very young and the urge to be someplace else was on me, I was assured by mature people that maturity would cure this itch. When years described me as mature, the remedy prescribed was middle age. In middle age, I was assured that greater age would calm my fever and now that I am fifty-eight perhaps senility will do the job. Nothing has worked. Four hoarse blasts of a ship's whistle still raise the hair on my neck and set my feet to tapping. The sound of a jet, an engine warming up, even the clopping of shod hooves on pavement brings on the ancient shudder, the dry mouth and vacant eye, the hot palms and the churn of stomach high up under the rib cage...I fear the disease is incurable."

Lying there on my back, with a million stars twinkling in the night sky, I realized that the adventure travel disease permeated every cell in my body.

KEY POINTS FROM THIS CHAPTER

1. You are in charge of your life and where and how you travel.
2. You can think up any means for your personal travel.
3. You could imitate the Coffin Man.
4. Always look for creative ways to make money and travel.

Chapter 7—Greatest adventure of all; search for personal truth

"I have always gone to other lands with one idea: to meet people and come to know them. I learn to sing their songs, dance their jigs and eat their food. I try to be one among the people in whose land I am living." Grace Halsell

Your intelligent life begins with the first words you hear as a child once you exit the womb. Growing up, you learn tens of thousands of words. From that network, you learn numbers, concepts, ideas and create your own thoughts. You become self-aware. You learn about the world and soon, by trial and error, you learn about yourself.

As an infant, you get your way. You enjoy unlimited attention from your parents. They provide everything for you. It's a party from ages one to twelve. When you reach your teen years, you learn about friends, bullies, prejudice, bias, sports, girls, boys, the Internet, cell phones, texting and a ton of interesting things happening around the planet. You will enter the world sooner than you realize as you graduate from high school.

In the 21st century, things are not as simple as they were 20 years ago. You face work, politics, environmental calamities, disasters, good people, obtuse people and a host of other dramas throughout humanity.

It's a wild ride and whether you like it or not, life thrusts you into living, experiencing and expressing. One of the greatest adventures of your life will be your journey toward finding your personal truths, your purpose for living on this planet and what it will mean to you.

Travel may be the perfect vehicle for you to gain ground on your quest to know yourself and a little bit more about humanity. Travel may help you realize that you possess the ability to become whatever you intend, whatever you choose and whatever you think in your mind. Additionally, travel creates purpose that harnesses your creativity.

Often, many children carry their emotional baggage with them into their adult lives. They may have suffered difficult childhoods by the way of abusive parents, poor schools, bullies that picked on them and a host of other childhood traumas.

I was a skinny kid. Tough guys picked on me and beat me up. I endured some very traumatic experiences in my teen years. However, once past them, I moved on. I took those experiences as well as defeats and used those encounters as true grit, self-confidence and self-acceptance to propel me into a positive attitude. I decided to face the tough challenges in my life with confidence. Please realize that very few individuals, no matter how rich, good looking, tall, short, skinny, fat, smart or otherwise—move through this life without failure, without emotional pain, without breaking a few bones and without facing their demons, whether real or imagined.

It's not the demons or harsh winds that defeat you. It's how you choose to handle them. Always maintain complete and total confidence in yourself as a person and as an adventurer. Like the famous sports advertisement says, "Just do it!"

TRAVEL ALLOWS INTROSPECTION AND PERSPECTIVE

Thankfully, you will gain tremendous perspective in your world travels. You will also shed a few tears at what you see in many countries where no one enjoys the advantages that you may take for granted: a hot shower, toilet, safe food, clean bed and personal safety.

Therefore, take time to educate yourself. Education gives life purpose and also prepares you with skills. Most important, education allows you to think critically and wisely by gaining perspective. Accent your intelligence and maximize your understanding of life. Advance your mind through education, reading, talking to others and learning a language. It enlightens you and encourages you toward a meaningful path.

Before traveling to specific countries, visit the library to check out CDs or tapes to learn French, German, Italian, Chinese, Japanese, Dutch, Portuguese, Swedish, Norwegian and other languages of countries you intend to visit. Also, bring a multiple language book so you can learn basic phrases and greetings. By knowing basics, you will bring a smile and many invitations from locals of a country—pleased with your efforts.

Make sure, also, that you practice unlimited patience in foreign countries. Remember that their cultures may be diametrically opposed to yours, especially when it comes to time. Thus, relax and go with the flow. It's not like you must get to work that day.

A SENSE OF BRAVERY

When I prepared to bicycle the entire length of South America, many friends worried and expressed their concerns about us getting killed or hurt along the way. Without a doubt, you must pick your destinations with care. You can get killed if you travel through countries that suffer armed conflict or highly corrupt governments.

Choose safe countries at first in order to enjoy a taste of being in a strange political environment. As you gain an understanding of politics and cultures, you will equip yourself with greater comprehension of what you face.

Personal courage, self-confidence and alertness go a long way when traveling around the world. Critical thinking and common sense keep you safer as to decisions. Without a doubt, a few characters out there wait in the shadows of every country, of every city and every village to trick you and relieve you of your possessions.

Let's face it, you wouldn't walk down the dark city streets at night alone in many American cities would you? You may avoid negative situations by maintaining your sixth sense, your awareness of your surroundings and taking appropriate actions.

You must be aware everywhere in the world. Yes, most people live honest lives and with great integrity. That's wonderful. Yet, it's the few that will slice your backpack or cut your camera strap or strip your passport within seconds if you become careless.

A MOMENT TO TALK ABOUT COURAGE

Courage may be easy for some and challenging for others. Some folks enjoy recklessness while others remain very cautious. I suffered anxious feelings and fears during my first forays into the world. You hear so much bias and prejudice about someone or some country.

Please remember that most folks go about their lives just like you do. They work, eat, play, sing, dance and laugh in every country in the world.

They get married, rear kids and care about their communities the same way you do in your hometown.

So, take that step into the unknown with a calm courage that will grow with each new positive experience in your adventures here in America or in some far-flung corner of the world.

Do you remember in the fabled movie "The Wizard of Oz," where the Lion searched for courage, the Tin Man for a heart and the Straw Man for a brain? As we all grew up, we encountered scary moments mostly concocted by our own imaginations. I remember I didn't dare let my hands or feet drop over the edge of the bed during the night because I thought something would pull me into the underworld. I have no understanding where I got the idea that some monster would grab me, but at that point in my life, I felt the reality of my fear.

In the darkness, your mind can dream up anything. When I think of the horror movies out today, I am amazed kids aren't a train-wreck of fears and phobias brought about by those horror movies. I avoid watching them to keep those images out of my mind.

I used to walk down a 100-yard-long dirt driveway from my grandma's house back to my house after helping my grandfather milk cows. I carried a gallon of milk with me. Sometimes, I thought up some of the wildest animals jumping out of the bush to devour me. When I look back at that time at the age of 12, it scared the daylights out of me. Somehow, I kept putting one foot in front of the other and made it back to the house night after night. Today, I laugh at my youthful folly.

Therefore, maintain courage, sustain your sense of yourself and your purpose—to explore, discover and enjoy your journey into the unknown.

"You have plenty of courage, I am sure," answered the Wizard of Oz. "All you need is confidence in yourself. There is no living thing that is not afraid when it faces danger. The true courage is in facing danger when you are afraid, and that kind of courage you have in plenty."
L. Frank Baum (Wizard of Oz)

KEY POINTS FROM THIS CHAPTER

1. Your personal truth stems from learning from experiences.

2. Maintain calm and patience in every situation in a foreign country.
3. Learn how to travel with alertness and caution, yet enjoy yourself.
4. Your courage comes from your choices over fear.

Chapter 8—A frozen moment in Antarctica

"Great God, this is an awful place."Robert Falcon Scott, 1912

In the morning, a whiteout howled across McMurdo Station, Antarctica with 150 mile per hour winds and minus 80 degree temperatures. I had been confined to my barracks for two days as a "Condition One" storm worked its way over the icepack before me.

By late evening, the weather turned placid but a biting minus 40 degree temperature kept most people inside. I, however, bundled into my cold weather gear—insulated boots, heavy mittens, five Thermax layers, fleece, three hats, face protection, along with ski goggles—and headed out the door to ride my bicycle over the ice runway.

Yes, there were bicycles at the scientific station for me to ride. Operations reported some emperor penguins on the ice. I had to see them no matter what the cold. I jumped on the bike looking like an overstuffed bear with all my cold weather gear on. My breath vaporized as I pedaled toward the ice-covered ocean. My lungs burned with each inhalation of polar cold.

About a mile around the cove, the setting sun glinted off the roof of Robert Falcon Scott's Discovery Hut. He had died 90 years ago on his last attempt to reach the South Pole. The hut had stood on the point of McMurdo Sound since 1902. It gave mute testimony to the courage those men displayed in their polar adventures. This was a cold, miserable place.

I rode along a path that led toward the ice pack in the sound. It's hard to describe pack-ice, however, it is a bunch of jumbled, broken ice chards being heaved and smashed into multiple shapes such as triangles, domes, squares, tubulars, and wedges—like an Erector Set gone crazy. However, near the shore, it was reasonably smooth with a thin veneer of snow from the blizzard.

Above me, a gold and purple sky glowed brazenly in its final glory into the crevasses of the Royal Society Range across McMurdo Sound. For once, a rare quiet softened the bitter edge of the crystal white desert before me. One of the glaciers, more than ten miles across at its terminus, radiated liquid gold from the setting sun. Stepping through some shallow snow drifts, I sank knee deep until I pulled through and gained the edge of the ice. Even with polar weather gear protecting my body, the numbing cold crept through the air as if it were trying to find a way into my being.

The bike frame creaked at the cold and the tires made a popping sound on the snow. The big boots I wore made it hard to keep on the pedals. But I persevered and kept moving forward. Across the ice, I looked through the sunlight and saw four black figures approaching. I shaded my eyes with my gloved hand. They drew closer; their bodies were back-lit by the sun on the horizon. It was a family of Emperor penguins. I dismounted from my bike. From our survival classes, I learned to sit down so as not to frighten them. By appearing smaller than them, they might find me interesting.

Slowly, I lowered myself into the snow cross-legged like an Indian chief. Minute by minute, they waddled straight toward me. Three big birds, about 80 pounds each kept moving dead-on in my direction. The smallest followed behind them.

Another minute passed and they were within 30 feet of me. The lead Emperor carried himself like a king. His silky black head-color swept down the back of his body and through his tail. A bright crayon yellow/orange streaked along his beak like a Nike logo. Under his cheek, soft aspirin-white feathers poured downward glistening in lanolin. His wings were black on the outside and mixed with black/white on the front. He stood at least 40 inches tall and his enormous three-toed feet were a gray reptilian roughness with blunted talons sticking out. He rolled his head. He looked at me in a cockeyed fashion, as if I was the strangest creature he had ever seen.

I don't know what made me do it, but I slipped my right hand out of the glove and moved it slowly toward him. The rest of the penguins closed in. The big guy stuck his beak across the palm of my hand and twisted his head, as if to scratch himself against my skin. I felt glossy feathers against my hand. He uttered a muffled coo. The rest of the penguins cooed. Their mucus membranes slid like liquid soap over their eyes every few seconds.

I stared back, wanting to say something to them, but realized I could not speak their language. However, at that moment, we shared a consciousness of living.

My frozen breath vapors hung in the air briefly before descending as crystals toward the ground. I battled to keep from bursting with excitement. Within seconds, one of the other penguins pecked my new friend on the rump. He drew back. With that he turned and waddled away. Following the elders, the little one gave one last look at me, as if he too wanted to scratch my hand, but was afraid, and turned with his friends. As they retreated, their wings flailed outward, away from their bodies like children trying to catch the wind in their arms. The baby Emperor departed as the last to go.

My hand turned numb so I stuck it back into the glove. As I sat there, I remembered once when a hummingbird landed on my finger in the Rocky Mountains. I remembered the sheer delicacy nature shared with me that warm spring day in the wilderness. Here, in this frozen wasteland beyond the borders of my imagination where man does not belong, nature touched me again today with its pulsing heart and living warmth. I only hope my species learns as much respect for our fellow travelers as they show toward us.

I stood up, tightened my hood and looked for the penguins. They had vanished into the frozen white world in front of me. Only the pack-ice rumbled toward the horizon. I turned to my bike. It's hard to believe that two rubber tires laced together with spokes and rims, and attached to a metal frame could carry me from the Amazon Jungle, to Death Valley and on to where the bolt goes into the bottom of the globe.

That simple machine lying in the frozen snow had taken me to far flung places on this planet and it had allowed me magical moments beyond description. That moment with the penguins probably was the best it had ever done by me. I remounted it and turned toward the barracks.

The ride back didn't seem so cold.

KEY POINTS FROM THIS CHAPTER

1. No matter what the adversity, you can choose to move forward.
2. To explore the world, you must step into it with confidence.
3. Always prepare for an adventure to enjoy a positive outcome.
4. Learn from the adventure and expand your mind for greater pursuits.

Chapter 9—Adventure mode that turns your crank

"The purpose of life, after all, is to live it, to taste experience to the utmost, to reach out eagerly and without fear for newer and richer experiences." Eleanor Roosevelt

While starting my life on the farm, thanks to my U.S Marine Corps father, I traveled through 40 states and out of the country in my first 18 years. I lived an exciting life for an average farm boy. I remember his being stationed as a recruiter in Cadillac, Michigan for two years. My brothers and I milked cows, fed the chickens, helped with animal births, slopped the hogs, picked cucumbers and baled hay. I plowed the fields and cultivated the corn. Hard work! Low pay! Long hours! It gave us a sense of the value of a dollar. Since that time, I have worked two dozen jobs and each one propelled me to where I wanted to go. I have never had anything given to me.

But my dad and mom's greatest gift stemmed from our being dependents in the military. We lived on bases around the world. Each summer, the bus stopped by our house, picked us up and took us to dozens of Special Services activities.

We learned to play golf and tennis. We learned handball, paddle ball and racquetball. We learned how to bowl, swim and canoe. Next, scuba diving and ping pong. We attended pottery classes, sculpting and woodwork. We became Boy Scouts. We camped, backpacked and snorkeled. We lived on a beach in Hawaii for endless hours of adventure as we swam out to a lone island. We examined every kind of marine creature and we swam with the big rays. We climbed inside dormant volcanoes and rock climbed.

I rode a bicycle on my morning paper route for seven years. At the time, I didn't know it, but that bike became my trusty steed as I threw papers, watched deer in the woods, birds in the air and witnessed glorious sunrises on the eastern horizon. Little did I know that pedaling a bicycle turned my crank and prepared me for a life of pedaling two wheels.

We played baseball, basketball, football, soccer and badminton.

I learned to dance in classes in the sixth grade. I learned swing, cha cha, salsa, tango, country & western and ballroom. From those classes, I have been a dancer all my life. Men, learn to dance. You will always enjoy the nicest girls on your arms. Why? Most men won't learn to dance. They would rather stand around the dance floor drinking a brew watching you dance with all the pretty girls. I never could figure out why, but it never bothered me.

I have danced with women in the Galapagos Islands, Greek Islands, Alaska, Norway, Italy, Australia, Rio de Janeiro and more. Learn to dance men and you will find more fun on your world travels than you ever thought possible. Learn six count swing also known as jitterbug. It's easy and you can teach any lady quickly how to follow you on any dance floor in the world.

Later, I jumped into windsurfing, triathlons, skiing, motorcycling, bicycle touring, rafting, mountain bike racing, horseback riding, road racing and mountain climbing.

As you can imagine, that kind of a youth prepared me to be a participant in every kind of activity and each one prepared me in different ways to become an adventurer. To this day, you might say I am a dilettante. I participate in everything life offers.

How do you find out what turns your crank?

Most youth do not enjoy such a fortunate childhood. That's not a problem. Create it yourself at any age. Create a list of all the sports or activities out there in the world. Go try them out, one by one, day by day and week by week. Take classes and learn how to excel in any activity. Learn to bowl on a bowling team. Take dance classes. Take ski lessons. Take a course in scuba diving which will allow you to dive in the oceans all over the planet. Take a course as a Water Safety Instructor to teach swimming classes. Learn how to be a short order cook. Learn how to become a bartender. That job will carry you around the world on a cruise ship or have you slinging drinks at a ski resort. Additionally, use your dance abilities to teach dance in the USA or any foreign country.

Use your own talents or develop new talents to use at some later date.

Everything you engage in will pop up to your advantage in the future. Most importantly, the more you learn and place those activities in your experience quiver, the more you prepare yourself for amazing opportunities all over the globe.

"Twenty years from now, you will be more disappointed by the things you didn't do, than by the things you did do. So throw off the bowlines. Sail away from the safe harbor. Catch the trade winds in your sails." Mark Twain

KEY POINTS FROM THIS CHAPTER

1. Explore as much as you can at every moment in your life.
2. Hang with others who enjoy specific athletic or activity pursuits.
3. Open yourself to opportunities that come your way.
4. Learn specific jobs to further your travel plans.

Chapter 10—Winter mountaineering adventure at 13,000 feet

"You cannot stay on the summit forever; you have to come down again. So why bother in the first place? Just this: What is above knows what is below, but what is below does not know what is above. One climbs, one sees. One descends, one sees no longer, but one has seen. There is an art of conducting oneself in the lower regions by the memory of what one saw higher up. When one can no longer see, one can at least still know." Rene Daumal

Have you ever strapped on a 45-pound pack, stepped onto skinny skis and trudged off into the wilderness like the mountain man Jeremiah Johnson? Have you ever made a winter ascent of a 13,209-foot peak on skis with screaming winds and frigid temperatures tearing at your body? No? Don't feel like the lone ranger.

Enter intrepid mountaineers named Greg, Nick and Frosty. Fearless travelers? Or crazy guys that don't have the common sense of a Canadian goose?

After driving through the Eisenhower Tunnel west of Denver, Colorado, Greg drove into a snow-white world on the western side of Loveland Pass. Later, we drove over Battle Mountain Summit Pass, continued on through 10th Mountain Division Camp Hale in a wide valley before pushing over Tennessee Pass. Just over the other side, we stopped at a parking lot on an old country road.

Greg's car made first tracks in five inches of fresh snow. Around us, startling blue sky, deep green pines and majestic white peaks pushed their jagged rocks into the heavens. A few gray jays perched in the trees while some crows flapped overhead.

We pulled our gear out of the car, stacked the skis and warmed up with Gore-Tex, vests and gloves. In a few minutes, we slung the packs onto our shoulders and walked up the road with skis and poles ready for the five-mile trek into the wilderness. We expected to ski from 9,000 feet to our destination at 11,300 feet near the tree line. From there, we would establish base camp for our summit attempt of Homestake Peak at 13,209 feet.

After a quarter mile, we reached the trailhead for the 10th Mountain Hut. The hut organization found its name after the brave soldiers of the 10th Mountain Division in WWII. They trained in Colorado and fought in the Italian Alps.

Around us, 10-foot snow banks gave an idea of how much snow fell in that area. A local said, "We usually get 30 feet of snow by this time every year, but only 20 this year so far."

Fortunately, as we slipped into our skis, another group of skiers had cut the trail before us. That made it easier to follow those tracks instead of breaking trail, which takes more energy. While we made our way, we snapped several pictures of our 45-pound packs, cold weather gear and skis. With our red jackets, we made colorful contrasts in a world of white garnished with green and topped off with an azure sky.

Nick said, "I feel like I just pulled on a 50-pound sack of cement."

Much like the mountain men depicted in the movie "Jeremiah Johnson" starring Robert Redford from the 1850s, a mountaineering skier must be prepared for basic survival living. Men and women have died from trips exactly like the one we attempted. We could get caught in a blizzard. Someone might break a leg or arm in a crash. We could suffer an avalanche.

Soon, three heavily-loaded mountaineering skiers slogged through a mountain meadow. While the summers featured blooming wildflowers in a riot of colors, the winter offered white snows sparkling like millions of diamonds lit by sunshine.

The trail led into ever-steepening mountain terrain. Leafless aspen stood quietly while lodge pole pines shot straight into the blue sky. We marveled at the pristine beauty all around us.

Trail chatter proceeded with three of us sharing adventures from past times. Amazing how each of us enjoyed a totally different story with unique circumstances. We talked about travel to foreign lands, about our jobs and the latest news reports.

The trail climbed into thicker woods and steepening inclines. Looking skyward brought astounding beauty with fresh snow falling from branches that mingled with crystallized air. We breathed deeply and exhaled vapor clouds.

We crested a ridge. The trail shot quickly down through the trees. I looked like Ichabod Crane on the trail behind Greg. He nearly crashed taking a hairpin turn so I veered off into the trees for a safer ride. Unfortunately, I caught the crust of the snow for a major face plant. Snow penetrated my glasses, eyes, ears, nostrils and mouth.

After regaining my orientation, I said, "Wow! That tastes like an ice sandwich."

I surveyed my circumstances. One ski stuck under my body. The second one stuck straight up into the sky. My pack fell to my side and my two ski poles crossed under my body. I could barely move to release my hands from the ski poles. Next, I unbuckled my pack. I broke loose from the second pole. I rolled to my side as I pulled the one ski out of the snow. With great effort, I pulled my body to my knees and let the pack straps slide off to the side. I straightened the skis. I raised myself up, pulled up the pack, slung it over my shoulder and hoisted it onto my back. I brushed the snow off my face and glasses. I tried to regain my dignity while I slipped my hands through the straps.

"Gosh, that was more fun than jumping out of my car at 60 miles per hour," I muttered to myself.

"Are you okay?" Greg yelled from far below.

"Yeah, I just stopped for a mouthful of snow," I yelled back.

I skied down very carefully to meet my mates.

"Taking a siesta?" Greg said.

"Yeah," I said. "I ate a snow bank to cool off from sweating so much."

We continued through uncommon beauty. Trees befriended us at every turn. A clear sky blazed across sunlit peaks in all directions. A mantle of trees swept down from distant 13,000 and 14,000-foot peaks at the tree line.

We kept pushing through deep snow with wind blowing the crystals like sand blowing across a desert. The sun neared the horizon as the day fell away. Along the way, we took two rest and food breaks to regain our energy.

As we climbed, we felt increasing pressure on our hips from the heavy packs and constant slogging forward into the incline of the mountain sides.

In the late afternoon, our shadows lengthened to 20 feet from the sun setting in the west. We snapped several pictures of our elongated bodies. We also experienced weariness. Slogging through snow, traveling 2,000 feet of vertical climb upward into the rarefied air, steals oxygen from the body.

Around 5:00 p.m., a huge open meadow led toward Homestake Peak in front of us at 13,209 feet. Shadows cast the woods into darkness while snow tornadoes swirled from distant peaks. The wind picked up as it blew hard into our faces. Sharp crystal snow bullets beat into us as we pushed forward. We changed our gloves to mittens to give more warmth.

Around the next corner of trees the stark outline of a cabin emerged from the woods.

"Straight ahead," I said.

"Hot chocolate," Nick said.

"Works for me," Greg said.

We slogged up the slope with renewed excitement. As we drew closer, a large cabin, capable of sleeping 20 people, rose above the deep snow. Featuring dark brown wood and laced with huge picture windows—it looked like home. It sank into six feet of snow, which covered the bottom windows halfway up.

On the front deck, we shed our packs and skis. We walked inside to a big kitchen, three picnic dining tables and at the far end of the cabin, a horseshoe shaped wood couch that featured a pot bellied black stove in the middle. A half dozen ski boots dried around it and "skins" hung from hangers. Mountaineering skiers use skins to create traction for moving uphill. Once on top of a hill, they tear off the skins from the bottoms of their skis, pack them and ski down.

In back, an outhouse appeared to be buried in ten feet of snow.

We introduced ourselves to Jen and Josh, and a man named Chris. Several other skiers prepared to leave. We carried our packs to our bunks on the second floor.

The sun set over Homestake Peak with pink alpenglow bursting against the clouds and on distant mountains. We stepped outside to take pictures. Magical and majestic! Soon, darkness swept across the high country. Stars appeared one by one, 10 by 10 and then, millions sparkled across the ink-black of space. Orion appeared, followed by the Big Dipper, Saturn, the North Star, Andromeda, Corona Borealis and galaxies beyond our imagination.

Back in the cabin, hot chocolate was first on the menu. Umm, good, after freezing our butts off for five hours on the climb up to the cabin. At dinner, we cooked up freeze-dried pasta primavera and raspberry crumble.

"It doesn't get any better than this," Greg said.

After sitting around the fire for fine conversation, we decided to make a starlight cruise under the night sky. Once outside, the frigid air startled us, but undeterred, we strapped on our skis and pushed into the stillness.

Above, a star-filled sky blanketed us from mountain peaks to mountain peaks. Each constellation proved magical, mysterious and awe-inspiring. We looked up through the trees. We slogged through glistening snows. A deep quiet engulfed us. There wasn't much to say since such wonder provoked only reverence. We cracked first tracks through virgin snow. It was like exploring as the first humans through unknown territory.

Under that magical canopy we saw the universe twinkle. Planets moved, stars radiated and the gloaming of the universe raced outward to forever.

"Look," said Nick. "A shooting star."

Sure enough, a white hot trail blazed across the darkness, making a distinctive exclamation point to punctuate the day.

After 30 minutes, we skied full circle and moved back toward the cabin. Once inside, another hot chocolate.

"Thanks for a day well lived," I toasted my friends.

"It doesn't get any better than this," Greg said.

We climbed the stairs to the second floor of the bunk house. We rested our heads back upon pillows while looking out the windows to stars twinkling in the night sky. In moments, our eyes closed and we faded into the bosom of nature's peace.

Next day, we woke up to a fantastically sunny day. Looking out the giant bay windows offered white shark teeth mountains biting at a marvelously blue sky.

Our cabin featured two sinks, two gas stoves, various silverware, pots, pans and paper towels. The unfinished wood gave the interior of the cabin a rustic look. The walls featured 10th Mountain Division plaques of soldiers who served. A small library offered books.

A trip to the outhouse offered a new sensation. Sitting down on an oval icicle adds a most exciting experience to going to the bathroom.

After a sumptuous breakfast, we bundled-up for our attempt to summit that distant peak. Far away, at 13,209 feet on the southern skyline we gazed at Homestake Peak. A long 1.2 mile ridge cut like a knife across the sky.

"Let's go," Greg said.

"I'm with you," I said.

A brisk breeze met us when we stepped outside the cabin. We decided to ski along a ridge through the trees that would carry us toward the base of the peak. It couldn't be more than 1.5 miles. Soon, we plowed through deep snow, each of us taking our turn breaking tracks.

We swept out of the tree line into a mountain meadow. We witnessed endless white everywhere.

The Yukon poet Robert Service:

The winter! The brightness that blinds you,
The white land locked tight as a drum,
The cold fear that follows and finds you,
The silence that bludgeons you dumb.

The snows that are older than history,
The woods where the weird shadows slant;
The stillness, the moonlight, the mystery,
I've bade 'em good-bye---but I can't.

There's a land where the mountains are nameless,
And the rivers all run God knows where;
There are lives that are erring and aimless,
And deaths that just hang by a hair;

There are hardships that nobody reckons;
There are valleys unpeopled and still;
There's a land—oh, it beckons and beckons,
And I want to go back—and I will.

Soon, we climbed toward the ridge. Nick powered up the mountain while we followed in his ski tracks. After an hour, we reached the start of the climb that would carry us from 11,300 feet to 13,209 feet.

As beautiful as our surroundings, we faced a bloody beast of a climb with wicked winds racing over the crest of the ridge we followed. We slogged upwards into 40 mile per hour winds. Swirling snow-devils caught our attention in the steep canyons sweeping down on both sides of the ridge we followed. The higher we slogged, the more astoundingly the blue sky blazed overheard. Distant peaks chewed into the sky like sharks in a feeding frenzy.

In front of us, a white ridge featuring a raging wind pressed to blow us off the mountain. Off to our right, gapping snow fields swept downward a thousand feet. In front, a far-away summit brushed the sky with powerful grace.

We skied past two rock fields breaking out of the snow drifts. Below, green pines splattered in interesting patterns on a white world. Above, an elegant sky soared ever pure and pristine. We lived on the raw, rugged and riveting edge of life.

After breaking for a rest, we dug in our poles, braced against our skis and held ourselves against a violent wind. Again, we moved forward. We gained altitude, which meant less oxygen. That exhausted us so we stopped to catch our breaths. After recovering, we pressed onward. Increment by increment, we pushed toward the summit. The higher we pushed, the harder the surface. It was almost ice-like. I slipped and crashed.

Two hours later, slowly, painstakingly and determined, we reached 150 meters short of the summit. The wind howled. An ice patch separated us from the top. We shed our skis.

With our poles, we stomped our way to the summit. The wind tore at our bodies. In the face of blistering cold and violent winds, our resolve drove us forward to our destiny to stand on the peak. Without hesitation, we plodded the final steps.

"Yahoo!" Nick said upon reaching the top.

"Yippee ki yo ki yay!" I yelled with arms outstretched.

Greg arrived to take pictures while we marveled at our stunning 360-degree view of the world. To us, it felt like standing on top of Mount Everest. To make a winter ascent felt deeply fulfilling.

"We're on top of the world," Nick yelled as the winds howled around us.

"Couldn't agree more," Greg said.

We looked over the ledge to cliffs and cornices filled with snow. We talked about skiing down the faces, but that would probably be fatal. Twenty minutes later, we grabbed our poles to make our way down to the skis. From there, we walked a half mile until we reached a major snow field. Greg and Nick strapped on their skis. They shot down into a glorious bowl, untracked, untouched and flawless.

I felt safer to drop down into a lesser bowl. I strapped on my skis. Unfortunately, the windblown hard pack failed to respond to my skis. I couldn't bite into the snow enough to turn. As my speed increased, I tried to slow, but couldn't get enough bite from the edges. I tumbled and smashed into the snow in a jumbled heap.

"Ouch!" I yelled, along with a few other choice words.

Below, Greg and Nick skied across the bottom of my run. I cut across the snow, but crashed again. I got up and crossed a steep grade only to crash again. I picked myself up. I felt like a mountain goat on a vertical cliff. One wrong crash and I could tumble down the mountain like a runaway snowball. After six crashes, I made my way down to my mates for a lunch break. I didn't have to eat. I ate enough snow to fill me up.

We laughed as we skied back to the cabin. Several at the hut watched us descend the peak. They noted their laughter at my many crashes.

"Oh, the cruelty of humor at another's pain," I said.

That night, we cooked delicious dinners and drank hot chocolate. Good friends, good times and a good life.

In the morning, we awoke to heavy snows falling outside the windows. Six inches had fallen in the night with more coming down. We savored hot oatmeal breakfasts with more steaming chocolate drinks. After packing our gear, washing our dishes and saying good-bye, we stepped out into heavy snowfall.

The ski tracks leading to the cabin had vanished. We must slog through virgin snows with our lifeline, the blue diamonds, nailed to trees that would guide us out of the Rocky Mountains.

"Gentlemen," I said. "This is a most excellent adventure."

We three mountaineers, laden with memories, pushed through the snows on the backside of our grand adventure. We looked one more time at the cabin covered in fresh snow. We saw the folks inside looking back at us. They waved. We turned to the task at hand. The eternal snows fell upon us with a softness of spirit that lifted us into their glorious beauty.

The Yukon poet Robert Service:

Have you known the Great White Silence,
not a snow-gemmed twig aquiver?
Have you broken trail on snowshoes?
Mushed your huskies up the river?

Dared the unknown, led the way,
and clutched the prize?
Have you marked the map's void spaces?
Mingled with all the races,

Felt the savage strength of brute in every thew?
And though grim as hell the worst is,
can you round it off with curses?
Then hearken to the Wild—it's calling you.

Let us probe the silent places, let us seek what luck betide us;
Let us journey to a lonely land I know.
There's a whisper on the night wind, there's a star agleam to guide us,
And the Wild is calling, calling...let us go.

KEY POINTS FROM THIS CHAPTER

1. Adventure awaits you no matter where you live.
2. Enjoy adventure in winter, spring, summer and fall.
3. Join friends for adventures to make them more fun.
4. Be prepared for hardship by maintaining top conditioning.
5. Buy top-quality gear for top-quality experiences.

Chapter 11—Why some people quest for adventure

"Keep your thoughts positive because your thoughts become your words. Keep your words positive because your words become your behaviors. Keep your behaviors positive because your behaviors become your habits. Keep your habits positive because your habits become your values. Keep your values positive because your values become your destiny." Gandhi

In Chapter Five, you read about a dozen people who created unimaginable and astounding adventures with their lives. At the time of their quests, they didn't think much about what they were doing. They busied themselves in their passions for a particular quest. Some may have become famous, while others enjoyed themselves regardless of any notoriety or fame.

For certain, if you pursue various adventures, you will enjoy being interviewed on camera and in the newspapers. It's nice to enjoy those clippings.

However the question remains: why do some people quest for adventure whereas most people live average lives?

THE ENTHUSIASTIC LIFE

From my perspective, life equals enthusiasm. What about enthusiastic people? What excites them? How come some become exceptionally engaged while others bide their time? Are extroverts enthusiastic and introverts not?

It's impossible to make any judgment about anyone based on their size, sex, height, education, race, creed or color. Everyone enters this world with a certain energy that moves into an intellectual or emotional grid that may give them extraordinary vitality or optimism or otherwise. Their outlook propels them into many kinds of adventure. That's why I stated at the beginning of the book that your adventure might be macramé or bowling or curling. Did you notice in the last Olympics in Vancouver, BC? Ardent curling fans packed the stands with wild enthusiasm. You could cut the air with a knife from the tension with each throw of the curling rocks. Tell me they weren't as wild and crazy about their sport as any NBA, NHA and NFL crowd you ever saw. People bring enthusiasm to their sport or activity.

It doesn't matter if you are a quiet type or an energetic person. You may express your enthusiasm loudly or quietly, in writing or song, in painting or sculpturing. You are a fountain of creative energy. You may guide that creative process by harnessing your mind. You will learn how to accomplish your goals within the pages of this book.

Again, these concepts or philosophical propensities can be used by you to explore your highest and best potential. But that doesn't guarantee anything. I once met a guy named Stan at a rest stop on the eastern side of the Grand Canyon. He possessed a sobering demeanor and harsh outlook on life. He had bicycled from the Arctic Ocean in Alaska all the way to the bottom of South America, some 18,000 miles. His stories mesmerized us. But his attitude stunned us.

"Life ain't so hot," he said. "You can be high one moment and your wife dies of cancer the next. You can be having a good day and a bunch of police can throw you into prison the next. I ain't getting too excited about life because it doesn't make any sense. Chances are, we're better off right now around this campfire tonight than we will be tomorrow. You just never know. I don't count on anything, except what's right now."

For certain, Stan lived in the here and how. For 13 years, he hammered those pedals to see the world. While he proved ornery and cranky, he delighted in telling his stories. I asked him about his funniest moment. Please note that he always traveled with his cat named Little Chum.

"Well, every night before I go to bed, I always put my false teeth in a cup at the back of my tent," Stan said. "But I got tired of knocking over the cup each night, so I put the cup outside the tent. Mind you, Little Chum sleeps all day in the milk crate and prowls outside all night while I sleep. One morning, in Mexico, I woke up to find my teeth gone. In a panic, I yelled to Little Chum. I had him sniff the cup and pleaded with him to go find my teeth. Well, he wandered around the campsite until he made his way over to a pile about 25 feet from the tent. He started digging. I got over there and started digging into a pack rat's den. About 10 inches into the hole, I uncovered my dental work smiling back up at me. I thanked Little Chum, rinsed my teeth and popped them back into my mouth. Breakfast never tasted so good."

We howled about that one.

But more than that, it showed that Stan, a confirmed curmudgeon, expressed his enthusiasm for telling stories. So, in his own way, he loved his life and expressed his joy in sharing his adventures. Bless Little Chum for finding Stan's dentures.

Thus, creative energy expresses through all of creation and all creatures. For humans, we enjoy an amazing expression called enthusiasm. That enthusiasm could be about macramé, knitting, painting, poetry, sculpting, rearing your kids, cheering your home team onward or it could mean exploring this planet in a variety of ways.

ENERGY, VITALITY, VIVACITY, GUSTO, DRIVE, VERVE, SPIRIT

Everyone possesses some kind of energy for something that enthralls them. That's why you will find people attracted to Spam throwing contests or underwater hockey.

To give you an idea of the craziness out there, here are nine unusual sports contests:

1. The annual Man versus Horse Marathon requires stamina and agility. Taking place in the Welsh town of Llanwrtyd Wells, the marathon places human contestants up against mounted horses. It started in 1980 when a landlord decided to hold the event after hearing two men arguing about whether or not a man could beat a horse in a cross country race.

2. First introduced in Finland, wife-carrying is an actual sport in which male competitors race while carrying a female teammate. The objective is for the male to carry the female with her legs locked around his neck as she hangs down his backside through a special obstacle course. Major competitions

are held in Sonkajarvi, Finland as well as Monona, Wisconsin and in Marquette, Michigan.

3. Bog snorkeling is a sporting event in which competitors swim in a water-filled trench cut through a peat bog. Competitors must wear snorkels and flippers and can only complete the course by swimming with their flippers. The World Bog Snorkeling Championships take place every August Bank Holiday in a dense peat bog near Llanwrtyd Wells, in Wales.

4. Toe wrestling is now a competitive sport. The World Toe Wrestling Competition first started at a pub in Derbyshire, UK in 1976. Locals thought it would be a great idea to hold a competition where individuals lock toes and force their opponent's foot to the ground. The organizers applied in 1997 to get the sport included in the Olympics, but it was not accepted.

5. Fistball is an old sport that's practiced all over the world. Like tennis and volleyball, the purpose of the sport is to hit the ball with your fist or arm and place it in the opponent's half where they won't get to it. After passing the net, the ball may be contacted up to three times (bounces are allowed) by the five players on each team.

6. Octopush, also known as underwater hockey, is a non-contact sport in which two teams compete to maneuver a puck across the bottom of a swimming pool and into "goals". Just like hockey but underwater, the game has actually become popular in countries like the UK, Australia, Canada, New Zealand and South Africa.

7. Kickball is played on a baseball diamond using a big rubber ball that gets pitched and kicked instead of hitting with a bat. The popular playground game has now become a competitive sport with the creation of the World Adult Kickball Association.

8. Chess boxing combines strength and brains. The sport is a combination of boxing and chess with the different games alternating after each round. A match between two individuals lasts up to eleven rounds, each starting with a four minute chess round and followed by two minutes of boxing. The sport is governed by the World Chess Boxing Organization whose motto is: "Fighting is done in the ring and wars are waged on the board."

9. Body rolling is probably one of the simplest sports out there. From the top of hill, a round of Double Gloucester cheese is rolled and competitors chase after it. The first individual across the finish line at the bottom of the hill wins the cheese. Competitors aim to catch the rolling cheese but this rarely happens as it has a one second head start and can reach speeds up to 112 km/hr. In 1997, the cheese took a wrong turn down the hill and accidentally injured a spectator.

On one of my West Coast bicycle tours, I rode through Angel Camp, California, the town of the "Celebrated Jumping Frog of Calaveras County" written by Mark Twain. They constructed a statue commemorating the frog. I laughed and smiled the whole time. Locals replay the famous contest annually. info@gocalaveras.com

In the end, why do people quest in so many ways? That's the magic of individual passions. You may possess one or dozens of interests. As can be imagined, some sports prove easy, fun and relaxing while other activities can get you killed or busted up pretty badly—such as bronco riding, running of the bulls, kick boxing, motorcycle racing, downhill skiing and surfing the big waves.

KEY POINTS FROM THIS CHAPTER

1. Creative energy in a person defines enthusiasm.
2. Introverts and extroverts enjoy enthusiasm for their passions.
3. Nine strange sports played with enthusiasm.
4. You get to choose your sport or games that match your interests.

*C*hapter 12—*The voluptuousness of living*

"It is only in adventure that some people succeed in knowing themselves - in finding themselves." André Gide

Riding east on Route 155, we neared a pass through the Greenhorn Mountains of the Sierras. Flat terrain near Delano, California gave way to peaks that cut the sky into wrinkled shapes across the horizon. Wildflowers bloomed along our route, which grew steeper with every crank of the pedals.

John, Mike, Kevin and I pedaled on a cross-continent journey. John, hailing from the coastal town of Kiama near Sydney, Australia, proved a charmer. His voice and wit had gotten us invited into three families' homes within the last week. The night before, we sat in a restaurant devouring the "all-you-can-eat" salad bar. A couple overheard John talking about the southern California climate. Before we knew it, John, who could be as charming as a Koala bear on one of those airline commercials, had gotten us invited into Larry and Valerie Johnson's home for the evening. Our hosts couldn't do enough for us and they loved to hear about our experiences. It's as if the price of admission was sharing our lives.

Being invited into complete strangers' homes may seem awkward, even unheard of by most travelers, but we had been asked into peoples' homes often during our tours. It may be the vulnerability of a bicycle rider. People feel we are honest. They sometimes give us the keys to their homes and cars.

On one tour, a man stopped me on the highway and invited me to his home. He tossed me his house keys before driving off to a ball game. When I arrived at his home a half-hour later, there were two bags of fruits and vegetables on the table and a note saying, "Help yourself."

I'm not sure why people think a touring bicyclist is trustworthy. Maybe they believe it takes depth of character for someone to pedal a bike for long distances—that someone who earns every mile with hard work and sweat must be honest. Anyone with less character would never tour on a bicycle, because it's not a free ride. It takes guts to pound the pedals mile after mile, mountain pass after mountain pass. My legs burn and I'm always hungry. I'm soaked in sweat and exhausted at the end of the day. It's not for those with weak physical resolve. However, age makes no difference because I have met men and women in their seventies on world bicycle tours. Attitude creates amazing strength and resolve.

Being asked into homes also has to do with a cheery disposition and the sparkle in their eyes as well as my own. Some folks get a kick out of living and they can spot it in others. They enjoy connecting with another life-force person who returns the energy. For that and other reasons, I've enjoyed many memorable evenings in peoples' homes around the world.

But that day, the heat and the climb had exhausted me. John climbed with ferocious power. Mike stayed with him. Kevin and I followed them. From flats to hills to bigger hills to mountains! I pushed my bicycle into the Sierras. By the afternoon, I had climbed 1,000, 2,000, 3,000 and was headed for 4,000 feet. Even with my 24 to 34 gearing, (number of teeth on the chain ring and freewheel) my legs took a beating.

The constant power strokes with no rest kept my muscles pumped and full of lactic acid. Kevin wasn't faring much better. The grade caused me to sweat profusely so I stopped to drink often. Each time, the cool afternoon air dried me quickly. Minutes later, more sweat moistened the dried salt. Passing cars threw dust on me, which locked onto the sweat. At the next water stop, it dried again, leaving me feeling like a mud-covered ball of dirt.

When I reached 5,000 feet, darkness crept over the mountains. A gray mist slipped down from the summit, cutting visibility. By that time, we labored through tighter curves that hugged the mountainside. I was ready to call it quits.

"John is probably at the top of the pass right now," I grumbled.

"I wouldn't doubt it," Kevin said.

"It's another 3,000 feet, but we'll have to do it in the dark for the next half hour," I said. "I'm blown out right now. You want to keep riding?"

"My knee is acting up," Kevin said. "But I can do another fifteen minutes."

Kevin and I slipped our feet into the toe-clips and shoved our bikes into motion. We continued upward into the mist. Sweat soaked my shirt. A few minutes later, a car passed us going downhill. I didn't think much of it until the car swung around and slowed beside us. The electric window slipped down.

"Good evening, mates," said John Brown. "How would you boys like a nice hot shower and dinner compliments of my new friend Ross?"

"Only if you promise never to drag me up a mountain again," I said.

"But you wouldn't be getting a hot shower," said John. "So why would you be upset?"

"Because you dragged us up this mountain all day and I'm going to die," I said.

"If we hadn't gotten this far, we wouldn't have met Ross and his nice shower," said John.

"You're right, John," Kevin broke in. "We'll just bend your spokes after the shower."

"Fair enough, boys," John said. "Follow me another mile."

"All the hot water you want, too," said Ross from the far side of the car.

"I'm going to live for it," I said as my body continued lathering up with mud-laden sweat.

Ross and John drove away. I felt weary and caked with dust, but the thought of a hot shower kept me going. I dreamed about it as I pedaled the last mile up the dark, winding highway. Even though I was tired, that single thought kept me going. It seemed to make the next fifteen minutes go faster, because I was feeling the soothing droplets massage my skin. The cranking seemed easier. Kevin started talking about the shower. Sweating like two horses and steaming in the cool night air, we reached the guest ranch sign John had mentioned.

Ross operated a summer kid's ranch. He gave us kitchen privileges. He led us to a row of six showerheads.

"Plenty of hot water," he said.

John, Kevin, Mike and I slipped off our shoes and walked into the shower room. After adjusting the temperature, we walked under them with our socks, shorts, shirts and gloves on. I've never heard so much groaning and laughing. Everyone soaped up.

Hot water streamed over my aching muscles. As the first rush of water doused my head, it cascaded over my face and streamed down my shoulders. I tore off my shirt and slapped it down on the tile. I peeled off my socks and shorts. The water ran down my body in waves, taking away the dirt and grime. Soothing steam filled my nostrils. I grabbed a bar of soap and lathered up my hair.

The soap and water did more than clean me. The whole day's hardship vanished in moments. I was in the middle of one of the greatest showers of my life. I had felt so worn out coming up the mountain, but now I felt tingling in every cell. As I stood there, transformed in the spray, I became aware of my friends' shouts at our good fortune of having a hot shower at the end of a tough day. From those gut-busting power cranks on the pedals, we enjoyed watery ecstasy.

As I stood there, I thought about my good fortune.

We enjoy 70-80 years to fill up our lives and I want to fill them up with the voluptuousness of living. I could be climbing a mountain, surfing or riding a bicycle. I want to be aware of pain, of joy, of potential within myself—of being excited for every leaf on a tree as it flutters in the wind, or watching a hawk rip down from the sky to grab a mouse, or the delight of discovering a ladybug landing on my leg in the early spring. I love gazing upon a mountain as it pierces the clouds.

It leads me to a kind of rage too, which is the blood sister of love— because the people of this world make it a charming, insane, exciting and confusing place. I want to maintain the ability to deal with them, with my mind, and my spirit—at full bore. To see is to know, and to know is to fall in love with what is known.

What's this? My shower just turned cold. The hot water ran out. I jumped back. The cold water shocked my skin. My friends and I headed for the towels. We dried our bodies and gathered our belongings. We ate a hardy dinner.

The next day, we loaded our bikes with food and water. Within seconds, sweat glistened on our bodies. Was it a lot of hard work? We call it hard fun. We pedaled into another glorious day of adventure across America on two wheels.

Have I made the right choice? Is it worth the agony and sweat of climbing a 9,000-foot pass or one at 15,500 feet through a blizzard in

Bolivia? You betcha! I want to fill up my life with living. Even when I'm home working five days a week, I make every day a positive experience. Daily life is an adventure. Weekends are a grand adventure. Each sustains the balance.

One night while sitting around a campfire, John and I, both being teachers, invented the ABC Concept. It fits our philosophies for happy living. The message is a simple attitude that anyone can choose to follow. With any life activity, a person can "go for it" and enjoy it before/during/after. That's the strategy of the ABC concept:

AIM—Take aim on life like Terry Fox who suffered from cancer, but ran on one leg across Canada to attract attention to the disease before he died. Fight for what you believe in like David Brower or John Muir when they brought their environmental message to Americans long before it was in vogue. Diane Fossey tried to save the gorillas. Ann Kanabe rode her bicycle from the top of North America to the bottom of South America. Anyone with a passion can work toward fulfilling his or her dream.

BUOYANCY—Keep buoyant in the challenging waters of living. Maintain motivation with a positive attitude. Keep light hearted against heavy odds. Lightness travels well and long. Bob Wieland, walking across America on his hands, epitomizes buoyancy. He didn't stop at that success, either. Later, he completed the Boston Marathon and the Ironman Triathlon in Hawaii.

CELEBRATE—Jump up and shout about being alive. Celebrate life! Stand up to be counted. Show your energy and excitement. Jump into a cold stream when you want a bath. Laugh at the hill you are about to climb. Remember that riding through the mountains is like a dance. Let the mountain lead and you follow. Enlarge that special photograph and hang it on your wall. Relish your excitement. Reach beyond your boundaries. Finally, avoid being afraid to fail. Failure can lead to success if you never give up.

"The secret of health for both mind and body is not to mourn for the past, not to worry about the future, or not to anticipate troubles, but to live in the present moment wisely and earnestly."
Buddha

KEY POINTS FROM THIS CHAPTER

1. Always keep a positive disposition; it will take you further.
2. Always write down your ideas in your notebook when they occur.
3. The harder the climb, the greater the reward mentally, physically and spiritually.

*C*hapter 13—*How to make money to pursue your adventures*

"When we are alone on a starlit night, when by chance we see the migrating birds in autumn descending on a grove of junipers to rest and eat; when we see children in a moment when they are really children, when we know love in our own hearts; or when, like the Japanese poet, Basho, we hear an old frog land in a quiet pond with a solitary splash--at such times the awakening, the turning inside out of all values, the newness, the emptiness and the purity of vision that make themselves evident, all these provide a glimpse of the cosmic dance." Thomas Merton

For the first 12 chapters of this book, you enjoyed some foundational information, several adventure stories and how to discover what you like. You also met regular people like you who created their own adventure-filled lives.

How in the heck did they do it? How did they make the money and find the time? How did they surpass the average life-path for most Americans? What is that path you ask?

Many of those adventure stories involved individuals living lives not too dissimilar from the one you may find yourself living. Almost 90 percent of Americans live similar lives. They get married, raise kids and enjoy weekend adventures during the year. They take two or three weeks of vacation annually.

Nonetheless, you may be looking for more adventure.

You may find yourself already along the standard path. You may choose to finish your child-rearing years before you begin your adventure life. But please hear this: married couples with kids do find ways to travel the world in a variety of creative outlets. Let's cover that subject.

JOBS AROUND THE WORLD FOR MARRIED COUPLES AND SINGLES

The Peace Corps offers anyone the opportunity to work around the world as singles or married couples. They train you for two-year stints in Africa, South America, Mexico, Middle East, Asia, Central Asia and the Pacific Islands. Any of those locations will present you with an excellent adventure. www.peacecorps.gov

You may apply to work on a cruise ship as a Licensed Practical Nurse, Registered Nurse, doctor, maid, busboy, bellhop, dance teacher, chef, concierge, maitre d', diesel mechanic, life guard, chiropractor, casino card dealer and dozens of other jobs. www.internationaljobs.com

Schools around the world need teachers to teach English in their own countries. They pay pretty well and you enjoy a beautiful bonding with your students as you teach them to speak and write English. Not only that, you may learn their language, so in the end, they did you a big favor. I spent time in Japan and they loved the way I talked and threw a bit of my personality into teaching. They said, "Mr. Frosty, you are a wild and crazy guy."

Become an airline flight attendant on international flights. That job will take you all over the world for an amazing life of adventure. I know one lady friend who visited 100 countries by the time she was 35 years of age. She spoke five languages. Start learning languages if you want that job.

Become a roadie with a traveling circus or rock band or rodeo or bicycle touring company. You may be pitching big tents, fixing rides or selling cotton candy. You can work yourself up to ring master or any number of jobs that you will learn and turn into a needed skill. You could become a clown. Most of all, you will be traveling around the country and learning the ins and outs of travel. It's all adventure and it's all good.

If you join the Navy or other military services, you will be shipped to bases all over the world. From there, you can learn the local language, take trips on weekends and thoroughly enjoy many adventures in foreign lands. You may take your dependents with you, which will enrich their lives immeasurably.

My military dad took us to Hawaii for three years. We lived on a beach.

We swam, enjoyed scuba diving, traveled all over the Hawaiian Islands and learned native dances. We enjoyed festivals and history. We hiked across ancient volcanoes and visited Pearl Harbor. We surfed at Waikiki beach. My dad took us fishing, sailing, surfing and snorkeling.

You may join a company that sends its workers all over the world. That means you must obtain a specific trade or enjoy a talent that some company needs. Almost always, you may take your family with you. I know a married couple right now living and working in South Africa as he works on power plants and she lounges on the beach. His specific talent opened the door. His next stop will be in Finland.

Are you a teacher with a family? Do you own or rent a house? You can enjoy a complete year of teacher exchange in another country, depending on whether or not you can speak the language of the country where you want to teach. You simply exchange teaching jobs with another teacher in a far-away land like Australia. You inhabit their home and they inhabit your house. You teach their classes and they teach your classes.

My friend Paula took off to Australia for a year of teaching. With her summer off, she explored all of Australia. She dove on the Great Barrier Reef, bicycled the Great Ocean Road, enjoyed a play at the Sydney Opera House, played golf with kangaroos hopping around the golf course with her, visited Ayers Rock and spent time in Tasmania with the Tasmanian Devil. She learned the idioms and customs of Australia. She returned home with a boatload of stories and memories. Later, she and her husband taught in Great Britain, New Zealand and Chile.

Additionally, you can teach school on over 700 U.S. military bases around the world and take your family.

WORLD ADVENTURE FOR SINGLE PERSONS

Instead of following the married-with-kids route, you may decide to spend your roaring twenties in a single mode. By remaining single, you may enjoy independence and latitude to travel as you wish, when you wish and how you wish. Additionally, it opens numerous opportunities for you to meet other people, other travelers and other lifestyles.

I chose to remain single throughout my 20s, 30s and 40s for maximum world adventure freedoms. You enjoy much more autonomy to take specific adventures with someone who enjoys a particular travel mode or style. If you find yourself hooked up with someone that likes to ski, but won't paddle a canoe down the Mississippi River, you're limited. If you remain single, you can find someone that will paddle down the Mississippi River with you, or bicycle across Asia or climb in Nepal.

Additionally, if you intend a lot of adventure before settling down, or if perhaps you don't want to settle down, you can do much more without children. You can accomplish more uncivilized adventures that require hardship, endurance or months on the road. Besides, you may find a variety of friends of both sexes along the way that you wouldn't have shared with if you were married.

Another bonus for staying single through your twenties is this idea. Most young people do not possess a clue as to what they want to do with their lives. They do not know what kind of work fulfills them. They do not know themselves or what they want in their early twenties. They wander aimlessly, and many times, fruitlessly through their younger years.

As you can imagine, once married, those two individuals must deal with each other whether they like or dislike several or many traits in their mate. By 25, many people change radically from where they were at eighteen.

Those who remain single discover their greatest talents and how they tick. By 25, they begin to understand what they like and don't like, especially in work, and, more importantly in the long run, the kind of person of the opposite sex they enjoy and like to be around. Therefore, the added bonus for staying single means you allow yourself a huge opportunity to discover the best possible you and figure out what other kinds of people you genuinely like to be around.

By the time you reach your mid-twenties, your wisdom and experiences will give you ample ability to make wiser choices as to your life-mate and friends. You will be wiser as to marriage and bringing children into the world. You will be a much better spouse and parent with the experiences and wisdom you learned by being single through your mid-twenties.

MAKING MONEY: FULL TIME, SEASONAL, WORKING THROUGH THE ADVENTURE

You need money and time to travel long distances. If you make a lot of money in a job, you usually do not enjoy a lot of time. If you enjoy a lot of time, you probably do not enjoy a big bank account.

From the aforementioned ideas for making money while traveling, perhaps you intend to travel totally unfettered by job constraints. You need to find jobs that make you a lot of money that allows you to resign without causing the company problems.

If you're a whiz kid with a college degree, you may command any number of jobs like repairing computers at $100.00 an hour or copiers at $50.00 per hour or diesel mechanic at $45.00 per hour. You can become a handyman at $48.00 an hour or construction worker at $35.00 an hour. A plumber makes $50.00 an hour. A furniture truck driver makes $40.00 per hour.

Further down the work chain, waitresses make $20.00 to $30.00 an hour.

Top ten blue collar jobs:

1.Elevator Installer and Repairer

Average salary: $87,518
Average hourly wage: $42.00
Average work week: 40 hours

2. Electrical and Electronics Repairer -- Powerhouse, Substation and Relay

Average salary: $68,084
Average hourly wage: $32.75
Average work week: 40 hours

3.Power Plant Operator, Distributor and Dispatcher

Average salary: $65,846
Average hourly wage: $31.50
Average work week: 40 hours

Gas Plant Operator

Average salary: $63,872
Average hourly wage: $30.71
Average work week: 40 hours

Locomotive Engineer

Average salary: $63,125

Average hourly wage: $28.27
Average work week: 42.5 hours

6. Electrical Power Line Installer and Repairer

Average salary: $60,354
Average hourly wage: $29.02
Average work week: 40 hours

7. Structural Iron and Steel Worker

Average salary: $59,224
Average hourly wage: $28.55
Average work week: 39.9 hours

8. Construction and Building Inspector

Average salary: $59,144
Average hourly wage: $28.31
Average work week: 40.2 hours

9. Ship and Boat Captain and Operator

Average salary: $57,910
Average hourly wage: $24.86
Average work week: 51.8 hours

10. Radio and Telecommunications Equipment Installer

Average salary: $57,149
Average hourly wage: $27.48
Average work week: 39.9 hours

Top white color jobs:

Top Paying Jobs Overall

* Physicians and surgeons: $147,000
* Aircraft pilots: $133,500

* Chief executives: $116,000
* Electrical and electronic engineers: $112,000
* Lawyers and judges: $99,800
* Dentists: $90,000
* Pharmacists: $85,500
* Management analysts: $84,700
* Computer and information system managers: $83,000
* Financial analysts, managers and advisors: $84,000
* Marketing and sales managers: $80,000
* Education administrators: $80,000

Top Paying Jobs That Do Not Require a High School Degree

These jobs tend to require substantial on-the-job training and work experience rather than formal education and schooling:

* Industrial production managers: $36,000
* Bailiffs, correctional officers and jailers: $36,400
* Drafters: $36,000
* Construction manager: $33,600
* Electricians: $31,900

Top Paying Jobs for High School Graduates

These occupations emphasize work experience and on-the-job training:

* Computer software engineers: $58,900
* Computer/information systems managers: $56,400
* Computer programmers: $55,000
* Network systems and data communications analysts: $49,000
* General and operations managers: $48,000
* Database, network and computer systems administrators: $48,000

Top Paying Jobs for a Two-Year College Degree

The following jobs tend to be technical in nature, skills developed on the job as well as job-specific training and certifications:

* Healthcare practitioners: $66,000

* Business analysts: $58,000
* Electrical and electronic engineers: $57,000
* Mechanical engineers: $56,800
* General and operations managers: $54,000
* Computer and information systems managers: $50,400

Notice that professional jobs will require long-term commitment. You won't be able to work and resign too many times, so please be aware of that condition. The key to all these jobs remains to save while you earn. You must live frugally in order to save the most money in the shortest amount of time. However, the longer you want to travel around the world—say one, two or three years, the more money you will want to save to carry you through your entire travel time span.

On one of my rides down the West Coast, I met a cyclist on his way to Seattle, Washington. Robert had worked a regular engineering job from age 22 to 35. At 35, he had piled up enough money to take a 10 year bicycle trip around the world. When he reached 45, he ran out of money, but he had lived a maximum adventure lifestyle for 10 years.

Robert said, "I wanted to see the world on a bicycle because it was cheap, easy and I was young enough to do it. I wouldn't trade a moment of the last ten years."

He headed up to Seattle to take another engineering job. Robert had the biggest grin on his face of anyone I have ever met on a bicycle.

As a teacher, I made $5,400.00 a year for nine months of work. Not only did I earn a pittance, I did not have much money to travel each summer. My brother Rex recommended me to a moving company for summer work. After making $25,000 in one summer of moving furniture as a trucker, I quit teaching to work three months a year with nine months off. That work proved arduous and physical. It demanded 90 to 100 hours a week all summer long. Nonetheless, it allowed me nine months of unlimited travel around the world with plenty of money for expenses.

SEASONAL JOBS FOR MAXIMUM TIME OFF

If you slap on your creative thinking cap, you will discover seasonal jobs that pay a lot of money and allow you to take off for six months at a time. As teacher, I enjoyed three months off every year, but poor finances. Later, I drove a furniture truck that paid five times as much and I only worked three to four months every year. All my brothers drove furniture trucks and they all traveled like I did. It depends on your own needs.

My friend Doug (standing on the right on the cover of this book) worked as a fisherman in Alaska during the crab and salmon season. He made himself so valuable, they welcomed him back every year. He has traveled all seven continents and has visited 130 countries to date. Another friend became a packer who walks into homes and packs household goods into boxes. It's great money for four to five months every summer. Once school starts, that job dwindles. Another friend returned to Antarctica for a six-months-on and six-months-off work schedule. He loved it. Another succeeded at seasonal sales of flower bulbs in the spring and summer. One friend, Bryan, (the blond guy on the left on the cover of this book) became a ski instructor all winter. He traveled the other six months of the year. One of my old buddies, Phil, became a tax advisor and worked four months a year at peak tax season and took off for the rest of the year.

OTHER MODES OF MAKING MONEY ON ADVENTURES

You can make money on specific jobs that render great adventure. Becoming a river raft guide will allow you to jump on with different outfitters, so that you can raft all the greatest rivers in the world and get paid for your work as well as your adventure. Refer to Chapter 53 on rafting at the back of the book.

You may want to become a bicycle guide to lead tours all over the world. You will enjoy pedaling a bicycle while getting paid and you get to see the world. Work for over 40 companies: www.bikeleague.org/links/touring. php Refer to Adventure Cyclist Magazine for dozens of bicycle touring companies nationally and internationally. www.AdventureCycling.org

You may want to become a mountain climbing guide to get paid for guiding mountain climbers up big or small mountains. www. alaskamountainguides.com

For those birders out there, I have enjoyed many expert birders who led birding excursions and got paid quite well for it. www.birding.com/ bestwebsites.asp

For those who love our National Parks, you may become a National Park Ranger and be assigned anywhere from the Grand Canyon to

Denali National Park in Alaska. You can also become a camp host. www.camphost.org

How did I travel to Antarctica? I found a job. They flew me down there and back. Along the way, I traveled all over New Zealand on my return. www.raytheon.com

MAKING MONEY AND RESIDUAL INCOME

Those persons enterprising enough, patient enough and talkative enough may work jobs that render a residual-income business. Once you gain a large clientele, you may take off for three to six months and enjoy more money in the bank than when you left for your adventure. After three to five years, you can make from $50,000.000 to $100,000.00 in annual income.

Such companies allow you tremendous latitude:

Melaleuca is a health and wellness company with $1 billion in sales. Really good and I am a director in that company. www.melaleuca.com
Mannatech is a health and wellness company. www.mannatech.com
Stem Tech is a health and wellness company. www.stemtech.com
Primerica agents show people how to save money, fix peoples' money problems, how to get out of debt, how to prepare for retirement and they teach people how to improve their financial conditions. www.primerica.com

Those are the four that I know work well for ambitious persons who want to make money and enjoy their freedom.

FRUGALITY, COMMON SENSE AND SAVINGS

When you're working to save money, that's your absolute intention. You may work two jobs at 80 hours a week, with only one day off, or if you're really enterprising, you may work seven days a week to get you to where you want to be financially, even sooner.

If you work seven days a week, it will become a mind game as you burn yourself out on several different levels. When I worked furniture, by the end of the summer, I found myself talking to the chairs and felt frustrated because of Murphy's Law, which resulted in damage claims.

But, as my emotional balance grew thin, August flowed into September. The peak season dropped off. By early September, my boss said, "This is your last run."

My emotions and spirit rose again. Before I knew it, I hopped out of the truck and bought a plane ticket for China or some other part of the world.

While you're working and making all that money, it's easy to slip and start buying things. Avoid that trap! Everything other than living expenses goes into the bank. Keep your eyes on the prize.

KEY POINTS FROM THIS CHAPTER

1. Jobs that make the most money.
2. Married person jobs.
3. Jobs for white collar.
4. Jobs for blue collar.
5. Keeping your eyes on the prize by saving money.
6. Marketing companies and residual income.
7. How to explore Antarctica.

Chapter 14—Raging and terrifying stretch of water in the Grand Canyon

"*Some of the days I have spent alone in the depths of the wilderness have shown me that immortal life beyond the grave is not essential for perfect happiness.*" *John Muir*

Dawn broke with a cool breeze over our camp. The sun, never visible for hours into the morning, lit up the high rock towers above us. A few yards from my tent on the beach, the waves slapped at the rafts lined up and roped together. I'm sitting here thinking about the thrill of Lava Falls.

It's the big one. It's the one to give the most excitement and the most danger. We humans are so capricious. We demand security and safety. Then, we run out into the wilderness seeking danger. We seek ways of testing, yes, even killing ourselves. Every weekend around the country, men and women run out to hang from thin ropes on vertical cliffs. They fall to break their bones and some die. Others mount bucking Brahma bulls that gore and stomp them to death. Motorcyclists jump, race and crash into each other like ping pong balls in a lottery. Others bungee jump and sometimes, the cord breaks and they cease to exist. Some jump out of planes riding a snowboard.

Jack London said, "I'd rather be a blazing meteor across the sky than a comfortable sleepy planet. Better to live my days than to extend them without passion or meaning."

That's what I call the "Voluptuousness of Living." You charge into the teeth of life and you gulp, grab, wrestle, sing, scream and jump off a cliff or ride a bicycle across a continent. You make it a point to live each day with a sense of passion.

That's why Lava Falls thrills seasoned rafters. It's their moment of glory or death.

Later, Strat and I got into a conversation by the river. He talked about his job as a wood craftsman. He struggled for money but his life was his own.

"No stress from above, or below," he said referring to no boss or employees.

Hollywood (my friend Gary) walked up.

"Hollywood had the same thing, but then he got married," Strat said with a sly smile.

"Yeah, I was newly retired and said to myself…hum, no more stress from the top, none from the bottom…guess I'll get married," Gary mused.

We laughed.

Brenda called out for breakfast.

Wocnis walked up to Badger with a cut in his left index finger. He had nearly sliced it off. Rick would have to row Lava Falls.

"I'll pray for both of you," Steve said.

We felt terrible that Wocnis cut himself so badly that he couldn't oar the boat. But secretly, I knew Rick yearned to row that rapid. He would get to captain the biggest, scariest rapid on the river. He showed his eagerness, too, like a true adventurer. He wanted to try the unknown. He purposely got out there on the edge of the cliff to peer over and crawl back. He inspected what was there, discovered not only the treasure, but discovered himself, tested himself and enjoyed himself. It's what took him to the top of Mount Rainier, Kilimanjaro and the tests he faced on the Zambezi. To top it off, he flames into life with a heck of a lot of laughter. Not even being a dish fairy could stop his tenacity in the face of deadly danger. He became a true river rat. His mother would be proud.

Wendell Barry said, "And the world cannot be discovered by a journey of miles, no matter how long, but only by a spiritual journey, a journey of one inch, very arduous and humbling and joyful, by which we arrive at the ground at our feet, and learn to be at home."

On August 25, 1869, Powell wrote: "Great quantities of lava are seen on either side; and then we come to an abrupt drop-off. Just over the fall a cinder cone, or extinct volcano stands on the very brink of the canyon.

What a conflict of water and fire there must have been here. Just imagine a river of molten rock running down into a river of melted snow. What a seething and boiling of the waters; what clouds of steam rolled into the heavens."

In the late morning, we reached Lava Falls at mile marker 179. Everyone tied up river right and hiked to the rapid. We witnessed an unholy, raging and terrifying stretch of 900 feet of pure seething white-water fury. We could hardly hear one another's voices.

I ran down through the rocks to take up a photo point near the huge hole at the end of the tongue. A thousand caged and angry lions could not have competed with the deafening roar of white water. Exhilaration coursed through my body. This watery fury excited every cell in my body. However, death beckons for the foolish or unlucky on Lava Falls.

One by one, everyone returned to their rafts and prepared themselves.

Badger and Steve rowed into the holocaust first. Steve hollered as Badger worked the oars. They hit the first hole and the boat shot skyward. Steve looked like a hood ornament on a 57 Pontiac.

I snapped a picture. It was nothing but a water white-out and their raft crashing through it. Outrageous!

They careened into the next hole and slid by Cheese Grater Rock. It's called that name because if you didn't pull away from it fast enough, you would be instantly grated like cheese. Moments later, they dropped into the calmness of an eddy.

Next, Ivan and Brenda slid down the maw of the green glassy tongue of the devil. They got caught in some laterals, which pushed Brenda to work the front of the boat. At the hole, Ivan's raft plowed through the pillow at the top, but as he did, the boat slid to the right. The seething froth sucked him further to the right and he headed straight into Cheese Grater Rock. He hit it, too, dead on. Ivan reefed on the oars, but the slant of the water nearly tossed him out of the boat. Brenda stepped to the high side to keep the boat from flipping.

Ivan gained the oars and powered them enough to pull the boat back into the rapids. Seconds later, they escaped.

Everyone cheered. Scary and even more thrilling!

I jumped up with adrenaline shooting through my body. I ran back to where Gary had streamlined his raft. He stashed all gear including the ammo boxes. I folded and secured the chairs. We cinched our helmets.

Where Hance Rapid scared me more than excited me, Lava excited and scared me to a fever pitch. If we lived, we lived. And if we died, well, we died.

"Let's do it," I said to Gary.

We drifted out behind Rick and Wocnis.

Behind us, Sally and Strat eased into the river. I detected a mischievous look on Sally's face—as if she dared the river to give her a wild ride—and confident that she would come out on top. She had the look of an 18-year old girl's excitement, encased in the wisdom of a woman of the world.

"Have a great run," Strat said.

"You the same," Gary said.

In the blink of an eye, Captain Rick positioned his boat near the big rock, swept past it into the left lateral and missed the big hole. He rowed with intelligence, but the kid in him screamed with pleasure. The boat, with Wocnis in front and holding his throbbing finger in the air, smashed through the waves, but headed too far to the right. They headed toward Cheese Grater Rock to seemingly be devoured and turned into taco condiment. But, at the last second, Rick pulled hard on the oars to bring the boat off to the left, but not enough to stop it from kissing Cheese Grater Rock. Whereby, Wocnis, in a moment of white-water delirium, stuck his hand out and touched Cheese Grater Rock in defiance.

The last we saw them, the boat fell over a huge wall of white and vanished down river.

"Rick made it." I yelled back at Gary as we too swept into the green stillness of the Lava Falls tongue.

Black lava comes up from hell and from the roar before us, it felt like we were being swallowed back into the devil's dungeon. But the dungeon was not fire and flame, but a white hot swirling tornado of screaming froth and boiling maelstrom. Nature at its best!

Into it we plunged.

Gary eased us into the middle and swung the River Slug into the first hole. I held on to both straps and pressed my feet onto the front air bladder of the raft.

Down, down, down until we crashed into the dead end at the bottom of the hole. The front end buckled my knees back at me like shock absorbers. The raft regained itself and began the climb out of the hole.

I held my breath.

At the top of the skyscraper of water, the river decided to throw a

40-gallon bucket of water into my face. I recoiled into the raft seat and clung to my straps. It felt like I was on the Andrea Gail in "The Perfect Storm."

Icy cold!

"YeeeeeeHaaaaaaa," I screamed.

We crashed through a world of roaring, screaming white water rage that swirled in every direction and carried us toward Cheese Grater Rock. Gary pulled on the oars until he got us away from the boulder. But his actions plunged us into three more skyscraper waves.

We smashed into them like a demolition derby and still came out the other side in one piece. I pulled the bucket out as 12 inches of water surrounded my feet.

"I'm bailing," I yelled. "Great job, Gary. You are the man."

Strat and Sally followed us into that wild mouse ride. I saw Sally ride the front end of the raft and she too, took that wall of white water and busted into it like Annie Oakley doing trick-shooting from her horse.

There wasn't a dry inch of skin on her body, but there was a Grand Canyon-wide-smile on her face.

We put in on a sandbar to celebrate with salmon, crackers, artichoke hearts, cookies and sodas for lunch. Lava Falls turned out to be a rite of passage—a portal into the club of river runners.

Everyone applauded each other's moment.

For me, I had faced my fear. Maybe not like Powell and his men faced fear—for theirs was a journey truly into the unknown. In fact, three of them left the adventure because of their fears.

But this was the 21st century. In my own way for my time, I looked the monster in the face and decided to go for it. I think every person in this life—at least those of us fortunate enough not to be starving to death in a country or culture that suffocates the human spirit—moves forward on an evolutionary trek. None of us knows what's going to happen tomorrow. Tomorrow is not guaranteed to anyone.

Thus, we move into the future with a sense of adventure because that is our nature.

Lava Falls still roars like a thousand lions this very minute. Day after day, century after century and through the ages. For a moment in time, I ran that rapid and didn't die. I lived and the thrill of it will remain with me for the rest of my life.

KEY POINTS FROM THIS CHAPTER

1. Courage comes with practice.
2. Hang with people who possess courage to gain courage.
3. Jump in with both feet.
4. High risk creates high energy.

*C*hapter 15—*How to find other adventurers*

"Follow your bliss. If you do follow your bliss, you put yourself on a kind of track that has been there all the while waiting for you, and the life you ought to be living is the one you are living. When you can see that, you begin to meet people who are in the field of your bliss, and they open the doors to you. I say, follow your bliss and don't be afraid...and doors will open where you didn't know they were going to be. If you follow your bliss, doors will open for you that wouldn't have opened for anyone else." Joseph Campbell

During your youth, you will run into many friends that live on the wild and crazy side of life. They can't wait to go on an adventure. Everything fires them up. That's them and that's you. In high school, teens travel to the wild side. They take off on weekend trips in the car. They travel to new places.

While living in South Georgia as a high school kid, I took off in cars to camp on the beach in Florida. My brother and I scuba dived in clear springs and board-sailed in the ocean off Panama City Beach.

During our college years in Michigan, we canoed, sailed, camped and lived some pretty fun times. At some point, things changed for all of us as we had to make a living.

In your own life, you may notice that most folks gravitate toward jobs, marriage and kids. A normal job and marriage trajectory changes everything. Our adventure friends fall away and vanish over night. For years, I found it challenging to find guys to ride to Alaska with me. Finding a ski buddy proved frustrating.

That changed with the advent of the Internet. You can find just about anybody to share any kind of adventure in the world. Additionally, you can search sport magazines to find partners for travel adventures.

WORLD ADVENTURE WEBSITES AND MAGAZINES

WWW.TUT.COM—This site provides you with great encouragement daily. I receive its "Notes from the Universe" every morning on my computer. I love them because every note sets my mind toward a happy day, adventure-filled life and expanded awareness.

Here is a note from the universe this site sent specifically to me: "Act with faith, Frosty. Prepare the way for your inevitable success. To the degree you can, behave as if your dreams have already come true, as if you already owned a bestselling book and speak on adventure, as if later today you were going to bicycle the boot of Italy. And you shall see the power you wield as the floodgates begin to tremble, the elements begin to conspire, people in your life begin to change, insights are summoned, comprehensions soar and clarity is born. Not to mention fierce, wild animals lying down when you pass by."

WWW.MEETUP.COM—Expanding into every city in the United States, you may join www.meetup.com in order to connect with folks whose style matches yours. Whether it's backpacking, horseback riding, mountain climbing, windsurfing, hiking, bicycling, rafting, camping, bird watching, falconry or photography—you will find a friend or group that shares your passions.

This site www.theadventureblog.blogspot.com connects you with adventurers around the world. You may find ideas, friends and travel to your liking.

This site www.adventuresummit.blogspot.com puts you in touch with top mountaineering friends who love to climb mountains in summer and winter.

This site www.oars.com brings you people who love to raft rivers and connections that take you on the Colorado, Selway, Yampa, Green and dozens of other rivers all over the country.

This site www.canoekayak.com furnishes you a wealth of information about canoeing and kayaking all over the world.

This site www.adventurecycling.org offers tips, ideas, stories and everything you need to know about long distance bicycle touring. If you need to find a bicycle touring partner, you may list your advertisement for free in their "companions wanted" section of the magazine. It's a great read each month on national and worldwide bicycle travel.

This site www.adventureworldmagazineonline.com offers a wealth of races, events, communities and ideas for your adventure kit.

This site www.outsidemagazine.com offers great stories on the national and international aspects of world adventure.

Let's say you can't find a club in your town that might cater to your interests. You may have exhausted ideas from this book. You may start your own club. Write up an advertisement and send it to the local newspaper for a meeting of anyone interested in snowshoeing, canoeing, high-wheeler bicycling or any of a dozen endeavors. Initiate a www.meetup.com in your area.

KEY POINTS FROM THIS CHAPTER

1. How to find people who like what you like.
2. Internet connections to link up with fellow adventure types.
3. Make sure you obtain daily "Notes from the Universe" for inspiration.
4. Create your own club as a last resort.

Chapter 16—Flying with condors at 16,000 feet in the Andes

"Whatever course you decide upon, there is always someone to tell you that you are wrong. There are always difficulties arising which tempt you to believe that your critics are right. To map out a course of action and follow it to an end requires courage." Ralph Waldo Emerson

"If you ride your bike into South America, there's a good chance you will be killed," said a guy at my bicycle club meeting. "They have gangs down there and violence."

"Thanks for the tip," I said.

"You're going to be sorry man," he said.

"Venture little, live little," I said.

Two of my buddies and I planned on riding the entire length of South America from Caracas, Venezuela to Tierra del Fuego at the bottom of the world and then back up into Paraguay and through the Brazilian rain forests to Rio de Janeiro. Would we get killed? Possibly! Would we enjoy a remarkable adventure? Probably!

As planned, we took our trip.

After one year and more than seven thousand miles, we pedaled our bicycles into the airport at Rio de Janeiro. I still feature a picture on my adventure wall of us making a fist-toast while astride our bikes with the Amazon rainforest behind us.

"Far better it is to dare mighty things, to win glorious triumphs even though checkered by failure, than to rank with those poor spirits who neither enjoy nor suffer much because they live in the gray twilight that knows neither victory nor defeat." President Theodore Roosevelt

On this journey, we rode into La Paz, Bolivia at 12,500-feet in the middle of the magnificent Andes. We suffered a hard ride on corrugated gravel roads over 14,000-foot passes that caused our butts incredible discomfort.

In La Paz, we rode a bus up to the highest ski resort in the world, called Chacaltaya, at 17,785 feet. Riding the bus up to the resort proved a life-and-death matter and we weren't looking forward to the trip down because buses enjoyed reputations for their brakes failing.

But on that day, we rented skis and shared a day skiing beside 21,000-foot peaks. Just blew my mind that I skied at such an altitude.

That day remains with me for my lifetime.

Later that week, we pedaled out of La Paz in a driving rain storm.

"You know, this is what we came for," my friend Doug said. "This is the toughest riding of my life. What's even better is that I think it's going to get worse."

He talked about a little-known dirt track cutting through the Andes from La Paz, Bolivia to Arica, Chile. It's called the El Camino Highway. It's rough, tricky, sometimes treacherous and always challenging. Nearly 300 miles long, it starts out at 12,500 feet, rises to 15,500 feet and plummets to sea level. This dirt road crosses astounding Andean landscapes on its way to the Pacific Ocean. It's not for the faint of heart and not for those who need a sag wagon. This bicycle expedition offers untamed adventure. Few roads in South America equal this ride for raw beauty.

We knew the route from La Paz, Bolivia to Arica, Chile featured gravel and rocks. It included altitude changes, severe weather patterns and no medical facilities. Food and water contamination proved a valid concern. A breakdown could end the ride for any of us. We beefed up our bikes with 40-spoke rims and bought the best racks available. We packed rain and cold weather gear along with spare chains and derailleurs. We could not find out about food supplies, so we carried six days of provisions. That amounted to 90 to 100 pounds of gear on each bike.

La Paz, Bolivia, population one million, sits in a valley that resembles a huge football stadium sunk into a gigantic hole. The city drops 1,000 feet below the altiplano. (The altiplano: a treeless, high altitude plain of land in Bolivia that averages 12,000 feet.) A four-lane expressway winds along the edge until it drops to the metropolis at the bottom. Two cultures exist. Poverty inhabits the rim above the city, while order and relatively clean conditions prevail below. Dramatic snowcapped 21,000 foot peaks surround La Paz. On a clear day, beautiful panoramas startle a first-time visitor.

We spent four days in La Paz. Toilets didn't work and we filtered our water. Buildings suffered disrepair—not much different from any metropolitan city in the USA. Cars ran until they dropped dead in their tracks. Even then, owners resurrected them like a cat with nine lives, with wire and tape. They pushed them back onto the road until they died again—beyond any hope of a tenth life.

We pedaled out of the city. On a sunny summer day, cold air prevailed. The Bolivians live their lives in a crisp, thin-air environment. Evenings turn chilly with the setting sun. Native costumes reflect the need for warm clothing. We rode past women dressed in heavy wool dresses with multiple layers of sweaters topped off with black fedora hats. Out in the middle of nowhere, shepherds sat near flocks of sheep or llamas. Although they never initiated a greeting, they replied to ours. Their small children stared at us. One young boy began crying when we stopped to rest near him. His mother grabbed him into her arms for security. He had probably never seen touring mountain bikes. Or, people our size! My friend Doug stands 6'4". My other riding buddy, Bryan, found the entire episode interesting as to how people reacted to us.

Bolivian men dressed in heavy wool pants and shirts. They wore ragged jackets but rarely a hat. Their jet-black hair, smooth dark skin and dark eyes fit the quietness of their demeanor. Everyone we passed plowed rocky ground or harvested crops within stone-fenced fields. Cows pulled one furrow plows and wagons featured wooden axles and wheels.

We pedaled on smooth blacktop, but it changed 24 miles out of town. Before turning off the main highway at Viacha, we stopped at a small gas station-grocery shop to fill our tires, water bottles and packs. Our six days' worth of provisions included rice, lentils, bread rolls, pasta, vegetables, oatmeal and cans of tuna. By the time we prepared to leave, a small group had gathered around the bikes. They crowded in close and handled everything on the cycles. In order to keep an eye on the gear, we stacked the bicycles in tandem and left one person standing guard.

Heavily loaded, we pedaled to the edge of town and headed west. The fat tires on our mountain bikes dropped onto the dirt. From one way of riding to another. We faced new rules and different dangers. We morphed into a new riding technique to deal with the rocky road.

When we first hit the gravel, flat land made pedaling easy. That changed when the serpentine road wound upward toward distant peaks shrouded in the clouds. Ruts and large puddles riddled the road bed. At times, we picked our way through a minefield of holes. We forded two small streams the first hour. We faced tricky riding. Bryan got stuck in the mud at one river crossing. Doug crashed in some soft sand and looked like a freshly plowed-up mouse.

"That happened so quick I couldn't put my foot out," he said, a bit dazed.

"Good thing I wasn't too close behind you," Bryan added. "I almost ran over you."

"Let's do another hour of riding and call it a day," I said. "What do you say we pitch our tents by a stream?"

"Sounds good to me," Doug said.

We found a knoll near a river, but out of the constant wind that blew softly throughout the day. I set my tent facing the sunset. The sun backlit the clouds as I watched the drama from between the nylon flaps. The end of the day brings peace when the last bird calls out its song and the sky fades into twilight. After eating, I took a sponge bath and slid into my sleeping bag. It's a fact that bicyclists rarely suffer from insomnia. Not so at 12,000 feet! We felt the effects of high altitude sickness called "serouche" by the Bolivians. No matter what time we went to bed or how tired we were, we woke up out of a dead sleep at three every morning until we became acclimated.

We filtered our water from the stream the next day before cranking up the winding road. Erosion-scarred hills drained down to the highway. Dark tundra grass covered the earth along a river valley that we followed. No reference points of humanity existed.

Later in the afternoon, after completing a climb, we faced a wide valley with a thunderstorm advancing from the south. In the distance, white summits peeked out of storm clouds, then vanished into gray mist. Darkness swallowed the valley with rain sweeping across the sky. Jagged lightning bolts slashed the air. I stopped to wait for my friends.

"That lightning scares the daylights out of me," Bryan said, riding up.

"It doesn't thrill me too much either," I said. "What do you think Doug?"

"It's passing to the east, so we should be all right if we wait a half hour."

"Let's eat while we're waiting," Bryan said.

We munched on sandwiches and watched the storm move away from us with rain falling on the tundra for miles. Soon, it looked safe enough to ride through a gap in the clouds. We coasted into the valley. Three miles later, we pedaled down a muddy, twisting road that led to a wide river. Riding became impossible in the muck, so we got off to walk the bikes. In seconds, clay squeezed up into our fenders and brakes, freezing the wheels. By the time we reached the river, we dragged our bikes. We spent an hour washing the soggy clay out of our tires, chains and rims.

With each day's ride, the land grew harsher. The road was pitched and rutted before us. We forded a dozen streams, sometimes getting stuck in the middle. At times, the deep sand washed over our rims.

We worried about our food supply because we ate a lot pedaling up hill. We reached a village where a walled compound housed a military unit. Passport check! They were enthralled that anybody would ride bicycles on a road as grueling as the El Camino.

A colonel came out to shake our hands, along with a captain who was surprised at the gear on our bikes. Fifteen minutes later, they let us go. The town looked abandoned, with no one in the muddy streets, so we didn't have much hope for finding food. A few blocks later, we looked through the dark doors of a mud house to discover carrots, onions and potatoes. What a find! The shopkeeper carried fresh bread and cans of peaches. We cleaned him out.

On the outskirts of town, we rode up to a transportation fiasco. Two large trucks had nose-dived into five feet deep of mud near the shoreline of a 150-foot-wide river. Dozens of men shoveled dirt, but the trucks sank deeper. We realized that this was the only supply route from Bolivia to the seaport. They were so poor; they couldn't afford one bridge over a river that was 150 feet wide and over two feet deep. We carried our bikes across.

Miles later, we climbed up a canyon. It took four hours and some gut-busting leg work. We crossed five more streams. At the top, cathedral-shaped boulders offered a dramatic skyline relief, but nothing compared to the huge summit called Mount Sajama west of us. It loomed 21,500 feet into the sky. Deep canyons along the road dropped a thousand feet below us. For two hours, we pedaled as the peak rose higher in front of us. We dodged hundreds of mud puddles, gully washouts and a few dozen mini-lakes in the road. Onward the El Camino stretched, ever reaching out in front of us like a ribbon in the wind, appearing and vanishing with the rolling contour of the land.

Near sunset, black clouds moved across the mountains. Lightning cracked the clouds into flashing sections and thunder rolled down from the alpine heights. It swirled over us and roared into the valley off the eastern face of Mount Sajama. Doug and Bryan ducked into a culvert beside the road. The lightning flashed closer. We were unprotected.

"We better camp right here," I said, riding up. "We will be miserable in the rain. I can't see riding for another hour. Let's call it a day."

"What about being exposed on this flat ground to the lightning?" Bryan asked.

"Once it moves out of the mountains, we don't have that much chance of being struck," I answered. "Although it can strike anywhere it wants."

"Great!" Doug lamented. "Let's get the tents up before the rain hits."

We laid the bikes down in the dirt and pulled our packs off. We pitched the tents as rain swept toward us. Electricity charged the air. We pulled the gear into our tents just as sleet, then hail, pounded us. The wind tore at our tents. Rain pounded our tents like rocks. With the last rays of the sun lighting the summits, the storm rolled across the valley.

We awoke to a cold, overcast morning. A gray shroud entombed the mountains. Tundra dominated the terrain around us.

Climbing into the higher elevations, we followed the meandering road as it slipped between two huge peaks. Behind us, Mount Sajama dominated the sky. Ahead, a row of five 19,000-footers made their own bids for the most awesome award. One cone-shaped volcanic peak, Mount Payachatas at 20,000 feet, jutted into a brilliant blue sky. We pedaled through a corridor of giants. Each one stood four miles high.

At one river fording, we decided to take baths in the glacial runoff, which was relatively warm. When I say relatively, that means above freezing. After four days of being skuzzy and disgusting, no matter how cold it was, we took baths. There's nothing quite like bathing in an icy river. It's like filling your bathtub with ice cubes and jumping into it for ten minutes. It lets you know you're alive because every cell in your body is screaming, "Cold pain!" It hurts so much that you question why you do things like that to yourself.

We followed the El Camino into a wide valley. Llamas grazed in small herds. Traveling on my bike carried me back thousands of years to a place where time wasn't marked by clocks or schedules. It was either morning, afternoon, or night. No calendars marked the progression of the year to the few mountain people who lived in thatch-roofed mud huts scattered along the valley. Only the weather expressed the time of year. A sense of peace flowed out of the timelessness.

Late in the day, we again stripped the bikes to portage them across another river too deep for our axles. At the Bolivian border check, we dismounted and walked into the office for our passport stamp. The man was casual. I used to worry about those guys, with all the stories about border officials, but so far we hadn't had any problems. We walked out and headed over to a small cafe. We ordered rice, tomatoes, potatoes and onions. A half-hour later, the cook filled our orders. The cafe was a shack with a wood burning stove in the rear and a few tables out front.

We made our final assault over the pass at 15,500 feet to the border of Chile. Bigger rocks bedeviled us as we continued climbing up the mountain. We suffered constant jolting and lurching through the rocky minefield. Sometimes we couldn't react fast enough and would take a tumble. Spokes were another worry. Constant pounding could break them, or warp a rim. This road was tough on bike and rider alike. After two more hours of solid climbing, we reached a plateau. Everywhere, broken rock greeted us. There was no vegetation or animals except a black condor soaring overhead. Laboring up the incline, we felt the effects of 15,500-foot altitude when we had to stand on the pedals. We gasped for air when our bodies needed extra oxygen, but it wasn't there—not in abundance.

On our left and right, Mount Payachatas, Mount Quisiquisini and Mount Guayatre punctuated the sky. Each was over 19,000 feet. Even at our altitude, those mountains dominated the corridor of giants that we had been riding through. By the time we reached the pass, broken rock lay everywhere upon the land. Grapefruit-sized rocks made riding difficult. Ahead, Lake Chungara filled a valley at the foot of Mount Payachatas, which we had now circled to its far side. At the crest, we coasted downhill toward the border station. We bounced and bucked all the way.

We stopped at the Chilean border, where we had to register the bikes and get our visas stamped. Because of bureaucratic paper shuffling, we were forced to stay five hours at the border for a maximum of 15 minutes work. But the one thing you avoid doing with civil servants is get them upset. They can hold you up for days, so you just keep smiling through your anger. Around 6:00 p.m., we were stamped, sealed and delivered. By that time, it was freezing. As we thanked the guards, cursing under our breaths, we walked the bikes out into what was becoming a blizzard. They smiled and wished us luck. After holding us five hours, they didn't seem to think we should mind that they had cost us lots of wasted time. At that late part of the day, we faced frigid misery.

Nonetheless, we started out with snow swirling around us. We were told there was a cabin two miles up the road. As we pedaled our bikes into the storm, I stopped to take a picture of Bryan and Doug vanishing into the snow. After taking the first shot of them, I noticed some interesting ducks near the lakeshore. They were black, with non-webbed feet, white and yellow beaks and two raised eye sockets. When I looked around, a half-dozen different kinds of birds floated in the water near the shore. They included black and white seagulls, diving ducks, gray ducks with long curved necks and some geese—all living on a lake at 15,500feet.

The icy water alone would dissuade the heartiest fowl, but add a few blizzards, and it is a wonder they would live there. By the time I finished shooting, heavy snow limited my visibility to 30 yards. I was cold, shivering and getting wetter as I rode. My gloves were soaked. I kept pedaling along; figuring two miles could mean anything from one to ten. If that cabin didn't come into view soon, I was going to pitch my tent and jump into my sleeping bag to save myself from freezing to death.

The road worsened, which meant I suffered jolts in rapid succession. Keeping my bicycle vertical was a major consideration. I continued riding through the gray mist and snowflakes, hoping for a glimpse of the cabin. It was an amazing feeling to be so high in the sky that I was not only in the snowstorm; I was in the clouds that created the storm. On my right, the lake was barely visible. Quick glances showed many of the black ducks still lining the shore, tucking their heads back into their feathers to keep warm. With one glance toward the water, I couldn't believe my eyes.

"What in the heck is that bird doing at this altitude?" I said to myself. "No, it can't be. I must be losing it."

I thought I saw a pink flamingo standing near the shore. No way! Not at 15,500 feet! I must be suffering from hypothermia. Upon a second glance, I saw not one, but three pink flamingos. Tropical birds! Why would they be living at this altitude and in such inhospitable conditions? No matter how cold I was, I had to get a shot. I uncovered my camera and snapped two pictures.

A short time later, I spied the cabin marking the boundary of Parks Louca National. Bryan stood in the door. By then, a mantle of white covered the ground. I was numb from the cold. I cooked some hot soup and retired.

We jumped out of our sleeping bags at sunrise. The sun had melted the snow at the lower elevations. Outside the cabin, Mount Payachatas rose into a crystal blue sky on the other side of the lake. Its regal white robe reflected off the still waters of Lake Chungara. On the shoreline, the black ducks turned out to be Tagua Gigante. Morning shadows moved across Mount Payachatas as the sun rose higher. Along the green moss-covered shoreline, four pink flamingos danced in the water. They danced to stir up the water for their food. We watched the ritual.

As we squatted for pictures Bryan said, "You know, as mad as I was yesterday at those border guards, I have to thank them for what we're seeing this morning. This is incredible. When I saw those flamingos through the snow yesterday, I thought I was suffering from altitude sickness."

"Me, too," I said. "I thought I was seeing things but here they are."

An hour later, Bryan and Doug rode a mile ahead of me. I was still sick in my guts from some kind of bacteria I had picked up in Peru when we hiked to Macchu Picchu. I had suffered the Inca Two-Step for weeks.

As I struggled along, I looked up into the sky to see two black dots around 17,000 feet. I pedaled at 15,500 feet. Seconds later, to my amazement, two condors with twelve-foot wing spans glided 30 feet off my handlebars and looked over at me. They flabbergasted me so much, I could hardly speak. They were curious as they looked over at me.

"Good grief!" I exclaimed. "You guys are enormous...like a couple of 747 jumbo jets."

They didn't make a sound. I wondered if they thought I was a piece of meat or just invading their air space. My first thought was to get my camera out and take a picture, but to my dismay, I had taken the last picture of the roll at the border.

Looking back at the two birds, I knew I had made a huge mistake in not reloading the camera. About 60 seconds later, they both tipped their wings northward and caught an updraft.

They vanished! Minutes later, they were two black specks in the sky. But for me, they will remain 30 feet off my handlebars for the rest of my life. They inspired me to name my touring expedition bike—"Condor." He has taken me to great heights and has helped me fly with the condors in the Andes of South America.

Several hours later, with clouds closing around the higher elevations of Mount Payachatas, I caught up to Doug and Bryan on a rest break. They were astounded at my story and wished they had been with me.

The gravel road wound around the backside of the mountain. Once past the volcano, the road climbed again onto a rocky plateau. We reached a high point on the highway. It quickly descended into dark green tundra grasses. We rode through alpine terrain. The road carried us through valleys along braided streams. Ducks lived in some of the tundra ponds while vicunas, a wild skinny version of the llamas, grazed on distant hills. Kangaroo-like-rats hopped across the road. Down we rumbled, bouncing along the rocks and ruts in the road. The canyon we traveled into grew wider as the road followed mountain flanks and descended into a large open area where we could see for miles to the west. Distinct changes in the vegetation were apparent at the lower elevation. The road hugged the steep sides of the mountains like a slithering serpent. We rarely pedaled as the road dropped.

From our lofty perches in the high mountains, we plunged downward along hairpin turns. Soon, the peaks became higher and more pronounced as we dropped lower. The only traffic consisted of an occasional rodent scurrying across the road. Trees grew along the route, then cactus. An hour later and several thousand feet down, we made our way onto a flat plain that opened into a rock-strewn sand dune valley. Before us, no vegetation, no birds, no animals, not even a fly. We witnessed utter desolation that looked like a moonscape of tan, brown and red canyons. We picked our way along the dirt until we rode onto asphalt.

For 54 miles, we sailed along the snaking highway that led through desert dunes. Nothing lived out there.

The wheels spun fast and free. Smiles spread wide across our faces. At 30 miles, a second canyon joined ours, giving us a muddy river to follow. We pedaled through a world of white dunes and blue sky.

We rode our bikes into the driest region in the world, the Atacama Desert of Chile. A few hours later, we reached the outskirts of Arica with the Pacific crashing against sandy beaches. In one day, we had gone from blizzards, glaciers, pink flamingos and condors to the utter desolation of a desert, by dropping from 15,500 feet to sea level.

Few raw adventures remain on this crowded planet—the Motto Grasso Jungle of Brazil, Antarctica, the Australian Outback, perhaps the deepest reaches of Africa and the El Camino International Highway of Bolivia and Chile. It was a merciless road that carried us back through time, up into pure mountain majesty and allowed us a glimpse into nature's showcase. We earned this adventure with each crank of the pedals and the pitching of our tents at every desolate campsite. But the campsites became the ultimate experience when we set our front flaps looking into the face of a howling storm over Mount Sajama or woke up to a mantle of white—covering Mount Payachatas—garnished with pink flamingos.

This ride was what we came for. It was the worst. It was the toughest. It was the best.

KEY POINTS FROM THIS CHAPTER

1. The roughest adventure can bring you the most magical moments.
2. The rougher the adventure, the greater stories for your life.
3. Sometimes adventure is not so comfortable, yet it's still adventure.
4. You learn true grit by adversity.

SECTION II –FIVE CONCEPTS THAT FOCUS YOUR ENERGIES TOWARD SUCCESS

The points in this section contain concepts that create pathways for you to live and express your most positive self-image, hopes and desires.

Read these chapters several times to incorporate the concepts into your brain's hard drive. The more you read and the more you re-script your brain toward success in your endeavors, the sooner you will meet with achievement on all levels. This process does not happen overnight. It takes practice. With intention and effort, you will begin seeing these concepts take hold in your life day by day.

Chapter 17—Thoughts thicken into things; things become reality

"I will not die an unlived life. I will not live in fear of falling or catching fire. I choose to inhabit my days, to allow my living to open me, to make me less afraid, more accessible, to loosen my heart until it becomes a wing, a torch, a promise. I choose to risk my significance; to live so that which comes to me as seed goes to the next as blossom and that which comes to me as blossom, goes on as fruit." Dawna Markova

CONVICTIONS LEAD TO EXPERIENCES

As the Greek philosopher Aristotle said, "You must have an idea of something before you can bring it into form."

He might have said, "Thoughts thicken into things. Things become reality."

That means invisible ideas come to visible form.

Ask the inventor of the light bulb, Thomas A. Edison, about his ideas. He brought 100 ideas to form as inventions. What about the uncommon architecture of Frank Lloyd Wright? His buildings still elicit wonder. How about Bill Gates or Mark Zuckerman with their work in the computer realm as to software and Facebook? They started with an idea. How about science fiction writers with amazing stories of other worlds? You all know about Gene Roddenberry and ***Star Trek***. We have all flown around the universe with Jean-Luc Picard and his crew on the starship Enterprise. Before him, Captain James T. Kirk explored the galaxies.

Everything we enjoy today started with imagination. This universe is your creative realm. As a human being, you are the only species on the planet that can engineer creative thinking.

CONCEPTS FOR LIVING YOUR INTENTIONS

1ST Concept—Thoughts thicken into things

Your thoughts and ideas or choices, acted upon, become your new reality. While attending school, if you choose to attend class, participate in discussions, study hard and take the tests—your intelligence and comprehension of the world will grow. Not only will you earn top grades, you will advance your intellectual talents toward higher learning, athletics and personal improvement.

Your thoughts, which drive your actions, will make you an excellent employer or employee. However, if you choose to be late to work or goof-off on the job, you will become another kind of employer or employee and soon be out of business or unemployed. When you come to work on time, perform with excellence and exhibit your talents, you will experience trust, better pay and added opportunities. In other words, your thoughts on how you will conduct yourself—thicken into your actions—and will result in your becoming an excellent addition to any organization with all of its rewards.

On the other hand, if you exhibit lazy behavior, become chronically late, irresponsible and other poor choices, your thoughts will thicken into a lifestyle of your choosing. Life will treat you commensurately as to your thoughts.

Positive thoughts lead to positive actions

Let's say you and your buddies decided to go camping on the weekend. Your thoughts thickened into the idea of going camping. From there, you made preparations to pack the car, filled it with gas, brought food, consulted a map and finally, traveled to your destination. Your thoughts thickened into a camping trip that you fulfilled.

All human beings possess minds with choices. We think. We decide. We change. We desire. We sense. We feel. We understand. We choose. We dream. We chase. We touch. We hear. We see. We smell. We react. We perceive. We extrapolate.

With all those amazing attributes, we find ourselves in a giant ocean of choices, possibilities and entanglements. We may organize those choices as we direct our minds to personal success of our dreams or intentions.

We drive our lives forward by thinking positively. Watch out! Very quickly, people will notice a spring in your step, a smile on your face and an energy bubbling up from within your body, mind and spirit.

Essentially, you begin working with the "Law of Positive Energy Exchange." That means the more positive energy you express daily toward yourself and others, the more that energy and human responses reverberate back to you.

"Creative living means optimizing your environment. Enthusiastic, successful people realize that life is a game; the hand they've been dealt is their environment, the result is optimization and their edge is creativity. They understand that overcoming obstacles is the natural state of human existence and represents the challenge that keeps life exciting." Ed Scott

When you read books that interest you and watch instructional movies, you will see your thought patterns change. Over time, your actions will evolve. Your mind and body will respond in ways you couldn't have imagined in the past.

Once you engage creative thinking, your thoughts thicken into things, skills, adventures, relationships and just about anything you can imagine.

KEY POINTS FROM THIS CHAPTER

1. Re-script your brain to positive thinking.
2. Thoughts thicken into things; sporting events, camping trips, good grades.
3. Begin practicing positive thinking for positive outcomes.

*C*hapter 18—Blank space on a mountain

"Life is an opportunity, benefit from it. Life is beauty, admire it. Life is bliss, taste it. Life is a dream, realize it. Life is a challenge, meet it. Life is a duty, complete it. Life is a game, play it. Life is a promise, fulfill it. Life is sorrow, overcome it. Life is a song, sing it. Life is a struggle, accept it. Life is a tragedy, confront it. Life is an adventure, dare it. Life is luck, make it. Life is too precious, do not destroy it. Life is life, fight for it." Mother Teresa

Verdant green lodge pole pines blanket the Mount Holy Cross Wilderness region west of Denver, Colorado. A cobalt sky profiles rolling mountain tundra while gray rock peaks push against the universe. In the valleys, snow-fed sparkling rivers cascade over boulders, while wildlife munches, stalks or chirps its way through the dark forests too silent to be real. In that wilderness, the circle of life maintains a certain perfection known only to those who dare enter that wild kingdom.

Driving along a dusty mountain road, my friend Al and I crossed over a frisky river leading into a quiet canyon. We followed that river for a half-dozen miles before stopping at a trailhead.

"This is it," I said. "Turn into that spot and let's get moving before that sun sets any further."

"Beautiful flowers," Al said, pointing to a group of red flowers.

We hoisted the packs onto our backs and stepped onto the rocky trail. Ahead of us, aspens, pines and wildflowers sparkled in the late afternoon sunshine. The trail, filled with tree roots and gray rock, climbed steeply.

A sign read, "Welcome to Mount Holy Cross Wilderness." Up we sped on our determined path toward the Walden Pond of the Rockies. The trail cut through pines and then through trembling aspens. Soon, it sliced through a meadow filled with white, red, pink, yellow, purple and orange wildflowers. We walked waist deep through one cut of flowers and deep vegetation. Purple bell shaped flowers reached four feet, but didn't give off any scent. However, all the flowers together wafted a delightful perfume across our nostrils.

To our right, a large meadow exploded with yellow, white and red flowers. But of course, the trail climbed steeply through them. We labored, took a short break and watched the sky shift from sunlight to deep blue with golden clouds tinged by the setting sun.

"Need to get our butts in gear," I said. "The darkness will be hitting within 45 minutes."

"I'm with you," Al said, grabbing a last swig of his water bottle.

We climbed from 8,500 feet toward our 11,000-foot base camp. The trail steepened again, but with determined efforts we made great time as we raced the sunset to our destination. Up, up we climbed to a beautiful, almost magical white-water stream tumbling over rocks and trees in front of us. Its white music played through the evening air.

After crossing the stream, we headed along a ridge until we reached heavy rock formations and a last stand of thick aspen. Inside the aspen, four-foot-high white, pie-faced flowers covered the forest floor as if someone had thrown a thousand white Frisbees. Every once in awhile, a purple bloom shot up into the field of white flowers, but the aspen trunks dominated, while green grass outlined every part of the woods.

Still higher, we hiked into deep forest pines, big rocks and fallen trees. A few squirrels chattered at us as we passed by them. Overhead, a lazy hawk soared into the last gleaming rays of the sun. The sky turned radiant blue with silver-gold clouds skidding across the heavens on the final chapter of the day's story.

"I smell the lake," I said. "I think we might beat the darkness to Magic Lake."

"I've got my miner's lamp," Al said. "So, I'm good to go."

After 20 minutes, we stepped over several dead logs until, up ahead, the last rays of light reflected off the glass-like waters of Magic Lake. In front, the perfectly still surface mirrored the snowfields at 13,000 feet above the lake. Tall pines surrounded the lake and they reflected their silence upon the water.

We stepped into a grassy spot near the shoreline.

Al said, "You weren't kidding...this is amazing...so utterly beautiful."

"Yup," I said. "This place pulls my spirit to center."

We pitched the tents, unrolled the air mattresses and opened the sleeping bags.

A fire made the perfect ending to a perfect day. Soon, the flames licked the night air as a slim stream of smoke curled into the pine canopy and on up toward the stars, now popping out one by one.

Soon after, we cooked up a steaming hot pasta primavera. While we waited for our dinner, the night sounds dominated.

How does hot pasta primavera taste after a two hour 2,000 foot climb with 40 pound packs?

"Uhmm, good," Al sighed. "Man, this is the answer."

"Yup, well," I said. "Wait until you taste my raspberry crumble."

"Can't wait," Al said.

I cooked up the freeze-dried concoction and served it to Al after he finished his pasta.

"Talk about a perfect taste treat after a perfect day," he said.

"You see that 13er (13,000-foot peak) reflecting off the lake?" I said. "You'll need the calories to reach the summit tomorrow."

"I'm ready," Al said.

We hit the sack as the Big Dipper, Orion, North Star and a million other twinkling galaxies spanned the ink black of space above us.

The next morning Al unzipped his tent to see the still glass-smooth waters of Magic Lake.

"It doesn't get any better than this," he said.

I crawled out of my tent, "You got that right."

We gobbled oatmeal and apples for breakfast. Later, we tore down camp and hung our packs in the trees for protection from animals. We carried all our food with us plus water. We looked beyond the lake to the notched mountain peak in front of us.

"You game?" Al said.

"I'm with you, dude," I said.

We hiked into the woods. Not finding a trail, we blazed our own. It climbed steadily upward until we crossed a small creek loaded with flowers and green grass. From there, we found a stash of purple columbine flowers.

Breaking out of the woods, we climbed toward a ridge that led toward the rocky peak ahead of us. Once there, we found ourselves engulfed with tiny mountain tundra flowers on our way into a rock field. Big ones, 50 tons, small ones, 10 tons and many others at five pounds! We picked our way through the rocks, into some snow fields, and back onto the rock scree.

Along the way, more flowers, lichens, butterflies and bees. Also, spider webs between rocks! Talk about positive attitude and expectation!

With every break in the rock fields, we hit a grassy area with thousands of pink, yellow, purple, white and red tundra flowers. All of them smaller than the head of a pin! Just amazing!

Upward we climbed, from rock to rock. We rested, then returned to the climb. We drank water, then returned to the climb. Step by step, hour after hour, we hammered toward the top. Around noon, we reached the summit of the notched mountain at 13,271 feet into the sky.

"Some folks left a small jar with a pencil and paper to sign your name," Al said, handing me the jar.

"Can't imagine too many people up here," I said. "I'll be darned. Quite a few folks reached the top in July already."

We signed it and sat down on top of our world. Around us, snow-capped peaks dominated. Mt. Massive, Mt. Elbert, Mt. Capitol and the Gore Range with thousands of peaks poked their jagged summits toward a raging blue sky. We ate, drank and talked about the climb. We filled that blank space with a story that never would have been told unless we had packed into the wilderness.

John Muir said, "Thousands of tired, nerve-shaken, over-civilized people are beginning to find out that going to the mountains is going home; that wildness is a necessity; and that mountain parks and reservations are fountains of life."

Mountain climbers fill in the blank spaces of unappreciated flowers or blazing sunsets. We herald the rising sun full of expectations. On the climb up, a marmot stood up, looked at us and said, "Welcome to my world."

Later, a pika squeaked his language and scurried back into his hole. Above us, hawks soared on thermals for the pure joy of a day of flying. As climbers, we become part of the wildness of the wilderness. We step into the dream, the fantasy and the reality. We make a story where none existed other than the indolent apathy of the universe to our presence.

While summiting a mountain creates tremendous satisfaction, we must all come down from that peak. We must slip back into the mainstream of our lives.

Al and I moved back down through the rock fields, past the flowers, into the snow fields, past the tundra, into the woods, down the steep embankments and soon we reached Magic Lake.

"I'm so sweaty, I've got to jump in," I said.

"Here's the perfect spot," Al said.

I stripped and dove into the ice cold, snow-fed waters of Magic Lake.

"Yeeehaaa," I gasped. "Not too bad."

Around me, I saw two-pound trout swimming past. Blue Stellar jays watched from the trees. Squirrels chattered like machine guns. Dragonflies danced in the air.

Later, we slung the packs back onto our shoulders for the hike back down the mountain. With one last look back at Magic Lake, we headed into the wilderness.

At the bottom, a little weary and thoroughly filled with visual and spiritual joy, we looked back at the high peaks. We created a tale where none existed until we stepped into the wilderness.

As my dear friend John Muir said, "How deep our sleep last night in the mountain's heart, beneath the trees and stars, hushed by solemn-sounding waterfalls and many small soothing voices in sweet accord whispering peace. And our first pure mountain day, warm, calm, cloudless, how immeasurable it seems, how serenely wild. I can remember its beginning. Along the river, over the hills, in the ground, in the sky, spring work is going on with joyful enthusiasm, new life, new beauty, unfolding, unrolling in glorious exuberant extravagance, new birds in their nests, new winged creatures in the air, and new leaves, new flowers, spreading, shining, rejoicing everywhere."

KEY POINTS FROM THIS CHAPTER

1. Take a friend on a camping trip.
2. Drink in the beauty of the silence.
3. Relish every bite of every meal.
4. Bring your body in sync with nature by exploring the wilderness.

Chapter 19—Reality starts in your mind

"This is the beginning of a new day. You have been given this day to use as you will. You can waste it or use it for good. What you do today is important because you are exchanging a day of your life for it. When tomorrow comes, this day will be gone forever; in its place is something that you have left behind...let it be something good." Author unknown

2nd Concept—Reality starts in your mind

What you perceive through your senses gives you an idea of what exists out there in the world. What you see is what you get. You've heard that statement dozens of times from others.

Most humans think that reality is visible and that visible reality is the only reality. As we discussed in Chapter 17, ideas create new realities and ideas change reality. Our minds create ideas. In fact, all reality started with an idea.

Therefore, your reality stems from your thinking processes and how you see or understand the world. It's called a "worldview." It's thrust upon you by your culture and parents along with your life experiences. Have you ever noticed that successful people tend to come from successful parents?

Successful parents imprint their children with positive self-concepts via their actions and their words. Children of loving parents gain security, sense of self and a worldview that allows them to go forth like a crusading knight to do battle with life and expect to triumph.

However, as an inner-city teacher, I saw the exact opposite of positive self-concepts in the children I taught. Many inner-city kids find themselves hammered by negative self-concepts from their parents and other kids with the same programming. Why? Their parents instilled in them negative self-concepts on multiple levels—because their parents succumbed to the same parent scripting.

"You're dumb! You're ugly! You're useless!" Those statements have been repeated millions of times in many homes. Additionally, because of unfortunate food choices, many children suffer obesity, diabetes and poor self-image. With violence, drugs and other negative behaviors, many children find themselves in uphill battles as to education, personal wellbeing and future outlook.

I won't sugar-coat their reality. It's unfortunate.

Nonetheless, some kids, no matter what their background, carry the spark of life in them that allows them to triumph over enormous difficulties. Oprah Winfrey provides a positive example.

Yes, you have read about rich kids whose lives turned to broken shambles because of drugs, sex and rock n' roll. Hold it! I like rock n' roll and I turned out okay. You have read about super stars falling into despair. Many celebrities must enter drug rehab numerous times. You may have discovered that perfect marriages shatter in a blink. You will discover that life guarantees us nothing. Not happiness, not money, not love!

Life only allows us opportunities. Those opportunities may yield positives or negatives. It's how we handle them that counts. You may have heard, "In life, we're all dealt a hand to play from the same deck of cards. Good or bad; it's how we play that hand. It's our choice."

INTENTIONS, INTENTIONS, INTENTIONS

If you experienced a hard luck past as some folks call it, you may change that past by rewriting your immediate life. Is it difficult? It depends on your courage, your intentions and your will to overcome. Finally, it depends on your will to succeed at whatever level you expect. You can rewrite the poor scripts of your past into a newer opportunity-filled reality of your present. Everything stands in the here and now. Your life begins anew each day.

Assume or accept that your intention has already manifested. Whether you are taking a test, working on a project, sewing a dress or building a car, think in your mind that you have already succeeded. As you travel adventure highway, act and see that you raised your hand at the top of

Mount McKinley in Alaska or walked on the Great Wall of China or canoed the Mississippi River or skied a whole winter in Colorado or painted a stunning piece of art…anything that you intend as your passion to accomplish.

Your dreams become true via your intentions. Intentions move the world, move with the law, move with your thoughts and take you wherever you intend to go.

YOU MAKE YOUR REALITY BY YOUR THOUGHTS AND ACTIONS

Finally, your mind creates your reality, good or otherwise. For a powerful example, I once lived near a lady named Elizabeth who loved to complain. When she didn't like the heat, she said, "I hate these hot days, day after day."

When it rained, she said, "I hate rainy days. They are so gloomy, so dark and so depressing." When the winter arrived, she said, "I hate snow. I just hate it."

One afternoon, on a fine summer day, I stood out in her front yard talking with her as she complained about the coming winter.

"I dread the cold and snow," she said.

I responded, "Elizabeth, have you ever thought about moving to Florida where it's warm all year around?"

"Oh, the humidity and bugs down there would just kill me," she said. "I just can't take the heat let alone the people."

Her mind created her reality. No matter where she lived, misery followed her and the world was a negative place.

How can you handle where you live in a positive way? If it's sunny, hot and humid, you can still take your bicycle ride in the morning and a shower afterwards. When the winter snow storms arrive, you can trade your canoe, bicycle, hiking shoes or kayak for cross country or downhill skis.

"Whatever the weather, I enjoy myself," says my friend Bob.

Fortunately, if you're reading this book, you probably enjoy a much more positive self- concept. Nonetheless, I wanted you to see the difference. Why? As you travel around many parts of the world, you will witness some nasty and ugly aspects of humanity. At first, their reality will knock your socks off when you see people starving and children dying with flies crawling all over them. You will see harsh realities not imagined in the United States and other western countries. You will see living conditions more brutal than any pictures. Such sights will drive you to despair and even depression. However, you will find a way to buck-up your emotions and accept what you cannot change. If you are affected enough, you may join the Peace Corps and change the world for the better. Every person reacts differently to his or her world experiences.

You cannot change the world; however, you can change your sphere in the world to move it toward a more positive future.

By living your adventures, you will find yourself exploring creative avenues. Your limits keep extending until you feel limitless. Your view of the world and your reality begin to grow to greater dimensions.

Remember this concept. Reality starts in your mind. Your thoughts create your reality. Your positive choices make for a better life.

KEY POINTS FROM THIS CHAPTER

1. You create your reality via your perceptions.
2. Changing your perceptions takes practice.
3. Work on self-concepts that push your limits.
4. As you see yourself as a world adventurer, you become one.

Chapter 20—Bear scare, or, is my hair standing up for no reason?

"Your own words are the bricks and mortar of the dreams you want to realize. Your words are the greatest power you have. The words you choose and their use establish the life you experience." Sonia Croquette

Adventure is not always comfortable; however, it's still adventure. It's not always safe, either. Whatever it is, it beats a couch, remote control and the indolent TV any day of the week.

Our first canoe trip of the summer provided green trees, blushing flowers, small wild animals, waterfowl and the delights of paddling around islands, past geese, dragonflies and under blue skies.

When we dipped the canoe into the autumn waters of Shadow Mountain Lake, the first hint of fall flashed before us in golden leaves sprinkling the forest landscape. For whatever reason, most of the boats of summer ceased their noise on our September weekend.

We threw our gear into the canoe after unloading it at the dock. We tossed in sleeping bags, tent, air mattresses, food, water and more camping gear. Sandi jumped into the front while I slid into the rear seat. Once again, peaceful, still waters curled past as we dug our paddles into the placid waters of that high mountain lake. All around, lodge pole pines swept upward along the mountain flanks creating a green theme. However, reddish brown needles from beetle blight sobered us with millions of dying trees.

Nonetheless, as John Muir said, "This grand show is eternal. It is always sunrise somewhere; the dew is never all dried at once; a shower is forever falling, vapor is ever rising. Eternal sunrise, eternal sunset, eternal dawn and gloaming--on sea and continents and islands, each in its turn, as the round earth rolls."

Sandi and I pressed the paddles of the ancient canoe, which has carried trappers, Indians, Hawaiians, South Americans and, really, most people of many civilizations around the planet.

We headed toward our favorite spot to watch the Canada geese and the magnificent pelicans on the west side of the lake. We pressed our canoe past three islands. As usual, majestic osprey flew past us or watched us go by from their perches in tall dead trees. Mallard ducks and diving ducks paddled around the islands as we swept past. A few squirrels, on their own private islands, chattered at us as we neared the shoreline. Before us, white, purple and yellow mountain daisies greeted us with their own beckoning beauty.

All of it slow, quiet and eternal. Can't quite describe the speed of a canoe, however, it's one that gives a sense of spiritual serenity.

What do you do in that canoe while paddling around the lake? For sure, you soak up the sky, the sun, the birds and the view. You fall back into your natural, spiritual speed. You talk about something, nothing and everything.

A big pelican walked across the water before taking flight to put on an air show for us. Several Canada geese descended before skidding to a landing. Several turtles sunned themselves on dead logs sticking out of the water.

Near dusk, we paddled toward a private lagoon. We pushed through giant cattails, through a narrow canal and into our own quiet, magical pond in the wilderness. Tall pines surrounded us.

We pitched camp, set up our chairs, table and fire place. Sandi pulled the tent, sleeping bags and air mattresses out of the bags. We strapped on our miner's lamps and warm sweaters. We stood on a small spit of a clearing that was 30 yards long and 10 yards back from the water. We pitched the tent near the water. We pulled the canoe onto the land near the tent. Sandi broke out the vegetarian meal which tasted like it came from a five star New York restaurant. We cooked it up and served it with onion-flavored soft bagels.

"This tastes good," I said.

Sandi agreed, "I love this food."

"Look," I pointed. "Honkers flying overhead in a chevron formation."

"Beautiful," Sandi said.

Then gone! All turned quiet.

We ate our steaming dinners with a glass of wine in our new wilderness wine glasses.

Winston Abbott said, "Twilight is a time for sharing, a time for remembering, sharing the fragrance of the cooling earth, the shadows of the gathering dusk. Here our two worlds meet and pass, the frantic sounds of man grow dimmer as the light recedes, the unhurried rhythm of the other world swells in volume as the darkness deepens.

"It is not strange that discord has no place in the great symphony of sound, it is not strange that a sense of peace descends upon all living things as the things of substance lose their line and form in the softness of the dark."

The night air cooled. While sipping on freshly prepared hot chocolates, we looked up at the night sky to see the Big Dipper, North Star, Little Dipper, Orion and many other magical constellations. Nothing like sitting up at night to see the universe as the ceiling over your head. It allows you to see forever.

Sandi rolled over on the fat mattress.

"Good night," she said.

"Sleep tight," I said.

As usual, I dropped off to sleep like a rock. Around 2:00 a.m., I heard Sandi unzip the tent to take a bathroom break. Moments later, I heard her unzip the tent and crawl back into her sleeping bag. I dropped off to sleep heaven.

"Harrumph! Harrumph!" a big sound from a big animal sounded not far from the tent.

I awoke with a rush of adrenaline that raced through my body like the cars at the Indy 500. Fear plowed through my mind like Hurricane Katrina. Whatever it was, it was big. I hadn't had that kind of fear since I faced a grizzly in Alaska in the 70s.

"Frosty," Sandi whispered.

"It sounds like a bear," I said.

"Where's the bear spray?" Sandi asked with her heart pounding out of her chest. She was scared to death. I wasn't too far behind her in my own fear.

"It's in the plastic box in the vestibule," I whispered. "I forgot to put it in the loft in the tent…not smart."

"Get it," she said.

"Harrumph! Harrumph!" the sound wasn't 20 feet away and coming closer.

I unzipped the tent. I grabbed my miner's lamp. I jammed it on my head. I grabbed the bear spray. I shoved my feet into my boots. I didn't want to face a 350 pound black bear in my stocking feet.

"What are you going to do?" Sandi asked.

"I'm going to face the bear and spray him with a load of this stuff," I said. "If we're going to die, we might as well give him a fight. No sense letting him maul us in the tent."

I unzipped the nylon door, turned on my light, stood up and looked 360 degrees while pointing the bear spray with the beam of light. Not 30 yards away, in the brush, along the lakeside, two big eyes reflected my miner's lamp. He crashed through the brush making a lot of sounds breaking off branches of small trees.

"Good grief!" I said to Sandi. "It's big!"

"What is it?" she said.

"I can't tell," I said. "It's moving away probably 100 feet and going east from here."

Soon, I couldn't see its eyes as it vanished into the night.

"I think it's gone," I said as I stepped back into the tent.

"My heart is pounding out of my chest," Sandi said with fear in her voice. "I first heard it when I took my potty break. I raced back into the tent. I didn't want to wake you up because I didn't know what to do."

"As soon as I heard that first sound," I said, "that startled me out of a sound sleep. It's probably just a black bear making his night rounds. I think we're okay now because he's headed east away from us. Let's hit the sack."

"I'm too scared to sleep," Sandi said.

"Okay," I said, "stay up until you fall asleep."

I dozed off. Suddenly, at 3:00 a.m., that same "Harrumph, Harrumph" sound startled me out of my sleep. This time, the breaking of branches added to the fear I felt. The animal got closer and closer while it busted through the underbrush and trees.

"It's coming back," Sandi said, clutching my arm. "What are you going to do?"

"Get your shoes on and prepare to run like a deer," I said. "I'll take the bear spray and fight him off as best I can. Head toward the lights of some cabin near the lake."

I unzipped the tent and about wet my pants I was so scared. I stood up and looked in the direction of the sound. My miner's lamp lit up the bushes and trees and, there, not 60 feet away, two big eyes headed right toward me without stopping.

"Good grief, it's coming right at us," I said. "Get your shoes and get ready to run if it attacks."

I looked at it. It looked at me. Two big eyes reflected my miner's lamp. I stood there in the wilderness with my little can of bear spray and wondering if I was going to live through the night. All my years in the wilderness, and finally, a bear was about to eat me for a late-night snack. Where's my Lazy Boy lounger and remote? Where's my safe bedroom in suburbia? Why didn't we order a motel?

In it came, steadily, "Harrumph, Harrumph, Harrumph" as it broke down more branches and plowed through bushes. It was less than 40 feet away when it broke through the clearing. It loomed bigger and bigger, scarier and scarier until my light shined not only on its eyes, but its whole body came into view, all 1,500 pounds of its body. Because I was expecting an awful monster of a bear, my eyes couldn't believe what it was until my mind switched gears to the sight before me—a magnificent bull moose with a four-foot wide rack on his head.

"I'll be darned," I yelled to Sandi. "It's a vegetarian...we're saved."

"What?" she cried out. "It's a what...a vegetarian? What are you talking about?"

"It's a bull moose," I said. "He's a vegetarian. He won't eat us."

The big guy walked right by the tent not 15 feet away. He looked at me, I looked at him, and he kept on walking until he vanished into the darkness.

"Incredible!" I said. "What a magnificent beast. Sure happy it wasn't a bear. Let's go to sleep."

"Tell me again why we love camping," Sandi said. "I'm scared to death."

We fell back to sleep, or at least I fell asleep, while Sandi clutched at my sleeping bag and squirmed in closer than ever before.

Next morning, ducks flew overhead, geese honked across the water, mist rose from the lagoon where we had camped. I opened up the fly to see the steam rolling in circles off the water. A golden aspen bloomed across the way.

"Ah, great to be alive," I said. "Let's fix breakfast."

We cooked oatmeal, prepared hot chocolate and sliced a few bananas for condiments. Lovely breakfast watching the steam rise off the lake! A cacophony of squirrels, osprey, crow, robins, geese and ducks made for an amazing breakfast full of wilderness.

That day, the sun rose high in the sky. We paddled to our hearts' content around the beautiful waters of Shadow Mountain Lake. Later, we headed the bow of our canoe toward the eastern shore. Sandi wanted to hike the east side of the lake, so we tied up and took a four mile hike through the magic of the wilderness.

Later, as the day faded, we paddled southward toward our take-out. We didn't see a boat on the lake. Quiet! Serene! Lovely! What a gift for us to sail away on placid waters teeming with birds, fish and vegetarian wildlife. In our memories—delicious eating by starlight, night sounds, birds, a vegetarian moose on his night rounds and the very special joy we shared with the coming of autumn as we paddled our ancient craft upon the magical waters of a high mountain lake.

The summer no sweeter than ever,
The sunshiny woods all athrill;
The grayling aleap in the river,
The bighorn asleep on the hill.

The strong life that never knows harness;
The wilds where the caribou call;
The freshness, the freedom, the farness—
O God! How I'm stuck on it all. Robert Service

KEY POINTS FROM THIS CHAPTER

1. Life feels better at a slow, natural pace.
2. Nothing like getting the daylights scared out of you once in awhile.
3. Fear lets you know you're alive.
4. Traveling over water soothes your spirit.
5. Carry your bear spray everywhere in the wilderness.

Chapter 21—Engage your creative subconscious

"Invariably, when big dreams come true, and I mean BIG, there is a total metamorphosis of one's life. Their thoughts change, their words change, decisions are made differently, gratitude is tossed about like rice at a wedding, priorities are rearranged, and optimism soars.... Yeah, they're almost annoying. You could have guessed all that, huh? Would you have guessed that these changes, invariably, come before, not after, their dream's manifestation?" Mike Dooley

3rd Concept—Engage your creative subconscious

This concept operates on all thought and executes the will of your mind to bring your ideas to form.

You must engage the positive creative process of your subconscious mind. To put it clearly, you must, in your conscious mind, create an idea of what you intend. Once you complete that task, your subconscious mind works on the particulars.

For example: when an architect draws plans for a building, he writes his ideas down on papers, which are known as blueprints. He places those instructions into the hands of the work crews, which act as his subconscious. They build the house. His ideas manifest as a building, bridge or skyscraper. In other words, his conscious and subconscious activities come to form or reality.

In the early part of the last century, a farm kid had to fetch water by walking outside the house to a big hand pump that sat on top of a deep well. He or she brought a full pail of water and an empty pail to the pump. Why? If the farm kid expected to pump water, he or she had to use the full pail of water to prime the pump. The farm kid poured the pail into the pump to create the necessary suction and sealing of the parts to begin drawing water up the long pipe that was sunk 100 feet into the ground. Once primed, the farm kid filled both pails and walked back to the house.

In other words, the farm kid had the conscious idea to procure two buckets of water. The kid primed the pump (subconscious) to secure the final result of two pails of water, which is the final product or end result stage. Even in the 21st century, if you visit a park with a hand pump over a water well, you will have to pour water into the top of it to prime it before you can pump any water out of it.

If you are an artist, you may think of a fantastic painting one evening. Your conscious mind thinks of the theme of the painting. That night, your subconscious mind dreams up all the extras that will make that painting your grand work. Once you conceive of an idea, you must let your subconscious "prime" your brain to work on the idea to bring it to fruition. The next day, you bring it to form by painting the actual work of art.

The same process works for any kind of an adventure that you hope to bring to reality. You first consciously think of what it is that you intend to bring into form. As you sleep at night, your subconscious brain fills in all the blank spots. In the days ahead, you fulfill your conscious and subconscious work by taking action to bring the adventure to reality.

This tells you that nothing can be anything unless you first conceive the idea in your mind. Your thoughts become the activities of your life whether you choose to paint, write, play sports, compose music or any other life activity.

Always accept your own creative talents and abilities with no comparison to others. You captain your own boat. The key to your success is to live your life at your highest creative energy and enjoy every second of it. Your thoughts give you a ticket to the future of your life.

"Your thoughts and your thoughts alone will set you in motion," said author Mike Dooley. "Your thoughts will yield the inspiration, creativity and determination you need. Your thoughts will orchestrate the magic and inspire the universe. Your thoughts will carry you to the finish line if you just keep thinking them. Never give up! Never waiver! Never doubt! Aim high!"

KEY POINTS FROM THIS CHAPTER

1. Allow your creative subconscious to work for you.
2. Intentions drive everything followed with action.
3. What you think is what you get.

Chapter 22—Those who follow all the rules all the time, miss out on all the fun

"If you are alive, you have to flap your wings; squawk a little and make some noise. Let people know you are here. Let them know you're alive. You see—life is the very opposite of death. Get out there and live it." Mel Brooks

With silver hair, aqua blue eyes, handsome face and a lean frame, in his early sixties, Charlie epitomized a soft-spoken polar adventurer in Antarctica. He'd snuck into a few illegal escapades at McMurdo, but none were the wiser because he never allowed himself to be caught.

As I spoke with him this night before Christmas at the Coffee House, we discussed the three skydivers who had died jumping over the South Pole two weeks before. He too had made more than one thousand jumps.

"They couldn't tell the ground was coming up because everything was white," he said. "They were probably stunned at breathing minus 60 degree air and from the lack of oxygen at that altitude."

"There are a bunch of extremists doing crazy things around the globe," I said. "I was reading in Sara Wheeler's book (**Terra Incognito** about Antarctica) that someone on this base had climbed Mount Erebus by himself. He could have died at 13,400 feet in a snowstorm and no one would have ever found him.

At that moment, his eyes lit up and he smiled a smile that I'd only seen when someone I knew had gotten away with something. Looking further into his mischievous face, it dawned on me that I was looking into the eyes of a legend. Was I mistaken? I didn't think so.

"It was you, wasn't it?" I said.

"Let's just say Katharine Hepburn said it best," he said.

"What's that?"

"She who follows all the rules all the time misses out on all the fun," Charlie said.

"You could have died," I said.

"So what," he said.

He told me how he had commandeered a snowmobile on a Saturday night and drove it up to 8,000 feet above sea level to a glacier coming off 13,400-foot Mount Erebus. That smoking volcano's name means "The Gates of Hell." He slung a survival pack over his shoulders and headed up the mountain. It took him six hours until he could no longer carry the pack. He ditched it and spent two more hours climbing with his ice ax. Once at the top, he took pictures and sat on the edge. He looked down at the smoking caldron below. It took him an hour to get back to his pack and six hours to get down to the snowmobile. He drove back to the base and hit the sack 32 hours after he had begun and reported for work the next day. I sat on the barstool with my tongue hanging out like a starving dog eyeing a pork chop.

Before the evening had finished, he invited me to ski out to Castle Rock, a four hour round trip, on the following Sunday. While walking away from the Coffee House that night, it did not dawn on me what I was getting myself into.

Saturday before New Year's, I checked out cross-country ski gear. They didn't carry my size 11 shoe, so I had to settle for a well broken-in size 10 oxford that would give no support. I barely squeezed my feet into the boots. The skis were old and wax-less with three pins and no cables. I was not a happy man walking out of the recreation gear room.

Antarctica's weather, although rarely nice, could sneak up on a person like a cat on a mouse. Temperatures once dropped 65 degrees in 12 minutes. I knew the Ice Continent could be merciless. When I arrived in October, it had been minus 90 degrees Fahrenheit a few days before I got off the plane.

As to experience, I had climbed thirty 14,000-foot Colorado peaks and had enjoyed much winter mountaineering skiing from hut to hut for years back home. Those experiences prepared me for the coming trek. I gathered my SPF 50 block sunscreen, glasses, film, cameras, extra cold weather gear, ice ax, rope, first aid kid, survival gear, food and water.

After a quick breakfast, Charlie met me at Derelict Junction in the middle of town. He carried a pack, boots and wilderness skis with cables. I slung my skis over my shoulders and walked up the volcanic black, rocky road out of town.

"Shouldn't we check in and grab a radio?" I said.

"Nope," he said, stone-faced. "We don't want those safety folks to get in a tizzy if we don't get back at our estimated time. By not checking in, we won't have to worry about it."

"Won't we get in trouble?" I said.

"It's Sunday and nobody cares," Charlie said.

As we climbed higher, we saw Mac Town's metal roofed buildings. It resembled a dreary mining town more than ever. A battleship-gray sky promised to break up as the day wore on. I made a note that it had been daylight for three months. Since it was January 1st, we wouldn't see a sunset for another eight weeks.

Like a snake, the road curled around a large hill that led toward distant snowfields. With each step, our elevation carried us higher above McMurdo Sound. To the north, glistening glaciers poured their ancient ice into the frozen ice pack and Mount Discovery jutted into a silver-blue sky. Once into the snowfields, we continued packing our skis until we saw a line of flags up ahead.

Red and orange storm flags stood every twenty feet to mark the trail. In a raging polar storm with 125 mile per hour winds, a person would be lucky to see 20 feet. The rules read to stay on that trail at all times—not only for safety, but because Search and Rescue teams hated breaking away from their beer parties to find frozen bodies in snow banks. Black flags meant imminent danger of crevasses swallowing a skier.

From where we snapped on our bindings, a long line of flags led up the mountain and over a ridge.

"I've heard people have died on Castle Rock," I said.

"Sure have," he said.

"How long will it take us on skis?" I asked.

"It's about two hours away," Charlie said.

"Let's get going," I said, adjusting my pack. "These shoes are a bit tight so I had to use thin socks to put them on."

"Hope the weather holds," he said. "Looks like it's going to be a nice day."

"Looks like it'll be fine to me, too."

The temperature hit minus five degrees Fahrenheit on that summer day with no wind. We skied along the flags until we passed a round red hut known as an apple (also tomato). That survival hut awaited anyone hiking out to Castle Rock who got caught in bad weather.

After an hour and a half, we crested a ridge. All around us, aspirin-white snowfields spread for as far as we could see. Antarctic veterans said, "One inch of powder, two miles of base." In some places, the ice thickened to three miles thick.

Up ahead, out of nowhere loomed a huge black mass of rock. I headed toward it following the flags. Several skiers lumbered ahead of us. As I headed up the trail, Charlie cut left and headed off toward the Sound's pack ice about a mile away. The snowfield dropped and he carved some turns with great skill.

"Follow me," he yelled back.

At that moment, a gut feeling wrenched up in my stomach telling me I was doing something regrettable. I could lose my job, get thrown off the continent, lose my work bonus and maybe, lose my life. Getting killed would really upset my mother. Gazing skyward, I watched for telltale signs of any storms. Luckily, the cirrus clouds streaked the cobalt sky with not a storm front in sight for a hundred miles to the horizon. Charlie's body grew smaller in the distance.

That's when I thought about Victim #1 and Victim #2 stuck in that crevasse until they froze to death. Their story was in the information pamphlet they gave us at orientation. The Search and Rescue team tried to pull them out to no avail. Their screams died in the night with their passing. I stood there for a moment. It was one of those times where you make a decision from your gut and not from your mind. You're pulled onward toward life by life. Even if life could get you killed, you must make a choice.

"Gees," I sighed. "Wonder what Katharine Hepburn would say to this deal?"

I took a deep breath. "I know what she would do," I muttered to myself.

Looking back, no one followed me. I couldn't see anyone up ahead in the ski tracks along the flag route. Another deep breath. Quick as a cat burglar, I cut left off the trail and dug my poles into the snow. I felt like Jesse James when he robbed his first train—queasy, heart pounding and that ill gut sensation knowing I was about to do something wrong.

Soon, I caught up with him as we crossed over a volcanic rock strewn field that seemed like we were skiing over the speckled coats of 101 Dalmatians. We dodged through the rocks until we reached a chute.

"Be careful on the way down," Charlie said. "It tightens up at the end where it meets the sea ice."

The chute snaked downward between large volcanic rock piles erupting through the snow like the stone sentinels on Eastern Island. Below, the river of snow worked its way toward a small opening into McMurdo Sound. Charlie patiently waited for me at the shoreline. I fell twice before making it down and my feet were feeling the pressure of the boots.

"Looks like we're in for a good day...must be near 10 degrees," he said when I skied up. "Sure gives us a nice view."

Across the sound, the Royal Society Range jutted into an azure sky. They resembled the mountains in Banff National Park, Canada, except for being pure white and not a tree in sight. For that matter, not one tree grew on the entire continent of 5,400,000 square miles. Off to our north, Mount Erebus broke through the clouds and a witch's brew steamed skyward from the caldron deep inside. It was Yellowstone all over again. To add to the drama of the sleeping giant, huge glaciers thrust their long, icy bodies down the slopes. Frozen rivers encased in frigid cold covered the terrain at the bottom of the world.

In front of us, speckled clouds gave a salt and pepper effect to the sea ice.

"You can't be too careful on this ice," Charlie warned as he probed the crystal cement, checking on its viability.

"I'm sticking like glue right behind you," I said.

A thick layer of snow covered the ice, which was cracked at angles and featured patterns resembling a spider web. In places, for us, it was as deadly—as if we were unsuspecting flies. Charlie pulled a 20-foot nylon rope from his pack.

"Just in case," he said. "We'll rope up if we come up on some wide cracks in the ice."

From there, we skied around a point (the land was to our right) with a large snow cornice, more than 120 feet high, hanging over the ice. It hovered over us. It was ominous and beautiful at the same time. As we turned the corner past the point, a new world opened before our eyes.

A 150-foot high ice cliff, tinged with indigo blue that would be the envy of Revlon's finest eye shadow, and more than a mile in the distance—had formed along the shoreline. The snow swept out over the cliff as if it were a gargantuan wave breaking on the beach. But in this scene, the wave broke toward the ocean and away from the land. The wave, frozen still, hovered 90 feet above the ground. Beneath the crest, facing the sun, thousands of icicles dripped into the snow. Ice stalagmites grew upward and in many places they met to form diamond columns with water streaming down their sides. The sun's radiation caused the melting. As we skied past, crystal columns from the icicles sparkled in red, blue, yellow and lavender. Every few seconds, layers of snow dropped down from under the wave crest like Frisbees falling from the sky.

"You better snap a few pictures," Charlie said. "It doesn't get much better than this."

After shooting a roll, I reloaded and we skied over a build-up of snow that led around another point. Right in front of our path, four Weddell seals snoozed near a crack in the ice. We skied along the crack until a seal resting in the water startled me. He looked at me, but quickly dove under the ice.

The four seals ahead of us perked their bodies and looked at us with their heads sideways, upside down and right side up. They sported blunt faces, long whiskers, golf ball-sized deep black eyes and brown fur mottled with white streaks on their bellies. They lay on their sides with one flipper hidden and the other skyward. Their two back feet looked more like a scuba diver's fins.

"What do you think they weigh?" I asked Charlie.

"They go three to four hundred pounds," he said.

At that point, one of them decided he wanted to move further onto the ice. He rolled over to his stomach and started undulating like an earth worm in the direction he wanted to go, but looked more like a slug-shaped waterbed splashing forward. Funniest thing I ever saw. Once he found the right spot, he rolled over on his side. He looked back at us and started chirping like a canary with short little chirps. Seconds later, he closed his eyes and fell asleep.

Not finding them any more interesting than forest slugs, we headed north along the ice cliffs. After a mile, we found ourselves facing a large three-foot crack in the ice. We followed it for awhile until it narrowed.

"Let's cross here," Charlie said. "We'd better rope up to be on the safe side."

"How are we gonna get back to the snowfield?" I asked. "Those cliffs are too vertical for us to climb."

"That ice wall will drop around that point ahead," he said, pointing a few miles away.

Charlie tied the rope around his wrist and I did the same. He stepped across with one ski and leaped to the other side. Just as I was crossing the crack, an Adelie penguin shot out of the water ten feet away from me. It surprised the daylights out of us. His buddy, like a piece of toast, popped up after him. As if we weren't there, both penguins kept moving along the ice either by waddling or dropping down on their bellies and pushing with their webbed feet. It looked like they were miniature black and white Mississippi River paddlewheel boats like Mark Twain used to captain.

"Where do you suppose they're going?" I asked.

"They've got full bellies and time on their hands," Charlie said. "They're probably out for a Sunday stroll just like us."

It reminded me of what John Muir wrote once, "How many hearts with warm red blood in them are beating under cover of the wilderness, and how many teeth and eyes are shining?! A multitude of animal people, intimately related to us, but about whose lives we know almost nothing are as busy about their own affairs as we are about ours."

We roped up three more times as we skied along the cliffs. Each section featured its own haunting beauty. Out there, two colors dominated: sky blue and aspirin-white snow. At times, indigo flavored the glacial ice and created delicate textures against the snows and the icicles glistened like clear uncut diamonds. There were no smells, sounds, trees, telephone poles, roads, lights, billboards, buildings or human references for thousands of miles in all directions. For the first time in my life, a mosquito or fly wasn't buzzing me. I was standing on ice that had known 150 mile-per-hour winds and minus 120-degree temperatures. At that frigid point, a glass of water thrown into the air, freezes before it hits the ground.

Antarctica was the last untamed, untouched place on earth. Yes, we had Plymouth Rock at McMurdo Station, but humanity cannot and was not meant to live in that brutal place. Its vast whiteness and eternal cold swallowed a man's imagination—like trying to figure out where the universe ends. At that moment, we were in the middle of it, and like the penguins, we were living and doing our thing with no thoughts other than what our vision provided us.

The afternoon wore on as we skied further and further away from Mac Town. Between the cliffs and sea ice, a three-foot swath of water opened where the tide broke the ice free from the warmer summer temperatures. In front, a Skua bird (a brown-white scavenger gull and the only one to fly that far south) glided along the crack on his dinner patrol.

When we arrived around the point where we should have been able to cross onto the snowfield, the cliffs had avalanched into the ice—buckling it. Broken snows formed cones, tubes, pyramids, blocks and flat shards poking in all directions. It looked like a scene from a six-year-old's playroom with tinker toys, erector sets, alphabet blocks and Legos scattered carelessly on the floor.

"That was our staircase off the ice," Charlie lamented.

"So what are we going to do?"

"Let's keep moving until the snowfield levels itself to the ice," he said.

"And if it doesn't?"

"We'll be forced to back track and I don't like to do that," he said.

"I'm with you."

We continued over the sea ice. In places, the snow was blown clean and we had to pole hard to make any speed. By that time, the small boots I wore crushed my feet. Because I hadn't skied in months, my elbows ached from the constant work. Around the next point, we spied a passage to the snowfields, but it was three miles away and looked like thirty.

We dug our poles into the pack ice and labored toward an almost visually mythical destination in the distance. The sky blended white with blue, which blurred into the ancient glacial ice. Ahead of us, a mosaic of drifting snows in the form of grandma's paisley curtains covered the glassy ice-rink surface. It was there in front of us, but I wouldn't bet my paycheck that it was real.

When we arrived hours later, the snow had swept down the mountain like a plush carpet spilling onto the ice. It was our ticket to the snowfields. We skied into some deep powder until we came to a gaping stop sign in the snow: a bottomless crevasse. We skied along it until we found a spot where we could safely cross. After ten minutes, we found a cornice that had swept over the crevasse, but there was a five to six foot gap we had to leap. We took our skis off and threw them to the other side of the crevasse. Charlie cut a step into the cornice with his ice ax. The tongue of the snow hung over the crevasse providing a dangerous diving board with no spring. I peered into the deep blue recess that quickly turned to black nothingness.

"Good grief," I said. "That's a long way down. I can't even tell where it ends."

"Could go five hundred feet and more," Charlie said. "We don't want to fall into it. No doubt, it would be our last fall into eternity."

"No kidding," I said, almost breathless thinking of the possibilities.

At that moment, it dawned on me why the rules, flags and protocol were so strictly enforced. What we were doing was about as close to the edge of living and dying as two men could get. Victim #1 and Victim #2 popped back into my thoughts. Those guys died ignoring the rules. My mind almost dove into a pool of fear without me being able to stop it. I pulled my fear back as best I could.

"That looks none too stable," I said.

Charlie cut a step into the cornice on our side of the gaping crack. It would be his launch point.

"We better rope up," Charlie said. "I'm lighter so I'll go first."

He tied the rope to his wrist and I wrapped it around my waist and sat back on my heels. I wasn't too keen on hauling a 160-pound man out of a deadly crevasse.

"Ready?" he asked.

"Whenever you are," I said.

In the blink of an eye, he stepped into the notch he had cut and kicked his body into the air. For a split second, I watched a man suspended over certain death, but with his momentum he made it to the other side and sprawled across the snow.

"Great!" I yelled, just about passing out with joy that he had made it.

"Let me dig my ax in and secure this line," Charlie said, stabbing his ax into the snow and tying the rope to it. "I'll need more help with your weight and you being downhill from me."

I threw my pack to the other side. Looking into that deep crevasse, a funny acid taste, (like the taste of bile after I have vomited), crept up my throat and bathed my tongue. I swallowed. My heart beat faster and a tinge of fear swept over my skin. Was this my punishment for breaking all the rules? In my mind, I asked Katharine Hepburn, "What happens when you're in the middle of breaking all the rules and having all this fun and you could die doing it? You got some answers here, lady?"

"Don't think about it," Charlie said. "Jump!"

With no more thinking needed as I was on the verge of being terrified out of my wits, I stepped into the notch with my right foot and kicked for all I was worth with my left foot. I soared into space over the bottomless crevasse. For that instant, my body ceased to feel that it was gliding over certain death. It moved quietly through the air. Below me, blue-black empty air—like the throat of the devil waiting to swallow me.

I hit the other side with a "Whompsh!"

I hugged the safety of the snowpack beneath me. Terra firma. Still breathing. Blood pumped wildly through my arteries. Yes, I lived.

"Just a bit exciting," Charlie said.

"No kidding," I said in relief to be on the other side.

While sitting up to catch my breath and let my body calm down, I looked into the awesome flank of Mount Erebus with its glacier strewn valleys and its fearsome smoking top hat. Across McMurdo Sound, mountains swept along the skyline and there we were: two tiny human beings out in the middle of nowhere, breaking all the rules so we wouldn't miss out on all the fun. I had to hand it to Katharine Hepburn and Charlie. They knew how to live because they weren't afraid to die.

There I sat on a glacier. But this one was at the bottom of the globe. It had been there for hundreds of thousands of years. It cared little that I was scurrying across it for but a blink of time. Muir wrote of these ice giants, "Glaciers, back in their cold solitudes, work apart from men, exerting their tremendous energies in silence and darkness. Outspread, spirit-like, they brood above the predestined landscapes, work on unwearied through immeasurable ages, until, in the fullness of time, the mountains and valleys are brought forth, these gentle crystal giants channel into basins and finally they drop into the deep arms of the sea where they shrink and vanish like summer clouds."

We snapped back into our skis and headed home. The hard pack swept upward a thousand feet to a ridge. The wind blew and my feet turned numb, which helped me with the pain. My elbows and shoulders hurt from the constant poling, but there was no 911-phone box to rescue me in that neck of the ice. I could have had a broken leg with frostbite eating me alive, but I would be responsible for getting myself back to camp. Although the sky was still silver-blue, a storm front could be moving across the other side of the ridge and we'd never make it back. Antarctica was brutal, unforgiving, and above all, indifferent. It didn't care whether we lived or died.

When E.G. Oates, a member of Robert Scott's polar team that raced to the South Pole in 1912, stepped outside for the last time, he said to his mates, "Don't worry about me...I'll be gone for quite some time." His frost-bitten feet were rigid and his fingers swollen. Life drained from his body as ice crystallized his flesh. Like the noble man he was, he faced his death with dignity along with a sense of resignation, yet with a power known only to great spirits.

Not wanting to die like that, I followed Charlie up that ridge. We pushed against stiffening winds and dropping temperatures. At the top, the wind blew harder, but the view stretched forever. To the south, we looked over the vast Ross Ice Shelf of glaciers hundreds of miles long. We stopped for pictures, a drink of water and the last of our food.

"How about another PB and J?" I asked.

"That'll do for me," Charlie said.

"For good measure I grabbed two chocolate chip cookies from the galley," I said.

"Nothing like a cookie to make the trip complete," he said, grinning.

"How far from home?" I asked.

"Maybe three hours."

"Let's get moving before I turn into an ice sculpture," I said.

We put on extra layers and headed toward Castle Rock. A cloud shrouded it from our view. Although I hurt and my toes were frozen, I felt a sense of accomplishment. With Charlie leading the way, I imagined him as Robert Scott or Ernest Shackleton. Then I realized that I, too, in my own way was a Shackleton. I put myself at risk to realize a quest on the mighty crystal continent of Antarctica.

As my skis slid across the powdered-sugar snow, I looked back at Mount Erebus and my tracks. Those tracks would soon vanish under the ceaseless blowing wind and no one would know I had been there.

But Charlie and I knew and we would remember.

KEY POINTS FROM THIS CHAPTER

1. Hang with the big dogs if you want to see how it's done.
2. Prepare yourself with smaller experiences to go after bigger ones.
3. Keep a cool head at all times.
4. Expect to succeed and maintain fitness to succeed.

Chapter 23—Believe it, see it, do it, live it

"A large volume of adventures may be grasped within this little span of life by individuals who interest their hearts in everything."
Sterne

4ᵗʰ Concept—Believe it and you will see it

Imagine it, intend it, believe it and work toward it. You will realize it. Creative law operates by your imagination and as you think.

You may read a slew of self-help books and a few may possess these concepts. Some may capture your attention better than this book. You might read them to receive a different angle on these concepts. That's a good idea. Another writer may turn your crank better to provide you other compelling metaphors in a more logical or even emotional manner. That's why you will find a library of books inside this volume that will give you a leg-up to realize your dreams.

Additionally, read books by adventurers in your area of interest. They expose themselves without shame, without hesitation and without guilt. Whatever got them onto their adventures also bubbles out in their writing or pictures or poetry. (Check Chapter 43 for 99 of the all-time greatest adventure books.)

The eminent photographer Ansel Adams said, "I respect everything changing and the solemn beauty of life and death. I believe man will obtain freedom of spirit from society, and therefore while man walks amidst the imminent beauty of objective bodies, he must possess the capacity of self-perfection and must observe and represent his world with full confidence."

In many ways, Adams saw what he photographed before he took the shot. He waited, he pondered and he fidgeted with his camera settings. He took good shots and poor shots. He gleaned his good shots from his average shots. He learned from the mediocre shots and made adjustments. With each outing into the wilderness, he fine-tuned his talents.

You do the same thing as you work toward your dreams. You fidget with your life to make it work so you can see the picture you want to live. You may make any number of mistakes as to choices, friends and work. As you make those mistakes, honor your learning process. Every failure broadens your mind and allows you to proceed by making better choices in the future.

Adams talked about an energy or creative process that moves through all of us. We can engage it for our own needs.

"My private glimpses of some ideal reality create a lasting mood that has often been recalled in some of my photographs," said Adams. "The subtle change of light across a waterfall moved me as did a singular vista of a far-off mountain under a leaden sky. Others might well have not responded at all. Deep resonances of spirit exist, giving us glimpses of a reality far beyond our general appreciation and knowledge. No matter how many stars we see in a clear mountain sky, we now know that they are but a minuscule fragment of the total population of suns and planets in the billions of galaxies out there in the incomprehensible void."

Adams shares with you his visions while working in the wilderness. You enjoy the same capabilities. Like him, engage them in your own ways for your own interests. You are working with the creative human spirit inside you. The more you practice creative thought, the more it works for you on multiple levels.

SEE IT, DO IT, LIVE IT

In my own life, while not knowing my path in my early years, I stepped forward with idealistic enthusiasm. I made a number of mistakes. You will, too. So what! Not a single great man or woman in history enjoyed a perfect life, perfect path or perfect approach.

The great thinker, artist and inventor Leonardo da Vinci incorporated the seven principles of a creative life: curiosity of the mind, demonstration of ideas, expression of the senses, willingness to embrace uncertainty, development of art, logic and imagination, cultivation of grace, fitness and poise, and finally, recognition and appreciation for the interconnectedness of all things and phenomena.

All of us struggle, stumble, tussle and move along the same path he walked. We each carry our own challenges.

The key is to believe in yourself. Believe in your project. Believe that you will succeed. Then, get your nose into the wind. Move toward your dream with eagerness and curiosity. Move away from the shore and safety. Move toward the unknown until it becomes known. The more you see it—the more you do it—the more you live it.

Pretty soon, you will understand and know the unknown territory. You will learn to feel at ease in it at all times.

"Tentative efforts lead to tentative outcomes. Therefore, give yourself fully to your endeavors. Decide to construct your character through excellent actions and determine to pay the price of a worthy goal. The trials you encounter will introduce you to your strengths. Remain steadfast and one day you will build something that endures; something worthy of your potential." Epictetus, Roman philosopher

How long does that take? It depends. However, the best way to get your feet wet stems from living small adventures. Later, you can move up to bigger adventures.

1. Create weekend adventures.
2. Create week-long adventures.
3. Create two-week adventures.
4. Create a summer adventure.
5. As you create your smaller adventures, they will prepare you for your longer adventures and you will gain confidence to expand your horizons.
6. Please note that this process works for anyone who wants to play the piano, paint a picture, sculpt, draw, sing, dance or seek other life activities. You begin with baby steps until you are ready to advance.

For example: join a mountain club and climb a mountain with someone who will show you the ropes. Go camping with someone who knows the rules of the wilderness. If you want to learn windsurfing, you need instruction. If you don't take instruction, you will keep falling with no idea of how to correct your deficiencies. That applies to snowboarding, rock climbing or any sport as well as any creative process that requires a learning curve.

CREATIVE PROCESS CANNOT ACT ON A HOPE, WANT OR WISH

Creative process requires expectation and action.

You may have heard your friends lament, "I wish I had good grades...I wish I had a million dollars so I could live a great life...I wish I was smarter." Others have said, "I want a new car...I want to make the team...I hope to get a new bike...I hope the world stops being unfair."

Here's the kicker. The creative energy of the universe (creative realm) cannot act on a wish, want or hope. It can only act on intentions and actions. What happens with wishing, wanting and hoping? If you live in that realm, you become a victim, prey or quarry for life's vagaries.

When you switch gears, much like Ansel Adams talked about; you kick your mind into action, which in turn requires activities to ensure your intentions move toward fruition.

KEY POINTS FROM THIS CHAPTER

1. Intend your dream, see it, believe it, live it.
2. The universe also known as the creative realm cannot act on a wish, hope or want.
3. Make no comparisons of yourself with anyone; a certain energy thief.
4. Strive to make intentions reality in your life.

*C*hapter 24—*Teeth, claws and antlers*

"The hard life that never knows harness; The wilds where the caribou call; The freshness, the freedom, the farness--Oh God! How I'm stuck on it all." Robert Service

Ramshackle buildings with wooden boardwalks lined the streets as we pedaled into Dawson City, Yukon on a hot day in July. Stoop-shouldered, craggy-faced prospectors shuffled along in the dirt without giving us a nod. Bowie knives hung from their belts and they gripped rifles in their hands as easily as a Chicago businessman carries a briefcase. Their faces reflected a rough life that hadn't changed since the days of Jack London.

I am an optimist, but I didn't know how anyone could live in that place, where the winter winds bit like driven nails.

My brother Rex purchased a gold pan and caught up with me at the Klondike Grocery Store. I crammed apples into my panniers.

"Ready to camp?" Rex asked. "I'm itching to hit the stream for some gold panning."

"The storekeeper said we could find a place a mile from here on a tributary of the Yukon," I said.

"This buckaroo is gonna make the big strike," Rex said, joking.

We pedaled our fully-loaded mountain bikes out of town to an abandoned path overgrown with bushes. The rutted trail led through deep woods, and several times we got off the bikes to hoist them over fallen trees. We followed the path down a ravine until it stopped at a wide, shallow stream. A sandbar stood in the middle of the slowly gliding current. It was one of those places where tranquility kept a vigil and only the whisper of the wind broke the silence.

"This is the perfect place to start the next Klondike gold rush," Rex said, slapping his pan. "You want first chance?"

"Go ahead," I said. "I'll set up the tents."

Rex took off his shoes and waded into the water. I pulled the panniers from our bikes, pitched the tents and had camp set up in 30 minutes. After starting a fire with deadwood, I boiled some water for tea.

With a steaming cup in one hand, I grabbed my journal and walked down to the river's edge. Sitting against a rock with my socks off, I wasn't paying much attention to my gold panning brother. Overhead, white clouds skidded across the sky and a cool wind whispered through the pine trees. This was a serene place--the dark soil, the rocks, and a pine-scented forest--and beyond, a river that crawled between sandy banks like escaped quicksilver.

"You rich yet?" I yelled at Rex as he dumped another pan-full of muddy water.

"Any minute now," he said, standing up to rub his back. "This gold panning is hard on my back."

Rex continued his task while I wrote a few lines in my journal. That journal had been a part of my bicycling travels for 20 years, but every time I began writing, I still wondered what to write. That shatteringly beautiful waterfall we had seen last night, turned to molten gold by the sun? The slow dark glide of that bald eagle on his dinner patrol? The salmon lashing upstream toward birth and death?

So absorbed was I in my thoughts, I only partially heard the harsh crackling of nearby brush and breaking limbs. But what happened next brought me leaping to my feet and turned my blood to ice. The journal fell from my hands.

Terrifying roars and bellows filled the air, and sounds of snapping limbs echoed across the river. Whatever it was, it was big—and the battle was being joined.

"What the heck was that?" Rex shouted, dropping his pan and scrambling out of the water.

"I'm not sure," I said, as he stopped beside me, breathing hard.

"I don't think we should wait around," Rex said—and at that moment a bull moose stumbled into view, head erect and blood blackening on his torn shoulder. He lowered his rack, as an enormous grizzly rushed at him and swatted the antlers aside. The grizzly charged with his thick neck lowered and extended, and his jaws opened wide as he lunged for the moose's throat. Somehow, the moose avoided the grizzly's teeth, and dug in his haunches so that the muscles in his legs were cable-tight. He countered with a lunge at the bear's chest. Horn ripped through his brown hide, hit bone—and the grizzly roared, but the killing lust was on him.

In he charged again, half-rearing on his hind legs, both paws swatting at the moose like a boxer, staggering the animal. The moose bellowed, gave ground, but came back again--and suddenly both animals reared, hooves to fangs, one desperate to live, the other intent on killing.

"Let's get out of here," I whispered. "Leave the gear. We'll get it later. This is not time to worry about the small stuff."

Rex needed no urging, and although every nerve in my body, and probably Rex's, screamed at me to run, I forced myself to walk my bike into the tree line. There, back in the shadows, we watched the brutal drama unfolding on nature's stage.

The moose suffered the worst of things, yet he battled gallantly, keeping his antlered head low and catching the grizzly each time it charged. But the bear was the size of a VW Beetle, almost as heavy and as solid as the moose. He towered higher when he stood, so that he could strike downward with his razor sharp claws, ripping his prey's shoulders like a toreador lancing the forequarters of a bull to weaken it and make it lower its head for the matador's sword thrust.

A bull moose weighs a ton and a grizzly can reach 1,500 pounds. These two seemed evenly matched in size—which meant that the bear, with his four-inch claws and two-inch teeth, had an advantage. Barring some stupid move, like allowing his jugular to be pierced by an antler, the grizzly's victory was a certainty.

From our hidden vantage-point, looking out between the limbs of trees, we saw bright rivulets of blood running down the bear's chest. The moose was now a pitiful sight, staggering with weariness, backed into the shallows where the water was turning reddish brown, with a large piece of antler broken off by one mighty blow from the grizzly's paw. In came the bear again, roaring so fiercely it was almost a scream, and the exhausted moose bellowed back its defiance.

Now, however, the battle's balance had shifted. The bear's sharp claws ripped into the moose's ribs, laying them bare. Then the bear's teeth sank into the neck, and only by a supreme effort was the moose able to shake him off again.

I didn't want to watch any more, yet my fascinated eyes were ready for the final drama. After five minutes that seemed like hours, the bear made one last head-down charge—and sent the moose sprawling into the river. The moose made a final bellow, a last exhausted attempt to rise, but it was hopeless. The grizzly had him by the throat, and the moose thrashed erratically for a minute, then died.

"Oh," Rex whispered, gripping my arm.

The bear held his grip until the moose stopped quivering. Then, raising his massive anvil-shaped head, he let out a roar that shivered the forest air, and began feeding.

I felt as Rex did, as any human being would—it had been a frightening scene. Savage violence unleashed beside a beautiful stream in the wilderness. Yet no one had committed a crime. Life sustains life.

The grizzly, blood mixed with froth lathering his jaw, raised his head and looked right at us. Whether the wind had shifted or not, I was leaving.

"Come on," I whispered. "Let's get back to town, not that anyone there is going to believe what we saw."

In the morning, we rode back to find our gear still intact, but on the sandbar a partly devoured moose carcass was the only indication of the battle.

In silence, we folded the tents and packed our gear.

"I guess you're out a gold pan," I said.

"I don't care," Rex said. "Money can't buy what we saw yesterday."

We pedaled our way out of the woods. The gravel road wound through the mountains like a lazy serpent, bending and slithering its way along the Yukon River. We pedaled our bikes up a long grade to the Top of the World Highway. No telling what lay ahead. That's the way it's been for my bicycle and me—always the promise of a new adventure around the next bend.

KEY POINTS FROM THIS CHAPTER

1. While on an adventure, anything can happen.
2. In bear country, carry your bear spray.
3. Always use your safe camping techniques to give you the best chance of survival.
4. Sometimes, nature will scare the daylights out of you. Live it.
5. Sometimes, nature will show you her grandest sunsets. Enjoy them.

Chapter 25—The action ticket

"The sea is dangerous and its storms terrible, but these obstacles have never been sufficient reason to remain ashore. Unlike the mediocre, intrepid spirits seek victory over those things that seem impossible. It is with an iron will that they embark on the most daring of all endeavors. To meet the shadowy future without fear and conquer the unknown." Magellan

5ᵗʰ Concept —You must engage the action concept

We live in a causal universe. Advancement toward your dream(s) depends on ideas transformed into action. Once you create a plan, idea or image, creative energy works on it through you.

Bestselling author Dan Millman said that in order to enjoy ultimate success, "It takes effort over time."

You must kick into gear the "Action Concept." It may be an idea for an invention, trip, project, painting, cartoon, thesis or anything that excites you. Always remain true to your passions. At the same time, be open to ancillary activities and people who may add to your life adventure. Remember, too, that as you grow into your own adventure-filled life, you will mentor others who come into your sphere.

You must maintain a personal determination and persistence to see an effort through to the end.

"If I had to select one quality, one personal characteristic that I regard as being most highly correlated with success, whatever the field, I would pick the trait of persistence. The will to endure to the end, to get knocked down seventy times and get up off the floor saying, "Here comes number seventy-one." Richard Devos, successful businessman.

On my corkboard, a card reads, "The Idea Fairy may strike at any time. Make sure to be alert and write down her ideas, so she will visit often."

You probably remember years ago when some guy got the idea to manufacture rubber shoes with holes in them. He decided to manufacture them in a variety of colors. His main goal was to make them comfortable and reliable.

Naysayers said, "That idea is a crock!"

You got that right. But his idea became one of the largest selling summer shoes in the world. You will see countless people wearing colorful Crocs in the summer. They even sell fur-lined winter Crocs today. It all happened because of an idea. From the idea, he moved into action.

IDEAS MOVE THE WORLD—CLIMBING YOUR MOUNT EVEREST

George Mallory, believed to be the first man to climb Mount Everest, but who died on the descent said, "The first question which you will ask and which I must try to answer is this: what is the use of climbing Mount Everest? My answer must at once be: it is no use. There is not the slightest prospect of any gain whatsoever. Oh, we may learn a little about the behavior of the human body at high altitudes, and possibly medical men may turn our observation to some account for the purposes of aviation. But otherwise nothing will come of it. We shall not bring back a single bit of gold or silver, not a gem, nor any coal or iron. We shall not find a single foot of earth that can be planted with crops to raise food. It's no use. So, if you cannot understand that there is something in man which responds to the challenge of this mountain and goes out to meet it, that the struggle is the struggle of life itself upward and forever upward, then you won't see why we go. What we get from this adventure is just sheer joy. And joy is, after all, the end of life. We do not live to eat and make money. We eat and make money to be able to enjoy life. That is what life means and what life is for."

Let's look at regular people that lived or are living incredible adventures by taking action. Once they latched onto an idea, they carried through with the action concept.

Charles Lindbergh started with flying airplanes. Soon, as a barnstormer, he flew all over the country. Later, he flew the mail. Then, an idea struck him, "I will fly across the Atlantic Ocean."

The rest is history. He loved flying and he loved adventuring. After his historic flight, he barnstormed all over Mexico and South America in the Spirit of St. Louis. Visit the Smithsonian in Washington, DC, in the Air and Space Museum, to see stickers on the cowling of his plane from all the countries he explored.

Leonardo da Vinci, an exceptional adventurer, not only painted, he dissected cadavers to see how the human body worked. He invented flying machines, jet engine prototypes, weapons and a prototype for the bicycle. He excavated those ideas out of the fertile soil of his mind. He engaged the action concept.

Jack Hamilton, a police officer from Ohio, loves bicycling. On one of my rides across America, I met him riding his bike across the country. He told me how lucky I was to do it all in one trip because I enjoyed three months off to ride. Because he could only get two weeks off a year, he pedaled two weeks and then, returned home, but came back to the same spot where he left off the previous year and the next year to ride another two weeks. It took him six years to ride his bicycle across America. But, he can stand tall in any crowd with the knowledge that he bicycled across America. How? He worked his idea into smaller parts to create his final victory.

Amelia Earhart loved flying. On May 20, 1932, Amelia Earhart took off from Harbor Grace, Newfoundland, and landed the next day in Londonderry, Northern Ireland. She became the first woman to fly solo across the Atlantic.

"The most difficult thing is the decision to act; the rest is merely tenacity," said Earhart. "Please know I am quite aware of the hazards. I want to do it because I want to do it. Women must try to do things as men have tried. When they fail, their failure must be a challenge to other women."

Andrew Skurka skied, rafted and backpacked 4,600 miles across Alaska and the Yukon Territory in 2010. He stood his ground against charging grizzly bears and endless mosquitoes. He faced loneliness. Nonetheless, he pushed toward his ultimate destination. Was it easy? Try shouldering a 50 pound backpack for 4,600 miles to find out for yourself. In total, he has backpacked 30,000 miles through many of the world's most rugged backcountry and wilderness areas—the equivalent of traveling once around the planet at the equator. www.andrewskurka.com

In 2011, Anne Miltenberger of Boulder, Colorado, rowed her rowboat across the Atlantic Ocean. She competed in the Woodvale Challenge Atlantic Crossing, but her larger vision was to bring attention to the predicament of our oceans being polluted and fished to death by humanity. The enormity of her task boggles my mind. That's over 3,000 miles of monster ocean waves, treacherous storms, mind-numbing loneliness, physical challenges and the incredible expanse of the ocean. However, she rowed for the environment. She cares about this planet and she wants to make the world better for future generations. Her journey started with an idea. She put it into action. www.rowingfortheenvironment.com

Susan Butcher won the Alaska Iditarod dog sled race three years in a row against a mighty field of men. She suffered from dyslexia which dissuaded her from veterinary medicine. She took up dog sledding. After more experience, she decided to race in one of the toughest endurance races in the world. One thousand miles of cold, mountains, ice, harsh weather and danger confronted her, but she succeeded in her intentions. It all started with her passion for animals and an idea to race in the Iditarod. She engaged the action concept.

KEY POINTS FROM THIS CHAPTER

1. You must move on your plan by taking action.
2. Work to fulfill your idea with persistence.
3. Moving toward your "Mount Everest" takes determination.
4. Improve your plan by being open to new ideas that you write down.

*C*hapter 26—Face to face with a cobra

"The sublime and the ridiculous are so often nearly related, that it is difficult to class them separately. One step above the sublime makes the ridiculous, and one step above the ridiculous makes the sublime again." Thomas Paine

Mount Everest rises 29,035 feet into the sky over Nepal. Its Nepalese name Chumolungma means Earth Mother. For me, this culture rendered a dramatic change from any of my world experiences. Riding through the streets on my bicycle in Kathmandu, Bachtapu and Patan distressed my sense of balance. These cities teem with human misery beyond most westerners' comprehension. Even for those who have enough to eat, the squalid conditions of great numbers of people left me gasping for understanding.

Children with deformed bones and bodies looked up with pathetic eyes and uplifted hands for a few rupees from passersby. Trash and garbage lay everywhere in a profusion of chaos. Freshly killed chicken and water buffalo meat were presented to the public on wooden tables in the street, accompanied by a cloud of flies. In a short time, I had to swallow my sense of trying to understand this strange land, and accept it. Otherwise I would have been emotionally torn to pieces.

One of the good things in Kathmandu was the cheap price for lodging. My brother Howard and I stayed at the Four Star Hotel. We stayed a week, exploring the nooks and crannies of the city. Bright colors sprang from everywhere. Women's costumes brightened the market bazaar with reds, oranges, greens and yellows. Temples featured Buddha's eyes glaring at every person walking by. Vendors offered an array of fruits and vegetables we had never seen. Merchants displayed metal works, cloth and beads along the streets. Boys on tricycle taxis stared at us when we passed. The poverty overwhelmed us, but Howard pointed out that it wasn't any different than inner-city New York. He was right. Nearly every society has poignant forms of human misery.

We decided to ride to Pokara about 180 miles away. That city was the beginning of many major trekking routes into the Himalayan mountains of Nepal. The climb out of Kathmandu was a killer. Combine altitude with steep grades, and my lungs gasped for oxygen. My legs suffered, too.

The second day into the ride, we stopped along a river to watch a funeral (on the other side of the water) of a young Sherpa boy who had died from a fall. His family had placed him on top of a pile of sticks. He was bound in linen, except for his face, which was covered later. People walked by his body to pay their respects. His parents gave his belongings to relatives. They sang a song of celebration. No one seemed to be sad during the ceremony. Finally, they covered the boy's face before throwing more sticks on top of his body and lit a fire. It quickly consumed the corpse. After it was thoroughly burned, several men used poles to throw the remains into the river.

What we had seen was one of the most natural ways to dispose of the dead. The longer I stayed in Asia, the more I understood their customs. Those cultures may be thought of as the developing world, but they live in sublime connection with the nature. Their lives are basic to the earth and in balance with it. I felt a new kind of peacefulness in Nepal and a sense of present moment living that blended harmoniously with life.

Two days later, we rolled into Pokara. Around us, stunning mountain scenery with snow-covered peaks jutted into a clear blue sky. The sun's intensity bore down on us and we were hungry as we moved into the city center.

"Let's get a good hot meal," Howard suggested, as we rolled through the dirt streets.

"There's a place that looks as good as any," I said, motioning off to our left.

"Let's do it," Howard added.

We stacked the bikes in tandem against the glass windows of the restaurant. Stacking made theft more difficult. We could never allow our bikes to be not watched for a second. Gear vanished when unattended.

Howard grabbed a table before I walked into the cafe. Wooden tables and chairs were the only furniture on a dirt floor. I threw my camera down on the seat next to me. A bearded fellow came over to take our order. We asked for Dahl Bot, a plate of rice, bean and leaf green food. It was the standard staple for most people in Nepal. They allowed extra helpings which was the custom. It was less than 50 cents a meal. Add some unleavened bread, and we were happy riders.

When our waiter walked away, a thin man dressed in a white turban and linen serape walked through the door carrying a stick over his shoulder. At the end of it hung a medium sized wicker basket secured with rope. The Indian man sat down ten feet away from us. He placed the basket in front of his folded legs. At first, we didn't pay much attention, but then something caught Howard's eye.

"What the heck," he blurted out, pointing down at the man.

"Look at that thing flare up," I gasped. "Is this a joke? Look how big it is. Hey, Howard, that thing's coming our way."

Before us, slithering ever closer, a six-foot-long, fully flared cobra held our complete, undivided and total attention. It kept moving closer, flicking its tongue. We sat there, a captive audience of two, looking into the snake's eyes, transfixed by the motion, solidly riveted to our chairs.

"What's the deal here?" I spoke ever so clearly. "This guy would be arrested back home."

"We're not home," said Howard.

I was transfixed by the snake. It crawled across the dirt floor of the restaurant toward us. What were we supposed to do? Nothing in my life ever prepared me for being in this scene. I was taken by surprise, unable to react. This stuff happens to Indiana Jones in the Temple of Doom, but not to a couple of small-town bicycle riders. Right? Wrong!

Seconds later, because we hadn't responded, the man let the snake crawl to within 24 inches of our legs, which brought an immediate response from both of us. We leaped up, sticking the chairs in front of us to fend off the cobra.

"What's the next move?" I asked, totally confused.

"No moves at all, unless you wanna die," Howard said.

"What is this guy's problem?"

As if to help us understand, the man thrust his free hand into the air jingling a few rupees.

"Money, ah yes, the bottom line, he wants money," Howard said.

"Give him whatever he wants," I said.

At that point, I would have given him my last dime, just to save our lives. We faced extortion by terror. We slapped a pocketful of coins onto the chair and shoved it toward him. He grabbed the money, then gripped the snake by the back of the head and shoved it into the basket. Seconds later, he tied the knot, stood up and walked out to the street. He vanished quickly into the crowd. It happened so fast, my cocked camera remained on the table, leaving me with the only pictures in my mind.

KEY POINTS FROM THIS CHAPTER

1. You never know what might happen in a developing country.
2. Accept every country, its customs and its surprises.
3. Enjoy such an amazing moment when it happens to you.

SECTION III – SIX PRACTICES TO MOVE YOU TOWARD YOUR DREAMS: HOW TO GIT 'ER DONE

While you may be inspired by other people living their adventure-filled lives, you are interested in how you can get started. Since you possess the five basic concepts that lay the foundation of your mind-set from the Section II, you may incorporate the following six practices that will move you toward your intentions, dreams and goals.

Chapter 27—Delete self-deprecating feelings

"Life is known only by those who have found a way to be comfortable with change and the unknown. Given the nature of life, there may be no security, but only adventure." Rachel Naomi Remen

1ˢᵗ Practice—Delete self-deprecating words, feelings or thoughts about yourself

Years ago, my college roommate chastised himself whenever he made a mistake, spilled a glass of milk, tripped or fumbled something. He would scream at himself, "You stupid…." At other times, he would say, "You dumb…."

"Jack," I said after taking a psychology class. "My instructor said your brain is like a computer. It can't tell the difference between a positive word or negative word about yourself. If you keep telling your brain that you're dumb, stupid or clumsy, guess what dude, your brain will respond by becoming dumb, stupid and clumsy. How about after you make a mistake, you say something like, "I'm going to get better at this…I'm improving…I'm going to change this for the better."

Jack, a math major and always logical, said, "Frosty, you're right. I will always speak highly of myself no matter what kind of a mistake I make in the future. Think well, be well. That's me. Thanks, dude."

From that day, he never said anything negative about himself again.

I have brought that practice to many people in my life after asking them for permission to present an idea for them to ponder. I've enjoyed many a "thank you" from folks over the years.

Once people stop berating themselves, it frees their minds to become positively productive on multiple levels. It brings serenity to their minds, bodies and spirits.

What's the lesson here? You can choose to mentally and emotionally move beyond self-deprecating concepts. Think positively. Act positively. Feel positively. In the end, you will become a positive, productive and happy person.

If someone came up to you and asked, "Can you name five positive things about yourself?"

Could you? Would you? I hope so. It's good to possess a positive self-image. It carries lighter in your life backpack and it thrusts you into greater possibilities. So, yes, answer them with, "I'm having a great day, I'm funny, I'm excited, I'm smart, I'm interesting, I love life…."

If you look out on our society and you watch all the inane television programs where the scenes show guys and gals in petty group situations, it shows you extraordinarily trivial and mean-spirited tit-for-tat conversations. The guys get into yelling matches. Later, the girls break down in sobs, apologizing and suffering from guilt.

They solve nothing and walk away having learned zilch. But they all leave with one thing intact: their negative self-concepts.

As a young man, I read a book by Thomas Harris: ***I'm OK, You're OK.*** He described four ways people feel about themselves. I'm OK, You're OK. Such a person lives a balanced life and enjoys a healthy outlook. I'm not OK, You're OK. Such a person feels negative self-concepts, but everyone else is OK. I'm OK, You're not OK. Such a person sees himself OK, but everybody else as negative. I'm not OK, You're not OK. Such a person sees himself and everyone as all screwed up. According to that book, many Americans live their lives with an "I'm not OK feeling."

You see them in bars drinking themselves into oblivion. You may see them eating themselves into their own torment. Look at the obesity epidemic in this country for a harsh dose of unhealthy self-concepts. They may smoke, drink endless coffee and watch countless hours of television. Others visit shrinks for $100.00 an hour for years to try to find themselves.

Many people never move to self-acceptance. What constitutes self-acceptance? It means you accept your height, weight, size, looks, mind, abilities and everything about you. You compare yourself to no one. You move through the world on your terms with a sense of self-confidence and enjoyment of the very fact that you're alive, healthy and living. You feel equal to every other human being on earth and you wish all humans and other creatures good will.

How do you get to self-acceptance? You make choices based on new knowledge. This book provides you with opportunities. At the same time, I am offering many other writers that may resonate with you better with their ideas for self-acceptance and success. Either way, you win.

My dad used to say, "I don't care how tough it is or what it takes or how hard you think it is, you can do it. You just decide to stand your ground. Stand tall and speak up or speak out. Accept who and what you are. Just realize that there are hundreds of others too afraid, too timid or too fearful to try. So, decide to do it, make your plans and make it happen."

From this point onward when facing challenges, you may say, "I can do that, I will do that, I am doing that."

KEY POINTS FROM THIS CHAPTER

1. Delete negative self-concepts.
2. Accept yourself as a whole, complete and capable person.
3. Enjoy every potential moment for a positive life experience.
4. Finally, you can say, "I can do that."

*C*hapter 28—*Wildflowers in the mist*

"A person should set his goals as early as he can and devote all his energy and talent to getting there. With enough effort, he may achieve it. Or he may find something that is even more rewarding. But in the end, no matter what the outcome, he will know he has been alive." Walt Disney

Magic mingles in the mist, especially at 14,000 feet, where nature pampers itself with waterfalls, rocks, trees and wildflowers. The mountain mists await, so let's hoist that heavy pack onto our shoulders and tread into the mountain throne room of the wilderness.

The door bell rang and my friend Paul ambled into the front room.

"Dude," he said. "Let's get moving up that road, times a wasting, move it!"

"Just getting my gear squared away," I said.

In the front room, I finished the last of my packing.

My backpack felt like 50 pounds. Nonetheless, we looked forward to a big adventure to climb four 14ers in a five-day pack trip in the San Juan Mountains of Colorado.

We talked about climbing those 14ers near Durango in the spring. A train ride on the Durango-Silverton narrow gauge railroad to the Needleton stop would dispatch us into some rugged wilderness where cool winds whisper through tall pines and the white music from cascading waters frolics across bucolic meadows.

I threw my gear into Paul's car and we sped off at nightfall. We talked philosophy for the next six hours before we stopped to see a heavy meteor shower lacerating the night sky.

"Did you see that one?" I said.

We shared lots of laughter as we watched white hot meteor tails ripping through the ink black of space.

The ride from Montrose down the Million Dollar Highway kept us swerving through endless curves. We watched the dark mountain peaks as if they were monster waves lapping at the night sky. Those mountains provide an endless opportunity for wilderness playground magic.

Next morning, we leaped out of the sleeping bags with our eyeballs dragging off the tent floor nylon after only three hours sleep. In town, we bought last-minute supplies and fruit. Later, we grabbed our packs and headed toward the steam locomotive—some 100 years old and still chugging up mountain grades.

The old train made quite a sight. Its black engine belched smoke out of the stack and steam released from the valves like a tea pot in the morning. It made us feel good and a bit old fashioned with a slower pace to match our spirits.

The brakeman heaved our packs into the box car and moments later, the clang, clang, clang of the engineer signaled the jerking start of the journey to the drop-off point at Needleton. A shrill blast split the morning air as people waved from the sidewalks. The whistle blew that lonesome call to adventure that I've heard around this planet many times, and once again, I sped off with a dear friend on a new journey.

People waved from intersections and gravel road crossings as our train chugged toward the mountains. The cars jostled back and forth in a rhythm that settled well into my soul. It didn't take long for the train to grind into steep climbs that carried us into a deep canyon along the Animas River. At one moment, we rode beside white-water and watched the swirling currents crashing over rocks. The next we soared high above the water that reflected blue-green far below us. Everyone snapped pictures of themselves and the scenery. The view up the canyon showed us needle-pointed peaks and barren cliffs. Always, the rushing water of the river sounded steady and peaceful.

Two hours into the trip, we stopped at Needleton where we grabbed our gear and walked over a narrow foot-bridge. We slapped each other's hand in a high-five and headed into the wilderness along a dirt trail. Tall lodge-pole pines and undergrowth allowed no views of the high peaks, but their presence seemed to vibrate around us. We reached a river that became our constant companion for the next six hours.

The trail cut through deep woods where wild flowers bloomed sporadically—orange paint brush, golden daisies and deep crimson lilies.

Paul, always the speedier hiker, vanished into the woods ahead. I came upon him when he stopped near a waterfall where a foot bridge crossed a rampaging river. We took pictures and devoured pieces of fruit.

The climb steepened and I creaked under the weight of my pack, but each footfall, however labored, brought me nearer to my destination. I am fascinated at my mental state when I work hard to climb a mountain with a heavy pack. It's hard exertion, yet I bear the burden with a smile.

I breathed deeply and relished vividly clean air. The stillness calmed my soul.

Two and one-half hours into Chicago Basin, the forest opened to a huge panorama of cliffs on my right and a large waterfall on the river below me. Above, snow dotted the tundra in patches while rock slides cascaded everywhere. I stopped to watch a marmot on a rock who gazed at me with indolent interest. After 15 minutes, he decided to skedaddle and I pulled on my pack for my continued journey.

Crossing a newly formed avalanche chute, I witnessed where 15-inch pines by the hundreds had been snapped at the base and swept along in a violent river of snow. It's an awesome feeling walking in the wake of something so powerful that had occurred only a few months earlier.

Into the woods again, the climb steepened until I broke through a meadow where a riot of wildflowers glistened with dewdrops reflected in the sun. A small stream cut through the verdant field.

I danced through endless colors, butterflies and hummingbirds. I snapped a dozen pictures.

On the other side of that flower meadow, I met up with Paul who had chosen a nice spot seven miles into the valley in a pine grove overlooking a river. Above us, raging waterfalls roared down the rock faces of the high mountains surrounding us. Through the evening light, more wildflowers waved in the breeze that sifted through the valley.

We cooked two pots of food and laughed at our good fortune. Near dusk, the high ridges near the 14ers lit up with the last light of the day. It gave a roller-coaster light affect to the highest rock faces. The sun finally dropped below the horizon. The peaks turned to dark profiles butting up against the night sky.

I sat on a rock watching the stars come out one by one when Paul walked up to talk. He relaxed on a rock ledge. A meteor shower cut the darkness with white lines slicing across the sky. We both stared up at a million twinkling stars.

We talked about everything and nothing—like two friends might do when they spend time together.

We retired to our tents.

A cool wind blew gray wisps up the valley in the morning. A light rain cleansed the air. It also cooled it. We pulled on sweaters and jackets.

After breakfast, we packed our gear and took off. We faced an immediate steep climb beside a waterfall that cascaded down the rocks before us. The dense undergrowth and wildflowers sparkled in the morning dew. Waterfalls converged upon us from every visual angle. The shelves of snow provided their sources and the valley filled with white music. I call it white music because it maintains a constant melody of splashing that produces a sublime serenity. White music can be heard and seen at the same time. This renders pleasant sounds and even more spectacular sights—to immerse the spirit in the harmonics of Mother Nature. It's a satori experience at the 7th level.

We broke through the 12,000 foot tree-line and climbed ever higher into the flower- speckled alpine tundra. Above us, Rocky Mountain goats traversed along a trail near the rock line where grasses stopped growing. We listened for the pika rodents and watched a couple of marmots chasing each other through the boulders. Clouds enshrouded the gray giants above us, but quickly released them for our visual pleasure. Nature played a game of hide and seek on a grand scale.

We marched up a steep incline beside a thrashing white water stream when a bolt of lightning ripped across the valley. We dove for cover. Paul found a small overhang above us and we pushed toward it as the storm swept through the valley.

We propped ourselves against the rock with our jackets protecting us from the wind. The rain fell in plunging sheets across the valley, which changed from several miles of visibility to less than 100 yards. Soon, hail pelted us.

Later, nature sent us a few lightning bolts to keep us on the straight and narrow, and then, to keep us humble, a few million marble-sized hail stones dropped on our heads. John Muir, my idol, climbed a tree once and rode out a summer storm in the topmost branches in Yosemite. He wanted to see how the tree felt in a storm.

After the tempest passed, the valley grew in clarity, which only happens when the rain scrubs the air clean. Our climb brought us to a second plateau in the valley. To our left, a grassy incline reached up to vertical rock walls that poked into the sky. On our right, three sharply pointed mountain massifs struck like daggers into the mist. In front, two turquoise lakes, one with an iceberg floating in it, reflected the snow and mountains in a perfect mirror image.

We ascended a steep wall of broken rock. It carried us to a large saddle that overlooked the valley we had packed up the previous day. We enjoyed an eagle's eye view at 13,000 feet. We stood on broken rock fields spread all around us. Below, the eternal white water from waterfalls lined the valley like throbbing silver earrings on a movie star's ears. But in this case, more sensual in a natural way. The white water river formed under the falls converged in the middle of the valley and cut a sparkling liquid path through the dense green tundra.

Wildflower patches in burgundy, yellow, red and white spread across the rocky terrain. They grew in places that seemed impossible. Scanning upward, we watched the trees change to golf-course smooth green tundra that faded into gray rock. In turn, it swept dramatically upward to sheer rock cliffs that vanished in the mist. We climbed in a natural coliseum. They call them the Needle Mountains because their sharp projections stand like porcupine quills against the sky.

Minutes later, we resumed our climb through treacherous broken rock. We moved into the gray mist at 13,500 feet where I watched every footfall. The clean air and mist reminded me of standing on the Golden Gate Bridge in San Francisco. Our visibility remained less than 40 feet and the rock we climbed gave us the only assurance of being attached to the planet.

It's a mental experience to move into this part of a climb. Each footfall must be measured, every rock calculated for safety, every breath felt in my heaving lungs—life rushing through my blood and spreading throughout my body. This is a time where there are no ordinary moments, when satori takes over, when I create my life, each moment of it—where I am responsible for what I am, what I am doing and what I want. I can create a living sculpture in my spirit and that life-force moves through me and upward on this mountain. It might be called a positive ion nirvana high. This is where life mingles with death. To top it off in the shadowy recesses of this dark mist, I must make distinct judgments of where I will place my foot, how and what I grasp to keep me in touch with the rock. One mistake

149

would send me flying down the mountain without the use of wings. Surely it would be a one-way flight with a terminal landing.

I will remember this day with my friend. We lived it deeply. It was not routine, dull or ordinary. We lived a peak experience on a mountain in Colorado.

Nearing the top, the rocks steepened into columns, like needles piercing the sky. We saw only oblong-shaped dark rock or gray vapor. We couldn't see 10 feet because of the mist. Finally, we reached the top at 1:10 p.m. We saw the little silver medallion marker embedded in a rock. It denoted the peak with a tube filled with paper to sign that we had succeeded. Cold! We breathed inside a cloud.

I am amazed when I look up at clouds. They look so beautiful with puffs and billows surrounding peaks, but when I reach the top and become part of the beauty, it turns out to be gray, damp and cold mist. That adage about grass being greener on the other side may prove questionable. The greenest grass is where I choose to live. I stood in the grayest, cleanest cloud formation on that mountain on that day of my life. Paul and I conquered Windom Mountain at 14,082 feet.

Paul couldn't wait to get off the mountain, but I insisted on pictures. That picture of us shrouded in mist on the highest rock decorates my desk for me to remember daily. As I stood there for the picture, I looked down. It dropped vertically more than a thousand feet into nothingness.

Moments later, we methodically descended the mountain. About 800 feet down, we saw glimpses of Sunlight Mountain. It was our next quest. They named it because of the rock needle projections at its peak cause shadows and streams of light to pour down into the valley almost like sunlight through the skyscrapers in New York City. We crossed over a snowfield dotted with boulders. We heard the muffled roar of waterfalls under the rocks below us. We climbed in a world of rock, ice, water and sky. It made me wonder what the pikas and marmots ate.

We headed up a couloir toward the summit. A number of watermelon-sized boulders dislodged in the rock scree so we decided to climb on opposite sides. It's really tricky trying to dodge a 300-pound boulder crashing toward you.

We had nearly reached Sunlight's summit when lightning cracked the sky and hailstones pelted us. We jumped for cover. That's when Paul told me that lightning can travel 13 miles horizontally. We needed to keep our ice axes close to the ground so as not to attract nine million volts of electricity which would have turned us into a couple of vegetable shiskabobs.

While we neared the top, too much danger caused us to turn back. That's a mind-bender in itself—to be so close to the top of a 14er only to turn back.

Down the mountain we descended on scree and rock. We pushed into the snowfields and over the rivers. At one point, we walked across a 50-yard wide section of a lake. It felt like walking on water as we leaped from rock to rock. Again, the peaks grew higher and higher as we hiked down. We walked to the bottom of an immense mixing bowl strewn with boulders the size of Volkswagens. Patches of snow stood ten foot deep surrounded by crystal clear tundra ponds.

Near the end of the valley, we looked down a crevasse with white-water exploding from every crack. A multi-layered waterfall kept us in rapt attention with its wonderment. Below, the twin lakes with the iceberg came into view. Near my foot, a tiny patch of purple flowers resembled a pin cushion.

We made camp at sunset. The valley filled with white music while we cooked rice and lentils along with freeze dried tomatoes. Ah, night and sleep, 12 hours of it.

We awoke to an overcast sky, rain and dreariness. No climbing for us. Paul took off early, but I decided to stay and contemplate. I savored the last few hours of that day to enjoy writing and quiet in the middle of the wilderness. I relaxed in my tent and soaked up as much repose as humanly possible.

By noon, I needed to get moving. I packed my gear as a new storm rolled up the valley. Wildflowers rustled in the breeze. Soon, rains swept toward me. I picked up the campsite and set out along the trail. I looked back. It was as if I had never been there and that spot was only a dream. I slogged down the valley into the teeth of swirling clouds and pelting rains. Lightning struck intermittently. I hiked close to tall pines on my way across a meadow of wildflowers. At one point, just before the rain hit me, I grabbed my tripod and camera. I took a picture of me looking back up the valley. I liked being out in a storm just like John Muir in a tree. After I snapped the picture, I stuffed the camera into my pack. I looked back at the valley. I cried out in the storm, "I'll be back."

It was no ordinary moment in my life. I turned around, surrounded by a rainbow of wildflowers, and headed into the mist.

KEY POINTS FROM THIS CHAPTER

1. Adventure is not always safe.
2. You need to push past limits in order to experience more.
3. Yes, you can die on an adventure, but you most likely will live.
4. Explore the unknown so it becomes known to you.

Chapter 29—Choose your view

"It is not the critic who counts, not the man who points out how the strong man stumbles, or where the doer of deeds could have done them better. The credit belongs to the man in the arena, whose face is marred by dust and sweat and blood, who strives valiantly. Who knows the great enthusiasms, the great devotion; who spends himself in a worthy cause; who at best knows in the end the triumph of high achievement, and who at the worst, if he fails, at least fails while daring greatly, so that his place shall never be with those cold and timid souls who knew neither victory nor defeat." U.S. President Teddy Roosevelt

2nd *Practice—Choose your view*

No one else but you chooses your mental perspective or your life view. You may choose a positive, negative, neutral, fearful, dull or bored life attitude. You could choose an outlook such as, "I don't care." You can choose an outlook such as, "I will make a positive difference." You may become involved in life or uninvolved. It's up to you.

Please examine two basic views that will lift you toward an extraordinary life experience or an average life path.

Will you choose a worm's-eye view or an eagle's-eye view? Okay! I know what you're thinking. Worms don't have eyes to see. Work with me here. Which will you choose? If you think below the surface or think limitations or wallow in your muck from past conditions—your world will remain that of a worm's reality.

When I attended high school, I studied every night. I attended every class. I played sports. I joined clubs to connect with other students. I learned how to swing dance. I pitched newspapers to 80 customers on my paper route at 5:00 a.m. seven days a week. I kept my eyes on the prize.

WORM'S- EYE VIEW

At the same time, quite a few of my classmates hung out in the parking lot—smoking, drinking and wasting time doing nothing. They didn't complete their homework assignments. Many dropped out to work as tire changers, janitors or stock boys. None of them advanced to college or trade schools.

They guaranteed themselves mediocre lives. They chained themselves to the lowest financial rung of the ladder. They hung with each other so they thought their actions or lack of actions appeared normal. Intellectual mediocrity, lassitude and sloth rarely make for a fulfilling lifestyle.

Such a worm's-eye view ensures definite lifetime limitations. It limits mental and physical travel. It relegates such a person to trailer parks or housing projects. It means factory jobs, stocking grocery shelves, maid work and other minimum wage employment. It means few choices and scant satisfaction.

At my high school reunions, I couldn't help but wonder what would have happened if those dudes and dudettes had chosen to study hard, engage in high school, move on to college and live a more abundant life. Their eyes may have been as bright and shiny as those in our class who chose the eagle's-eye view. Be certain that you get to choose. When possible, choose your view early in life.

The creative process affords, however, that at any life juncture, a mental shift will produce stellar results. It's really up to you how dynamic a life you want to live. It can start at any time you choose to change to an eagle's-eye view.

EAGLE'S- EYE VIEW

For those who choose an eagle's-eye view, hold on to your hats. What a ride! When you put your heart, mind and spirit into the joy of living, you discover a passionate, purposeful and energy-filled life. It's whatever turns you on that thrusts your mind toward mental and emotional zeniths.

I met a young guy named Sandy on my adventure to Antarctica. He was spirited, exuberant and friendly. He worked his way through college to become a journalist and photographer. He possessed buckets of high energy. During his time in Antarctica, he raced in the Scott Hut Race in bitter cold. He jumped into the water in the 12 foot thick ice of the Southern Oceans. He raced around the world within 10 seconds at the South Pole.

I've watched him for 13 years. He learned to speak Japanese. He traveled to France to learn how to speak French. He traveled to China, South America, Australia and other regions on the planet. Later, he met a delightful lady. They decided on a family. Today, he's a father and loves it. He skis, rafts, climbs and races in marathons. He lives in the woods of New Hampshire.

Did he receive a special start in life? Not really. He's a country boy from Missouri. He earned everything through hard work and tenacity.

Sandy provides you with an example of an eagle's-eye view of living.

"The outward movement into form does not express itself with equal intensity in all people." said Eckhart Tolle, author of **Awakening to Your Life's Purpose**. "Some feel a strong urge to build, create, become involved, achieve and make an impact on the world."

Does an eagle's-eye view mean you must be excited or filled with high-energy?

No, not at all.

Quieter yet equally dynamic people may be called "frequency holders."

"They are more inward looking by nature," said Tolle. "Their role is just as vital as that of the creators, the doers and the reformers. They endow the seemingly insignificant with profound meaning. They affect the world much more deeply than is visible on the surface of their lives."

Another young man I met in Texas on my 2010 bicycle ride across America proved quiet yet dynamic. Davis walked up to me at a sandwich shop, "Are you the one riding that bike that says coast to coast?"

"Sure am," I said.

"Can I buy you dinner?" he said.

"Why would you buy me dinner?" I asked.

"I want to learn how you do it," he said.

As we talked, Davis said, "I don't want to live a boring life. I want to see the world. I don't want to be average."

What did I notice about him? He came across as a quiet 18-year-old with a thirst for knowledge to live a great life. He attends college where he reads and writes profusely. His mind expands toward the great events of his future. We keep in touch and I look forward to his unfolding life with an eagle's-eye view attitude.

When you decide to see the world from a higher calling, your intentions fly with your thoughts. In other words, your dreams become your reality. Let these concepts move you toward your dreams. You make the call. No matter what the pains of your past, forgive anyone that has ever hurt you and unload your emotional baggage so it doesn't burden your brain or emotions. Your current perceptions color your imagination and fulfillment.

Engage these points to adopt an eagle's-eye view.

1. Write down what will move your dream into motion.
2. Take inventory, improve, build upon and expand your talents and abilities to maximize your potential.
3. Think positively, optimistically, affirmatively and constructively.
4. Delete that other self in your brain that comes on negatively.
5. Identify any trepidation and neutralize it by positive mental decisions.
6. Think and see success, write it down on paper and repeat it aloud.
7. Keep and read affirmations on your desk, fridge, car dash, bathroom mirror and everywhere that will move your mind toward your intention.
8. Hang with others that enjoy your eagle's-eye view.

What does an eagle's-eye view feel like?

When I go skiing, I take the Panoramic Express chair lift in Winter Park, Colorado to the highest point on the mountain at 12,065 feet. Once off the lift, I spread my arms like the wings of an eagle and fly down the mountain with long graceful turns. Out front, the massive 13,000- foot Perry's Peak greets me and the Continental Divide cuts a rugged profile across the cobalt sky above me. Essentially, I am an eagle flying at great altitude.

However, you don't need to live in the mountains to enjoy an eagle's-eye view. You can ride your bicycle while flying down the road for the same feeling. You can choose a positive mental-emotional point of view. You may be scuba diving for that eagle's-eye view or perhaps taking a canoe trip. Whatever your activity, take it to your highest level of attitude and fulfillment.

Proceed toward tomorrow with an eagle's-eye view.

KEY POINTS FROM THIS CHAPTER

1. You may choose an eagle's-eye view or worm's-eye view.
2. Worm's-eye view keeps you below the surface.
3. Eagle's-eye view carries you to personal and physical success.
4. Engage the eight methods that take you to the eagle's-eye view.

Chapter 30—Eat dessert first, life is uncertain

"Cookies always taste better than meat and potatoes." A third grader

I couldn't have found a more perfect spot among tall evergreens and a pine needle-covered floor to pitch my tent this evening. Birds chirp above me as the light fades from the sky and a cool wind whispers through the trees making them creak as they sway back and forth. The campfire chases away the darkness.

I shall remember this day for the rest of my life.

Sunshine blessed us today as we bicycled the 49er Trail toward Sonora, California. Flowers bloomed along the road like a bouquet from a child's coloring book. But something happened today that fills my heart with sorrow.

When Doug and I awoke this morning, the sun had broken through the cloud cover, revealing immense forests shrouded in gray mist. A green mantle of pines swept toward towering peaks of the High Sierra. The mist swirled like giant pinwheels above the treetops while we ate our breakfast.

Doug and I eat foods that give us top performance. While touring, we buy seven-grain cereal and mix it with sunflower seeds, raisins and fresh fruit. A loaf of wheat bread hangs off our packs and we spread peanut butter over each slice. Water is the simplest liquid to keep and pour over the cereal. Because bicycling utilizes so much energy, breakfast is topped off with an apple or an orange. We eat our food from the same stainless steel pots used for cooking. After breakfast, we break camp and push the bikes out of the woods to the highway.

We had descended from a snowstorm at 6,000 feet out of Yosemite National Park. The rolling highway led us away from Yosemite through tall trees, high mountain beauty and spring colors. Dripping wet forest green glistened along every mile of the road. We dropped another 1,000 feet before stopping for lunch on a grassy spot near the road. Doug grabbed his food pack and I followed him with mine.

Our lunch ritual was the same each day. We bought groceries for two days riding. Complex carbohydrates in the form of fruits and vegetables, rice and lentils were our main staples. We celebrated lunch because hunger constantly stalks a cyclist. We sat in the shade, spread our towels and prepared sandwiches.

Doug eats more than I eat. No, let me clarify that statement. He inhales more food than a humpback whale. He makes a shark look tame when it comes to appetite. To give you an idea of how much Doug eats at a sitting, I'd lay bets on him in a pie-eating contest against the Pittsburgh Steelers. Doug would eat them under the table. If there was a word to describe how much food he consumes, it hasn't been invented yet. That's Doug, all 6'4"of him. Yet, through the modern miracle of bicycling, he's lean and clean.

He sat with his legs stretched out in a "V" shape. He laid out eight slices of bread, along with a bag of vegetables. He carries a cutting board which he washed off with his water bottle. Within minutes, he cut everything into slices. He stacked tomatoes, cucumbers and green peppers on top of each other before topping his sandwiches with mustard. His eyes lit up as he licked his lips in anticipation of the coming feast. Not to be outdone, I chopped with vigor.

Hunger is fun on a bicycle adventure because we love to eat. Food dazzles our taste buds. Thirty minutes later, we had polished off four bananas for dessert.

We were ready to go when I held us up for another minute because I had to take a bathroom break. Back on the road, we cranked up a hill with sweat dripping from our bodies. Not five minutes later, we saw a touring bicyclist coming the other way as we rolled into a valley. At the bottom, he coasted to a stop. Doug and I also slowed to a stop.

I was looking at the bike rider when I noticed he was carrying a black puppy on a platform on his rear rack. "What a nice..." I began to say. Before

I could finish my sentence, the puppy bounded off the platform and ran across the pavement toward us. I heard a vehicle coming, but before the driver or anyone could bat an eyelash, the puppy yelped in a death cry after being crushed by two sets of wheels from a pickup truck going 50 miles per hour.

From a happy disposition with blue sky and sunshine overhead, I was jerked into bewilderment. My first thought was for the fellow across the road who had seen his puppy crushed to death before his eyes.

"Oh no, oh no," I said in a withered voice.

It shocked my senses from a lovely day to a terrible moment that happened with no rhyme or reason. Only that moment! Had we eaten lunch for 30 seconds longer or had I waited to relieve myself, the timing of our meeting of that fellow bicyclist would have saved the puppy. I felt sick.

The rider got off his bike. He walked across the road, picked up the dog and walked up to us.

"I'm so sorry," I said with grief in my voice.

"Nothing you could do," he said. "It wasn't anyone's fault."

The driver stopped and ran back, "I'm sorry," he said. "I couldn't stop."

"There's nothing you could have done, sir," the bicyclist said. "Thanks for stopping."

"I'm sorry, son," the driver said as he walked away.

"I'm so sorry," I repeated. "Is there anything I can do?"

"No," he said. "I need to take Sierra for a walk in the woods."

As he carried the pup away toward the trees, I stood there, my heart crushed with anguish. He had lost a special friend, one he had run through the high country with, one who had sat by campfires with him.

A half-hour passed before I walked up to where he was burying Sierra. I introduced myself. His name was Bob and he began crying. I walked up and embraced him. His pain moved into me. I wept with tears running down my face onto his shirt. I held him tight. He talked with his face on my shoulders, sniffling through his nose, convulsing with gasps of air. Minutes later, we picked up rocks and finished covering Sierra's body. Bob and I walked back toward the road. Bob didn't look back, but his whole being was torn. I sensed the anguish ripping at his foundations.

"I don't understand why this happened," he said.

Neither Doug nor I said anything. What could we say? What could we do?

Nothing!

Bob decided to continue south. He wanted to figure out why this happened. I gave him one last hug. Doug hugged him, too. Bob walked across the road, picked up his bike and rode off.

"Do you know only one car has gone by us in the last 45 minutes?" Doug said.

"This just blows me away."

"Eat dessert first."

"What?"

"I read it on a climber's T-shirt in Yosemite. It said, 'Eat dessert first, life is uncertain.'"

"No kidding," I lamented. "Let's get going."

I pulled my bike up from the gravel shoulder and grasped the bars with both hands. Looking down, I slipped my right foot into the pedal strap. I pressed hard. The wheels gleamed as they advanced. For the first time in my life, I noticed that the spokes go forward and they go backward simultaneously. They rotate up as well as down while the bike travels along the road. There is no power stroke for the spokes. They merely carry the load placed upon them. On the end of the spokes, the wheel rolls around. Just like this planet revolves in space. No reason, other than that's the way it is. I don't know why Sierra died. No reason! I fell in behind Doug. I watched his free-wheel spin forward. I watched his derailleur as it dropped the chain into lower gears when we began climbing out of the valley. For the rest of the day, I watched his spinning back wheel.

Sitting here in this tent, the light has faded and the last bird has ruffled its feathers in silence. The mountain air slips through the trees and my candle flame flickers quietly. I shall never forget this day, nor its message—eat dessert first, for life is uncertain. Take it all in daily—joy and sorrow, good and bad times, confidence and uncertainty, smiles and tears, love and heartbreak. This is the best moment of life and present living. Nothing is guaranteed even five minutes into the future. At no time are any of us immune to misfortune no matter what our situation in life. You can be rich, famous, handsome and happy. It makes no difference. You can look at Princess Di, John Kennedy Jr., Derrick Thomas, Elvis Presley, Martin Luther King, Marilyn Monroe, James Dean and countless others. The grand parade of life marches on with or without you.

I eat dessert first. But tonight, I don't feel hungry.

KEY POINTS FROM THIS CHAPTER

1. Live every day with maximum joy.
2. Take precautions for your own safety.
3. Help others who may suffer loss.
4. Understand that every creature does the best it can in life.
5. You always have choices.

*C*hapter 31—Claim your highest and best

"*One final paragraph of advice: Do not burn yourself out. Be as I am – a reluctant enthusiast... a part time crusader, a half-hearted fanatic. Save the other half of yourselves and your lives for pleasure and adventure. It is not enough to fight for the land; it is even more important to enjoy it. While you can. While it is still there. So get out there and mess around with your friends, ramble out yonder and explore the forests, encounter the grizz, climb the mountains. Run the rivers, breathe deep of that yet sweet and lucid air, sit quietly for a while and contemplate the precious stillness, that lovely, mysterious and awesome space. Enjoy yourselves, keep your brain in your head and your head firmly attached to your body, the body active and alive, and I promise you this much: I promise you this one sweet victory over our enemies, over those deskbound people with their hearts in a safe deposit box and their eyes hypnotized by desk calculators. I promise you this: you will outlive them." Edward Abbey*

3rd Practice—Claim your highest and best

When you regularly use your talents, the ideas and creative process be ome second nature to you. You will discover that new ideas and possibilities fall into your lap even if you don't know what they are at the moment.

Everything becomes clearer as you move creatively forward. Does every person's life turn out to be a fairy-tale ending? That depends on luck, random chance and tenacity. It depends on the right place, right time and right attitude.

By your consistent work and planning, you will move toward your dreams, goals and intentions.

"Most of the important things in the world have been accomplished by people who kept on trying when there seemed to be no hope at all," said Dale Carnegie, author and industrialist.

Many of life's failures are people who did not realize how close they were to success when they gave up.

How did a farm boy from Michigan land in Antarctica? I worked for it, kept trying and it happened. I interviewed four years in a row only to be rejected each time. But the fifth time proved a charm. Had I quit after the fourth time, I would never have reached Antarctica.

On the literary front, I sent my book manuscripts into hundreds of publishers for 22 years before enjoying my first published book. Had I stopped at year 21, I would never have enjoyed success.

Therefore, always think, act and feel for your highest and best.

As you may notice all around you, not all people work toward an outstanding life.

For an example, it's been shown that a large percentage of Americans dislike their jobs. They may enjoy the money, but they don't care for the heartburn, headaches, stress and fatigue of an unhappy employment situation. Many others plod onward without hope or enthusiasm. Anyone can change his or her future by taking action in the present moment.

At the same time, some men and women try daredevil stunts. Are they crazy? What do they get out of them? Who are they?

What happens when they have an accident? Let's talk about a man who jumped off a cliff into Lake Powell and broke his back, suffering paralysis from the waist down. I know him. His name is Matt Feeney. He was born with glorious good looks. He possesses charisma and power in his being that most politicians would give their fortune to possess. After breaking his back, Matt didn't sit on his butt and die of depression. He refused to feel sorry for himself. He got back up from the bed and jumped into a wheelchair. In fact, he started racing in wheelchairs.

During the winter, he learned to race on a mono-ski. Still later, he bicycle raced (using his hands to pedal) and water skied at the Special Olympics. He supervised and taught at the National Sports Center for the Disabled in Winter Park, Colorado. Today, he runs his own adaptive skiing sports camps for the disabled. www.adaptiveadventures.org He's the kind of man and athlete that thousands of people look up to for guidance, power and inspiration. Even as he mobilizes in that wheelchair, he tackles life everyday—with power, gusto, passion and purpose.

It is my honor and privilege to be his friend. He has no idea how much I admire him, his courage and his actions as he leaps toward life. He chose his highest and best under difficult circumstances.

Instead of accepting his condition as a failure, Feeney engaged "metanoia" which means a total consciousness change. He moved from fear and defeat to courage. He moved toward the light.

Bethany Hamilton at 13, a top Hawaiian surfer, lost her arm to a shark attack in 2003. Today, she continues surfing and inspiring kids of all ages by her full participation in sports and life.

No matter what physical, emotional or mental difficulties you face, you can engage metanoia like Bob Wieland, Matt Feeney, Bethany Hamilton and many other persons struggling with difficulties. By choosing your highest and best, you will capture a meaningful life.

The following are possible avenues toward your highest and best:

1. Hunt for new experiences and activities.
2. Take college classes and attend seminars on personal growth.
3. Apply for different part-time jobs.
4. Check out an unusual hobby or interest.
5. Volunteer to help someone else or an organization.

In the end, highest and best means you maintain a positive attitude no matter how difficult the task or assignment. Few people enjoy an easy ride to their dreams. Go to any library and check out DVDs on Leonardo da Vinci, Ben Franklin, Susan B. Anthony, Dolly Madison, Thomas Jefferson, Jane Goodall, Nelson Mandela, Amelia Earhart, Gandhi, Abraham Lincoln, Dr. Martin Luther King, Mark Twain, Oprah Winfrey, George Washington and many of history's great figures. Every single one of them faced daunting challenges. What did they share in common? They all worked for their highest and best.

To cement these concepts, evolve your thinking:

1. Trust your instincts. Move with the flow of ideas. Begin with increasing your mental, spiritual and physical goals.
2. Think of yourself as happy, prosperous and well.
3. One great philosopher said, "Despair means you're looking the wrong way." Look in the positive direction of your intentions for a positive outcome.
4. The Greek word "metanoia" means total conscious change. Move from fear to courage. Cleanse your consciousness. Move toward the light.
5. The term "universe" means the creative realm of possibilities.

You may like to incorporate one of the best practices for this transformation of thought: affirmative quotes. You can see in every chapter quotes from dozens of top male and female adventurers. Choose a quote from your favorite person and place it on your mirror to be read each morning before you start the day and at the end of the day. You want those positive thoughts and intentions moving through your brain all day and all night. You can write your own affirmation and read it daily. One writer said, "What you seek is seeking you."

Napoleon Hill said, "Life is like a horse. Life can ride you as you become the horse. Or, you can ride while life becomes the horse. The choice as to whether one becomes the rider of life or life rides is the privilege of every person. But this much is certain. If you do not choose to become the rider of life, you are sure to be forced to become the horse. Life either rides or is ridden. It never stands still."

KEY POINTS FROM THIS CHAPTER

1. Think, act and feel for your highest and best.
2. Use these points to move toward your dreams.
3. Trust your instincts.
4. Repeat your affirmations created by you or from your heroes.
5. Metanoia means to change consciousness toward enlightenment.

Chapter 32—A rare phenomenon on Earth

"What a privilege to know the profound stillness and the peace of the land, to see star spangled skies, and to listen to the pulse of the universe." Jill Tremain

Even the dogs don't bark at bicyclists in New Zealand.

If ever there was a paradise for a touring bicycle rider, New Zealand takes the cake. The South Island, with its 12,000-foot glacier-covered summits, possesses extraordinary mountain vistas. But it doesn't end there. Animal life abounds along the rocky seacoast including countless shorebirds. On the domestic front, 21 million sheep outnumber the human population seven to one. Four-billion-year-old Meroki Boulders hatch out of the sand along the coast on the east side of the South Island. Kiwi birds hide in the darkness while penguins and sea lions frolic in the surf.

Doug and I spent three days in Christchurch. That lovely Victorian city features characters like the Wizard and the Bird Man. The former is a self-proclaimed theologian who walks into the city center daily and preaches a sermon on most any subject that catches his fancy. His sermons cause wild reactions among tourists. More mild mannered, the Bird Man provides a walking perch for hundreds of seagulls that inhabit the city. His avian friends trust him and fight for the honor of perching on his cap.

But paradise sometimes exacts a price. We rode south out of Christchurch with a brisk tailwind. Being blown down the road feels like a free ride. You get to laugh, sing and sit in the saddle with little effort. A hundred kilometers south, we headed west on Route 79 toward Mount Cook National Park. It was the heart of the highest mountains in New

Zealand. We pedaled with side winds blowing us across the highway, but that wasn't too bad. We made our way through a valley until we reached Route 8 in Farlie. A wide-open plain covered with brown grasses brought us to a vista overlooking the turquoise waters of Lake Tekapo. We cut across its lower end and coasted for the next few hours on a tailwind that whipped along at 50 miles per hour. We loved it until we hit Route 80 at Lake Pukaki. We headed directly into a 50-mile-an-hour zephyr. We pedaled into the granddaddy of headwinds. Sixty-mile-per-hour gusts thundered down from the canyons in front of us.

Twenty-four miles separated us from the camping area in the park. It might as well have been a 10,000-foot climb with 16-percent grades. We stopped for a drink at the intersection.

"You sure we want to do this?" Doug asked.

"No kidding, man," I said. "This is an inland hurricane. We're gonna be blown off the road. I don't know how we're gonna make it."

"We'll be in Granny gear the whole time," Doug said. "Let's get it done."

From there, our five-hour ordeal began. With the mountains in front and to our left, and the whitecaps on the lake, we cranked into a savage wind. An invisible force ripped at our bodies. Normally, we hammer out 24 miles in two hours. Not in that wind. We cranked along, heads down, hands gripping the bars and fighting for balance. Blasts of wind howled in our ears. For the first hour, a narrow canyon directed a cyclone at us. The road pointed straight for three miles, but looked like forever. We pedaled in Granny gear the whole time even on slight downhill grades. After six miles, we reached the storm-whipped waters of Lake Pukaki.

The wind intensified as it exploded off the flat surface of the water. We rode side by side, but one blast sent me crashing into Doug. After that, we kept a short distance between our bikes. We cranked into brutal gale-force winds. Up ahead, swirling clouds played wildly in the mountains at the end of the lake. We discovered the birthplace of that raging tempest. It thundered and howled at us. It ripped violent patterns into the surface of the lake. That wind did everything in its power to keep us from our destination. Hour after gut-busting hour, we fought our way into that tempest of sound and fury.

Near sunset, we dragged our weary bodies into the camp area of Mount Cook National Park. Doug decided to take a rest. I pitched my tent, tossed the panniers inside and grabbed my camera. The sun set high over the peaks. Shadows moved up the west face of the mountains to my left. Glaciers hung on craggy peaks above me. I wanted to catch the sun making its final lighting assault on the glaciers for the day. I ran along a huge glacial moraine with my pack bouncing on my shoulders. At the end of the camping area, it turned to bush and moss-covered rocks. I followed a primitive trail that meandered upward along a ridgeline. It climbed steeply, offering me a glimpse of five large glaciers. Further up the hill, a gray glacial river came into view below me. In front, an enormous canyon stretched into the distance—the result of a receding glacier whose foot was barely perceptible under the south face of 12,500-foot Mount Cook. The clouds broke momentarily, giving me a full-blown view of its south face. Brilliant mountain energy! Along the canyon, back toward me, on sheer vertical cliffs thousands of feet high, four glaciers clung to their rocky perches.

About a kilometer to my right, a large gravel avalanche chute cut its way through dark green vegetation. In front of me, where I stopped to sit on a rock, I enjoyed a grandstand view of the merging of two glacial canyons. The one closest to me sported 300-foot-high banks that resembled a canal trough. Gray rock protruded like broken glass shards. Along the rock fields, sinkholes made indentations and 500-ton boulders lay around like broken eggshells. On the left side of the canyon, nine glaciers in various formations poured like cake batter out of the mountains. Beneath each glacier and mingling around the base of the ice floes, dozens of waterfalls cascaded down jagged rock.

Above this grand mountain scene, white and gray twisting clouds folded into changing formations like ghosts in a Disney movie. The wind thrashed and thundered all around me. It rushed through the canyon to my right with the deafening roar of cannon fire. Each volley blasted the ridge where I sat. The explosions bellowed over the water of the glacial lakes below me. The wind ripped up the ridge and roared by me at 60 miles per hour. The squall nearly blew me over the ridge at one point. I dropped to my stomach to save myself. The raging wind blew the grasses so hard, they looked like water running over a dam.

As I watched this drama, wonder crept into my soul. I let out a yell. At times like that, when the wind blows and the ice cracks and rumbles, and rivers roar, and the mass of nature's moving parts unite to create a natural movie with a screen that stretches across the sky—it's at those times I know my life moves in delicate perfection. Living feels right and good. No doubts as I sat there in a howling wind with my spirit soaring and my eyes full of blue, gray, aqua, white, ice, water and mountains rising to collide with the sky.

Upon returning to camp, a Kiwi couple invited Doug and me into their van for dinner. We talked for two hours before the wind died. We walked out at 11:00 o'clock just as a full moon broke over the summit of Mount Wakefield just east of us. A slight drizzle fell west of us across the Seffron Glacier. What we witnessed, I've never seen before or since. Its existence requires the most exceptional of circumstances to occur. That night, we saw one of the rarest wonders of the world.

"Would you look at that," Doug said.

"Holy catfish," I said. "What do you call something like that?"

"I don't know," Doug answered. "It's not a rainbow, so it's got to be a...moonbow, yeah, that's it, a moonbow."

Across the sky to the west, created by the blazing light of a full moon, and a clear sky to the east—a fully arced rainbow swung from the ground, up over a mountain, into the night sky, back down into the white glacier field, and touched down again on the rocky ground in the distance. It shone in green and yellow, but red and purple glistened in the drizzle, too. Within the arc, a white mist curtain brightened the darkness.

"That is a once-in-a-lifetime happening," Doug said.

"You know, this makes everything we suffered today worth it," I said. "This is so amazing."

My friend and I stood there watching the moonbow. In the silence, we heard something else—the heartbeat of the universe.

KEY POINTS FROM THIS CHAPTER

1. Sometimes life provides tailwinds, which make for easy riding.
2. Sometimes life offers challenges like headwinds. Keep pedaling.
3. Sometimes when you persevere, life rewards with you with amazing moments.
4. Nature always provides stunning surprises for those willing to seek out her secrets.
5. Take a friend to share the experience.

*C*hapter 33—*Live brilliantly*

"Never forget that life can only be nobly inspired and rightly lived if you take it bravely and gallantly, as a splendid adventure in which you are setting out into an unknown country, to face many a danger, to meet many a joy, to find many a comrade, to win and lose many a battle." Annie Besant

4th Practice—Live brilliantly

Your life unfolds as you choose. You enjoy abundant opportunities with endless possibilities. Move from limitations and limited thinking to unlimited expectations and actions.

Focus, commit, act and engage.

Live brilliantly with your own special brand of passion, enthusiasm, verve, fervor, zest, gusto or any other name you might call it. Let it boil up in you and bubble over in your daily life. Anything positive can and will happen when you work with an expectant attitude.

Focus on your goal, your idea or your purpose. Few persons ever accomplish anything without focusing on their objective. Drive your mind, heart, body and soul toward whatever you expect to accomplish. Focus on it, write it down, say it verbally or any other way you find energizing for your life.

Commit to it by avoiding distractions. It's easy to fool around on your way toward your goal by goofing off, making excuses, finding someone that takes you off your path and any other number of distractions. Once you commit, you set your mind toward your final destination. It becomes easier the farther along the path you travel.

Action always speaks louder than anything else. Conviction without action turns into entertainment. Words vanish into thin air. A page full of "I hope to...." won't amount to a hill of beans without action from you. Take action toward your intention. It's simple, straightforward and direct.

For example: when my siblings and I were kids, we marched into the kitchen after playing outside and asked our mother for some cookies.

She said, "If you want some cookies, you make them and you bake them."

Within minutes, we pulled out the recipe, all the ingredients and turned up the oven to 350 degrees Fahrenheit. We happily took action that carried us to our final reward of gorging ourselves on chocolate chip cookies. We gobbled those cookies brilliantly. Mom didn't do it for us. Unknowingly, she gave us a valuable gift. If you desire something, take action.

Another time, I needed a bike for my paper route. My dad said, "You earn the money and you can buy it."

It took me several months of walking my paper route, but after saving up the money, I plunked down cash for a brand new bicycle. I took action toward my goal of riding a bike. During the time that I worked for it, as well as when I pedaled it on my morning newspaper route, I lived brilliantly with purpose, passion and high expectations.

Other parents give their kids everything they want. They buy them televisions, bicycles, cell phones, sports gear and clothes. That sets up a dynamic for the child of thinking that life will give him or her everything at no cost, with no responsibility or personal accountability. Such an upbringing will create challenges for that child when he or she reaches adulthood.

On the negative side, a lot of kids ask their parents for something and the parents respond with a resounding, "No, you can't have cookies or a new bike or a dress."

When a parent says "no" like that, it means to the child that "life" says, "No!" It doesn't matter what rationale the parent is using. Why? That's all a child understands. That "no" manifests in the child's mind as a negative concept. With endless "no's" a kid may buy into the reality that he or she is helpless to enjoy a cookie or any other yearning. It can also translate into the orientation that they can't do well in school, become a cheerleader or captain the chess team.

Of course, all kids learn that they may enjoy recess only when the bell rings. They can only go to eat when the lunch bell rings. All of us learn about our scheduling paradigms, responsibilities and personal behavior.

At the same time, many young kids today lack a sense of self-confidence. They are told they can't do something. The father might say, "I had a hard time in math class so you probably will find math difficult, too."

Kids respond by accepting that they have no power to succeed or take action. Finally, their outcome is failure or apathy. None of us can blame our parents because the same thing was done to them. It's called "cultural consciousness" or "traditions" of our society.

"Well, that's the way we've always done it around here," said the local man in charge. "If you don't like it, that's tough."

You can change that orientation by understanding what happened to you in your youth. You can rewrite the hard drive in your mind. You can decide to take action. You can move toward creating an edge.

"Edge" means to maximize yourself mentally, emotionally and physically. You may notice all great athletes maintain an edge in their sport. Great tennis players study their opponents on film or in person to discover their strengths and weaknesses. Great golfers see their ball dropping into the cup. Basketball players feel their shot swishing through the net. Great home-run hitters watch the ball all the way until it connects with the bat.

It's no different for you. Keep your edge by keeping a keen mind and concentrating on your intentions, work, play and goals.

Finally, as the starship Captain Jean-Luc Picard in **Star Trek** told Commander Data, "Set a course for the Zebulon sector...engage."

Everything falls into place as you work your mind toward success. You engage your entire being into the process of triumph through these practices.

Do you see a new pattern for your life emerging? While many enthusiastic people create energetic lives for themselves, many other quiet individuals also create fulfilling and happy lives at their levels of engagement. None possess a patent on what it means to live an adventure-filled life. That's why someone who loves to sculpt, play chess, paint or macramé may enjoy just as passionate a life as a mountain climber. Each of us gets turned on by something in our own mind.

At Iguassu Falls in Argentina, my friends and I stepped beside one of the grandest waterfalls in the world. It's not the tallest, but, oh my gosh, it proves to be one of the most spectacular. Around the roar of the falls, we watched toucan birds and brilliantly colored butterflies. Near the falls, we watched 10,000 black and yellow butterflies dancing on pink flowers. Can you imagine the color contrast and movement as the butterflies pollinated the flowers?

What made that experience more incredible? A man, sitting at a seven-foot-tall harp, played his music to "flow" with the butterflies. We sat on the grass watching him play while the butterflies danced to his music. Maybe his music danced to the butterflies. His passion translated into an amazing experience for him and for us.

Sure, I get high riding my bicycle, skiing down a bump run, canoeing, rafting and climbing mountains. This guy got high playing his harp with butterflies dancing to the music. By the look on his face, I swear he climbed to the top of his own Mount Everest in the musical realm. He lived brilliantly.

KEY POINTS FROM THIS CHAPTER

1. Live at your highest sense of wellbeing.
2. Choose to expect good things to happen in your life.
3. Expect good outcomes as a matter of habit.
4. Relish every minute along the way whether work, play or quiet time.

*C*hapter 34—Leap for life

"Fear holds us and binds us and keeps us from growing. It kills a small piece of us each day. It holds us to what we know and keeps us from what's possible, and it is our worst enemy. Fear doesn't announce itself; it's disguised, and it's subtle. It's choosing the safe course; most of us feel we have "rational" reasons to avoid taking risks. The brave man is not the one without fear, but the one who does what he must despite being afraid. To succeed, you must be willing to risk total failure; you must learn this. Then you will succeed." Unknown

Heading east on Route 92 out of Provo, Utah, Paula and I cranked hard through the afternoon. Above us, craggy 10,000 foot peaks poked into a cloudy sky. We sweated our way through deep canyons. We stopped for a rest area at a turnout.

"Sure is a lot different than the salt flats," Paula said, sucking on her water bottle.

"My legs are feeling this hill," I added. "Guess they forgot about climbing after so long on the flats."

"It's prettier up here."

"Sure is," I said. "These mountains inspire me."

A few minutes later, we coasted down a steep incline. I hate losing altitude, but it's useless to fight it. We coasted through endless curves. Ahead of us, on the crest of a climb, a large boulder had fallen onto the highway. I decided to move it off the road so it wouldn't smash a car's undercarriage to bits.

"Give me a minute," I said, laying my bike on the side of the road. "I'm going to get this rock off the road. It could get somebody killed."

"I need a rest anyway," said Paula.

At that moment, another small rock cracked down from overhead. It bounced across the road before slamming into the guardrail.

"Looks like we're under some falling rock," I said, hoisting the boulder to the side of the road.

"Look out!" Paula yelled.

A shower of small rocks bounced across the road. I looked up to see where it was coming from.

"Look at that," I said, pointing upward.

"It's a bighorn sheep," Paula said. "He's knocking those rocks down on us. He looks like he's in a tight spot."

About 150 feet above us, a bighorn sheep stood on a ledge. He was stuck because the path ended. His massive horns swept back from the top of his head. He looked a bit pensive as he nearly leaped forward, but stopped.

"He's going to jump, but there's no place to go," Paula said.

"Unless it's that ledge above him."

"That's gotta be more than 15 feet away and higher."

"Maybe that's why he's hesitating."

Without a second pause, the ram coiled his body before launching himself up and out to the ledge above him. His trajectory burst upward, but not quite high enough to reach the higher rock. Instead, his two front feet slid like skids on a flat rock. One rear leg caught the edge of the ledge. He was about to fall 150 feet to his death before our eyes. But in a split second, with his one leg locked onto the ledge, he threw his front legs upward and thrust his head back. He kicked with his one back leg to launch himself upside down, his hooves pointed to the sky, back toward his original ledge.

While in the middle of his flight back, he twisted his body like a cat before landing. But again, only his front legs made the lower ledge. But his one back hoof reached the rock. His front legs skidded onto the ledge again, but his rear end was not going to make it. With only a split second left before he slipped off the ledge, he bellowed as he kicked hard with his one back leg that had made the ledge. That thrust kicked the back of his body upward and with the momentum of the leap, spun his rump around until he fell sideways onto the ledge. He lay there stunned. Seconds later, he stood up and walked back the other way.

"Good heavens," Paula gasped.

"I felt that," I said.

John Muir, America's first environmentalist and creator of our national park systems said it best: "How many hearts with warm red blood in them are beating under the cover of the woods, and how many teeth and eyes are shining? A multitude of animal people, intimately related to us, but whose lives we know almost nothing, are as busy about their own lives as we are about ours."

While bicycling, we roll quietly into the last of the silence. It allows us to peek into their lives for surprising moments.

KEY POINTS FROM THIS CHAPTER

1. Enjoy the magic of moving through the wilderness.
2. By being quiet, you may see something missed by noisy people.

*C*hapter 35—Total dedication and receptivity

"Your own words are the bricks and mortar of the dreams you want to realize. Your words are the greatest power you have. The words you choose and their use establish the life you experience." Sonia Croquette

5ᵗʰ Practice—Total dedication and receptivity

The key to the adventure-car that you expect to drive throughout your life, whether you climb a mountain, raft a river, paint a picture, write a poem, create a sculpture or raise kids—depends on your dedication and receptivity.

Let me repeat this wise saying by the philosopher Goethe to drive it into your conscious and subconscious mind: "Until one is committed, there is hesitancy; the chance to draw back—always ineffectiveness. Concerning all acts of initiative and creation, there is one elementary truth: the ignorance of which kills countless ideas and splendid plans. That the moment one definitely commits oneself to a task, then providence moves, too. All sorts of things occur to help one that would never otherwise have occurred. A whole stream of events issues from the decision, raising in one's favor all manner of unforeseen incidents and meetings and material assistance, which no one could have dreamed would have come his or her way. Whatever you can do, or dream you can do, begin it. Boldness has genius, power and magic in it. Begin it now."

Those words echo the quote at the head of this chapter by Sonia

Croquette. You must possess total dedication and receptivity. It pertains to words that you choose and their use establishes the life you experience.

That means you may change your entire thinking and speaking patterns to expect and receive new ideas and attitudes. You may approach it emotionally or intellectually or both.

You can engage your mental thought waves with the creative energy of the universe.

Once you engage that creative energy, you will discover thoughts and ideas that will facilitate your goals and dreams. What dream has your name on it? That's for you to decide. Once you stamp your name on your dream, take action.

When you incorporate the nuances of these practices along with the concepts, you will find yourself thinking, speaking and acting in new and self-fulfilling ways. You are receptive to new ideas and people with creative and adventuresome lives. In fact, you will interest them and they will interest you.

If you climb a 14,000-foot peak, you will run into people that love the mountains, love adventure and love the outdoors. Without a doubt, it's challenging to climb a mountain. No question that a 100-mile bicycle ride taxes the heck out of you. Nonetheless, you ride with others who love the quest. More than likely they love other quests in the same realm.

Those experiences lead to ever greater possibilities through your commitment and receptivity to a person, place or thing.

KEY POINTS FROM THIS CHAPTER

1. Your intentions engage your receptivity.
2. Your thinking must be geared toward success at all times.
3. Expect success, live success, feel success and breathe success.
4. Draw people like you to your realm by your energy of success.

Chapter 36—Arctic Circle, Norway to Athens, Greece

"It was the lure of adventure, the appreciation of beauty. It lay beyond the descriptive words of men—where immortality is touched through danger, where life meets death, where man is more than man, and existence both supreme and valueless at the same time. What kind of man would live a life without daring? Is life so sweet that we should criticize men that seek adventure? Is there a better way to die." Charles Lindbergh, first to fly across the Atlantic Ocean

In a blink, the spokes, once reflecting the dawn's early light in the "Land of the Midnight Sun," fell silent in the garage after rolling 3,500 miles from Nord Cap, Norway to Athens, Greece. My bike, Condor, rests back at his usual spot hanging from the ceiling awaiting the next ride. My friends Gary, Denis, Bob and I rolled our bicycles across the European continent in one of the great bicycle adventures on the planet.

However, the memories and 2,500 pictures remain fresh in our minds. How can you describe so much laughter and amazing moments?

I can still see all four of us meeting in Nord Cap on a cool evening. We laughed, smiled and enjoyed great expectations. We unpacked the bikes, wrenched them together and locked on the panniers. We found a campsite near a swiftly moving stream.

The first morning, we awoke to softly falling snow drifting down from a gray sky. Nonetheless, we rode through reindeer land, Viking territory and into the land of the cuckoo bird. That crazy fowl became our morning alarm clock, "Cuckoo, cuckoo, cuckoo!"

After two weeks of good weather, the gray sky opened up. For seven days, we rode in cold rain. It wasn't much fun. At one point, I saw the look on Bob's face. He was a novice at long distance riding. Water soaked him from head to foot, nose to toes, front to back, butt to feet and up to down.

Rain pounded our tents at night. On the eighth day, the rain stopped. No wonder the Vikings were so tough. It rains all the time in Norway. We rode south never to see another drop of rain for the next three months.

We reached Denmark which runs flat as a pancake with windmills, farmland and nice people. We stopped into a 150-year-old windmill that stood along the road.

For food, Gary ate his way through the pastry shops of Europe. Denmark provided the world's best pastries. Every shop offered éclairs, doughnuts, cakes and cookies. Shop owners offered an unending presentation of fabulous baked goods. We stuffed ourselves and burned it off as we pedaled down the highway. We rode the North Sea Cycle Route into Germany.

Soon, we followed the Rhine River. It featured the feudal system with castles built on high cliffs. We discovered 2,000 year old cities, 1,000 year old churches, fantastic wines and delicious foods. My cycling friends Uwe and Claudia took us to old churches in Esslingen. More cycling friends Hans and Erika showed the best of Karlsruhe with lakes, music and concerts.

We pedaled to the source of the Rhine River at Lake Constance and into the Swiss Alps where we climbed high mountain passes. We descended 37 kilometers off Splugen Pass. It was like riding down through a can of angleworms with so many twists, turns and tunnels. We passed dozens of touring riders from all over the world.

Chiavenna, Italy started our tour in Italia as we moved through the Roman Empire in Venice and Florence with their statues, paintings and exquisite architecture. We saw where Leonardo da Vinci worked, played and created as well as Michelangelo. His statue of David is as fantastic as one can imagine. We visited Volterra and other walled cities. We walked beside the canals of Venice and took a ride in the gondolas. We tried to prop up the leaning tower of Pisa. We pedaled into Rome where we visited St. Mark's Cathedral and the Roman Forum. We walked along the ancient stone roads where Caesar guided his chariot. We visited where

St. Mark suffered death. We sat at the Fountain of Trevi and made wishes while throwing coins over our shoulders. We stood in the Sistine Chapel to see where Michelangelo's human being symbolizing humanity reached upward to touch the finger and breath of life from God.

We visited the Coliseum where one million men lost their lives in 200 years of gladiator games. It was all quiet and only non-violent tourists walked around the 60,000 seat structure. We walked on the Via Sacra (sacred road) that led into the heart of Rome and we walked where all the great historical figures walked. We strolled where Caesar, Brutus, Pilot, Aurelius and other Roman greats walked. It was a pretty heady experience to read about them and then, follow in their footsteps 2,000 years later.

We visited a mass gravesite in Italy near Anzio of soldiers from America and Great Britain who died in WWII. Most of them were 19 to 24. We slept above the cemetery that night. In the morning, I thanked all of them. It hit me to invite them to ride with me that morning in the early sunshine in the hills of Italy. So, I led a group of 520 spirited bicyclists out of their graves and onto a morning ride. They yelled and cheered at what fun they were having on that special day.

All over Italy, we pedaled through the past. We rode our bikes into the hills of Tuscany. We pedaled up and down the vineyard-covered valleys. We sweated across rivers and camped on cliffs to watch magnificent sunsets. One village stood on a high hill and was walled off over 1,200 years ago. It was absolutely amazing riding into a city that was hundreds of centuries old with people still living in brick houses from so long ago. As we labored into the village and past the walls, we came upon a fountain. We poured water from the fountain onto our heads in the hot sun.

A tall cathedral stood behind us where we heard children singing. We walked up the steps and walked inside a fabulous 1,200 year old church with a children's choir practicing. We sat down in a pew and listened to the songs rise to the rafters of that old church. We couldn't begin to tell you how touched we were by those children's voices in that cathedral on a hill.

We loved the Italians who cheered us and applauded our journey. We left Italy filled with history and grandeur. We reached the coast and caught a ferry from Ancona, Italy to Patras, Greece. We rode though the dry, hot, olive grove-covered mountains to the Oracle of Delphi. Their culture stands as magnificent from the times of Socrates, Aristotle and Plato. We were touched by history in those buildings, statues and museums. We pedaled on to Athens where we walked on the Parthenon and discovered ancient ruins. We ate Greek food in a restaurant overlooking the Aegean Sea. Greece is the cradle of thought. I now have statues of Hercules on my memory shelf along with the leaning Tower of Pisa.

Back home, our lives pace to the humdrum of life, the daily grind, the normal deal of work, movies and friends. But from that summer on bicycles, we carry extraordinary moments in our hearts and minds.

KEY POINTS FROM THIS CHAPTER

1. Be open to the new challenges of culture, language and people.
2. You may enjoy learning the language to speak to the people.

*C*hapter 37—*Steadfast conviction*

"If you think you can or can't, you're right." Henry Ford

Back in 1884, Thomas Stevens decided to ride his Penny Farthing high-wheeler bicycle around the world starting in San Francisco, California. He pedaled with no gears, little pack, less water and no support. All before him had failed similar attempts. However, he wired his brain with attitude, guts, determination and steadfast conviction. On December 17, 1886, he finished his bicycle ride around the world in San Francisco.

You may appreciate right now that adventure is not and never will be a walk in the park, a Sunday stroll or a bicycle ride around the lake on a paved path. If you ride a long distance touring bicycle, climb a mountain, canoe rivers, walk the entire Great Wall of China, explore Antarctica, walk the length of the Amazon River, or pack into the Grand Canyon—you must be prepared for some rough slogging, harsh weather, tough times, demonic insects, irritating companions and hard knocks.

When the going gets tough, the mentally and emotionally tough get going. No whining, complaining or feeling sorry for yourself. No sitting around in a pity party crying, "Nobody likes me, everybody hates me—I'm going to eat some worms. Big fat juicy ones, squishy soft greasy ones; I'm going to eat some worms."

Instead, dude or dudette, buck up. Saddle up. True grit. Get moving. It's not the easy times but the hard times that make an adventure most memorable. Some days as I cycled 17,000 kilometers around the perimeter of Australia in 120-degree Fahrenheit heat day in and day out, baking in the desert, with those demonic bush flies crawling into every orifice of my body and not a soul in sight—I felt utter desperation, loneliness and futility. I felt sweat draining out of my pores as I fell asleep in the scorching desert heat night after night. I stunk like a koala bear and suffered from thirst and cotton-mouth all day long.

Cycling around Australia may be one of the most miserable adventures of my life. Before I started, one Australian, when I talked about cycling across the Nullarbor Plains said, "Do you know how hot it is across the middle?"

"I'm going for the adventure," I said.

"That only proves one thing, mate," he said.

"What's that?" I asked.

"You must be dead from the neck up," he said.

He may have been right. A few times, I sat beside my tent, sweating like a pig, filthy with grime and so lonely that when I looked up, all I saw was the bottom of the bucket. On Christmas Day, one lady at a roadhouse said, "Wouldn't you like to be home with your friends right about now?"

"Sure, it would be nice to share Christmas with my friends and family," I said. "But then, I wouldn't be on this incredible adventure around Australia. They all wish they were me. I'm happy that I am me and living this adventure. Besides, I could easily jump on a plane and fly home. But that's not what I came for."

My dad once told me that when I put myself into a situation, it came from my choice and either I lived it out or I would regret not finishing what I started. I always call on a deep-down conviction that my dad planted in me at a young age. He implanted the power of steadfast conviction in my heart, mind and body.

During that Australian ride, I witnessed natural phenomenon and animals unknown to 99 percent of humanity. I witnessed a frilled lizard walk up to my tent and flare his frill at me like a space alien. It scared the daylights out of me. I rode my bike across the Nullarbor plains with a flightless bird named an Emu for two days. I watched kangaroos hop through the bush. I walked among the Pinnacles of Cervantes. I swam with the dolphins at Shark's Bay. I stood in the prison Boab tree in Northern Australia. A crocodile chased me in Darwin. I scuba dived on the Great Barrier Reef. I watched the Southern Cross fill the night sky during the whole journey. I live with those uncommon experiences inside my mind.

Andrew Skurka skied, rafted and backpacked 4,600 miles across Alaska and the Yukon Territory in 2010. He stood his ground against charging grizzly bears. He shouldered a heavy 50 pound pack up to 20 miles per day. He pushed toward his ultimate destination. Was it easy? What do you think?

It matters little whether you walk across America on your hands or walk around the world or climb a mountain peak. You must engage an uncommon tenacity to succeed at whatever your quest.

Those hard times that you will experience qualify for adventure rather than someone taking a casual bicycle ride around town or watching a movie about some adventure. Let's talk about what it takes to succeed in your quests.

6ᵗʰ *Practice—Steadfast conviction*

Returning to Thomas Stevens, few people can comprehend how much dedication it took to ride a Penny Farthing around the world. First of all, it's not easy to ride one. If you brake too hard, you can fly over the handlebars from eight feet above the ground. Pedaling one of those bikes over sandy, gravel or muddy roads must have been a living nightmare for Stevens. A rider can carry very little gear on that ungainly bicycle with a trailing little wheel.

Nonetheless, Stevens maintained steadfast conviction. His book astounded me in that he lived through it. He pedaled that bike across sand, gravel and muck. He nearly suffered death many times. He crossed the entire United States. After his initial success, he took off by sailing ship to Great Britain. From there, he cycled across Europe, the Middle East to India and China. He hopped all over the place before finally reaching San Francisco two years later. He maintained a steadfast conviction to complete the ride. Not only that, he later pedaled into Africa, rode a horse across Russia, traveled through India and much more. We're talking diseases, polluted water, people trying to kill him and a host of challenges beyond anything imagined today.

As a matter of record, my friend Doug Armstrong spent 16 months pedaling from Cape Town, South Africa to Cairo, Egypt. He almost got killed, too. It's not any safer today.

As a six continent-riding cyclist myself, I have benefited from 21 gears and a derailleur that made mountain climbing easy. I have enjoyed big rubber tires, mostly paved roads and plentiful filtered clean water and food. My travels, for the most part, even in developing countries, have been a party compared to Stevens. He walked up every hill because a Penny Farthing cannot negotiate much more than a five percent grade, and because of poor brakes, he walked down the other side of mountains.

He proved one tough hombre. With my gears, I can ride up 16,000-foot mountain passes on gravel, as I have in the Andes, and coast down the other side. Nonetheless, it's tough busting your butt, and you need true grit in spite of any adversity, to keep going—especially in headwinds, torrid heat or pouring rain.

Thomas, you, me or anyone choosing adventure must employ the same tenacity and determination to succeed in worldwide adventures. It's called steadfast conviction.

Whether you're working a tough job to earn the money for the adventure or during the adventure, you need steadfast conviction. If you suffer from heat, cold, rain or insects during an adventure, you need to maintain steadfast conviction that you own success. That's right. You live it, think it and feel it. You walk, run, skip or whatever it takes to get you to your intention, dream or goal.

An old sailor once said, "A smooth sea never made a skillful mariner, neither do uninterrupted prosperity and success qualify for usefulness and happiness. The storms of adversity, like those of the ocean, rouse the faculties, and excite the invention, prudence, skill and fortitude of the voyager. The mariners of ancient times, in bracing their minds to outward calamities, acquired a loftiness of purpose and moral heroism worth a lifetime of softness and security."

No one will care one way or the other if you succeed or otherwise. For the most part, human beings only care about their little corner of the world and their own situation. Some choose personal greatness while others choose average lives. If you choose a life of adventure, engage your own brand of personal tenacity that will carry you to a lifetime of achievement.

Therefore, decide to succeed, and, quite frankly, you will succeed with your steadfast conviction.

KEY POINTS FROM THIS CHAPTER

1. Steadfast conviction becomes your mindset.
2. True grit and determination must become a part of your being.
3. Your success depends on your positive mental attitude.
4. If you think you can't or can, you're right.

SECTION IV –NUTS AND BOLTS OF WORLD ADVENTURE

This section offers you everything you need to know as to preparation for travel, gear and contact information. You will discover how to use your conscious and subconscious mind to create an action plan for realizing your intentions. If you need more ideas, you will find them from other writers that provide a plethora of information. This section gives you ideas for your bucket list of travel and adventure options. The key is to prepare you in every way possible for your continuing success.

Chapter 38—Action plan

"Every man or woman ought to be inquisitive through every hour of this great adventure down to the day when he or she shall no longer cast a shadow in the sun. For if he or she dies without a question in the heart, what excuse is there for continuance?" Frank Colby

By now, you have read a number of my adventures from around the world via different kinds of exploits. Most prove mild while a few could have gotten me killed. Many other high risk adventure-seekers make my escapades look like a walk in the park. Again, no comparison as everybody chooses their level of risk and adventure.

Okay, you understand all the concepts and practices. You want to live your own adventures. How do you make your life work out the way you want it? How do you guide your life in the direction you want to travel? You need to create, plan and fulfill your intentions, dreams or goals.

USE YOUR BRAIN: THE MOST POWERFUL COMPUTER IN THE UNIVERSE

Let's imagine three levels across your head, all parallel and evenly spaced. Just imagine your brain with a first level, second level and third level.

1. First level—your conscious mind or creative mind operates on the top level. That's where you come up with ideas. Let's say that you imagine a ski trip. It may be a canoe trip, a mountain

climbing expedition or riding a bicycle 100 miles in a day. It could be anything that you love or intend to experience such as a painting, sculpture or other works of art.

Essentially, your top level may be considered the architect that draws the plans for a weekend adventure, weeklong adventure or year around the world adventure. Again, you may be trying to win a dance contest or triathlon event. Whatever your adventure, it births in the conscious level of your brain.

That architect draws everything into the plans for a successful adventure. It includes times, routes, gear, people, support, transport, shots, passport, visas and everything you need to enjoy a successful adventure.

During your waking hours, you prepare for the adventure by working a job, buying equipment, training, obtaining a passport and all other preparations needed to step into the adventure. In other words, you complete all the necessary details created by your architect mind on the top level.

You research books that cover every detail you need by those who have gone before you. Fill in the blanks by following check lists promoted by clubs, organizations and other entities that help you prepare for your adventure. Once your architect draws up the plans, you let them germinate in the second level or sub-conscious.

2. Second level—let's move to the second level or subconscious. Once you make a definite plan to engage a certain adventure or piece of artwork, your subconscious works on it while you sleep. You engage your subconscious mind or whatever you care to call it. You work with the creative flow.

As you sleep, your subconscious mind works on the details by making sure you move toward your goals or dreams—however you interpret them. As your subconscious works, you will pick up more ideas and think of things that will move you toward your goals.

Whether it takes you a week to prepare for a mountain climbing trip, skiing trip or canoeing trip—you learn what it takes by starting small and, with time, moving toward more ambitious adventures. You gain knowledge and know-how as you proceed through each check-down.

3. Third level—the third level becomes your fruition level where you live the adventure or finish a painting or run a race. During that experience, you gain valuable insights and understanding of what you did or didn't do to make your adventure successful. With each successful adventure, you may choose greater experiences in whatever arenas interest you.

KEY POINTS FROM THIS CHAPTER

1. Your conscious mind creates the idea or intention.
2. Your subconscious mind works on the details.
3. You fulfill the steps to make your dream a reality.
4. You live your dream, adventure or intention.

Chapter 39—Adventure lists for consideration

"It takes a lot of courage to release the familiar and seemingly secure, to embrace the new. But there is no real security in what is no longer meaningful. There is more security in the adventurous and exciting, for in movement there is life and in change there is power." Alan Cohen

Your lifespan provides as many adventures as you care to pursue. You may participate in some of the wildest, weirdest, craziest and zaniest activities ever invented by humanity. You will not live long enough to do everything on this planet, but you can make a huge dent in your bucket list.

While I cycled through Tasmania, Australia, I met a British man who had traveled through 181 countries out of the 193 or so countries on the planet. Well past 80, he inspired me. One lady, Elizabeth, also from London, England, hiked through Nepal with us. At 72, she carried her pack along with the rest of the group. Obviously, her bucket list needed more adventures before she would leave the planet.

You may travel, scuba dive, climb mountains, raft rivers, surf, cliff dive, explore caves, camp, ride horses, sail, compete in triathlons and about a gazillion other activities. Suit yourself as to the kind of adventure as well as intensity, frequency and danger.

Several years ago, Morgan Freeman and Jack Nicholson played two guys suffering from terminal cancer. Because they didn't want to drop into their graves without having done something amazing with their lives, they created a bucket list of adventures to pursue while they still lived. That list included sky diving, stock car racing, traveling to the pyramids, climbing the Great Wall of China, visiting the Taj Mahal, visiting Machu Picchu, climbing to the base camp of Mount Everest, taking an African safari and more.

At one point, as Freeman touched the blazing red finish of a 1965 Mustang, Nicholson asked, "Are you going to race it or buy it a dress?"

"Just getting to know each other," Freeman replied, running his hands across the finish.

"Do you hate me?" Nicholson asked.

"Not yet," Freeman said.

As they sashayed around the globe on their bucket list of adventures, at one point, Nicholson said, "We live, we die. The world keeps going round and round."

No question, you possess only so many minutes on this little blue-green planet somewhere in the outskirts of space. When it's over, it's over. No rerun, no second chance, no mulligan, no do-over and no re-take. You're out to capture the whole enchilada while you're living on the planet.

BUCKET LIST IN NO PARTICULAR ORDER

1. Raft trip down the Colorado River through the Grand Canyon. Lee's Ferry to Diamond Creek takeout or Lake Powell.
2. Hike the Appalachian Trail, 2,175 miles and five to six months from Georgia to Maine. Amazing journey through hill and dale, woods and water. Hike the Continental Divide from Canada to Mexico via Montana, Wyoming, Colorado and New Mexico. Hike the Colorado Trail for six weeks from Durango to Denver.
3. Climb all 54—14,000-foot peaks in Colorado. Climb all 14,000-foot peaks and higher all the way to Denali in Alaska at 20,329 feet.
4. Bicycle across America. Bicycle border to border via the West Coast from Canada to Mexico, Continental Divide Ride Canada to Mexico, East Coast of Maine to Key West, Florida. Follow the Lewis and Clark Trail from St. Lewis to the Oregon Coast. Seattle, Washington to the Arctic Ocean, Alaska. Pedal Route 66 for a nostalgic journey through the past. Any of a dozen other routes across America will bring you unlimited bicycle adventure. Bicycle seven continents.

5. Ballooning across America. Ballooning in New Mexico, Colorado and a dozen other states.

6. Mountain biking in Moab, Utah on Slickrock. Race in the Leadville 100 Race Across the Sky either by foot or bicycle. www.raceacrossthesky.com

7. Ride the Triple Bypass in Colorado. Ride the Rockies. Ride the RAGBRAI in Iowa.

8. Scuba dive the five Great Lakes. Dive in all the famous places in Florida and the Gulf of Mexico. Dive in the Galapagos Islands. Dive the Great Barrier Reef in Australia. Dive in all the oceans and seas of the world.

9. Bicycle tour Nord Cap, Norway to Athens, Greece in five months. Bicycle 17,000 kms around Australia in six months. Bicycle from the Arctic Ocean in Alaska to the bottom of South America in Ushuaia. Bicycle the North Sea Cycle Route.

10. Train ride on the Orient Express. Train over the highest railroad pass in the world from Lima, Peru to Juan Kio at 16,000 feet. Train ride across Canada. Train ride across America coast-to-coast. Train ride all over Europe. Endless opportunities await you anywhere in the world on a train.

11. Bag all seven of the highest peaks on all seven continents. Trek in Nepal, where you will visit ancient people, an ancient culture and astounding scenery.

12. Visit 193, give or take a few, countries in the world by any means you can discover.

13. Surf the big ones in Hawaii, Australia, Bali, Panama and just about anywhere big waves crash on any region of the planet.

14. Horseback ride across America or any continent. For more information: www.thelongridersguild.com

15. Ski the Andes, Pyrenees, Alaska Range, British Columbia, Rockies, Whistler's Mountain, Stowe, Swiss Alps, Bolivia and anywhere mountains welcome you.

16. Safari in Kenya, Tanzania or anywhere in Africa. Ride a camel around the pyramids or a horse.

17. Parasail, hang-glide and sky dive anywhere in the world. Bungee jumping for kicks.

18. Travel to Antarctica. Watch whales, penguins, seals and skua. Work and live at McMurdo Station.

19. Climb Half-Dome at Yosemite National Park. Hike all of Yosemite and the Sierra Range.
20. Hut to hut mountain ski trips in Colorado and many other states. www.huts.org , www.sanjuanhuts.com
21. Camel trek in Morocco, Africa. Additionally, you can cycle from Cape Town to Cairo, Egypt in about 16 months.
22. Bicycle tour the profile of the boot of Italy.
23. Play golf courses in all 50 states.
24. Raft the Nile River.
25. Explore the Amazon River, South America.
26. Walk the Congo River, Africa.
27. Raft the Yangtze River, China.
28. Climb Everest, K-2, McKinley, Kilimanjaro, Cook, Matterhorn, Rainier, Fuji, Vesuvius, Huascaran, Popocatepetl, Kenya, Ararat, Bromo, Grand Tetons, Baldy.
29. Dive in a submarine.
30. Fly a blimp, airplane, jet, hot air balloon.
31. Ride an elephant, camel, ostrich and wild bull.
32. Play a piano, guitar, horn.
33. Become a globetrotting photographer.
34. Learn unlimited numbers of languages.
35. Stand on the North and South Poles.
36. Walk around the world.
37. Read all the classics.
38. Ride or run Monument Valley at sunrise or sunset.
39. Backpack into Chicago Basin, Colorado.
40. Walk or run the Boulder Bolder in Boulder, Colorado.

Top 110 adventures in the United States

Alaska

Complete a NOLS course
Explore ANWR
Heli-Ski the Chugach Mountains
Tree-climb Chilkat
Float the Tatshenshini-Alsek River
Trek Wrangell-St. Elias National Park & Preserve
Climb Mount McKinley
Camp with Alaska brown bears

Canoe the Yukon River
Bicycle the Richardson Highway
Bicycle the Dalton Highway across the Arctic Circle

Arizona

Row down the Grand Canyon
Hike Buckskin Gulch (& Utah)
Bicycle Monument Valley

California

Surf the Lost Coast
Bike the Death Ride
Hike Half Dome
Hike the Sierra High Route
Paddle Santa Cruz Island
Mountain Bike the Tahoe Rim Trail (& Nevada)
Bodysurf the Wedge
Raft the Forks of the Kern
Ski Mountaineer Mount Shasta
Hike the John Muir Trail

Colorado

Bike From Durango to Moab (& Utah)
Climb Ouray
Ski Scar Face
Hike the Colorado Trail
Run the Trans-Rockies
Ski Silverton Mountain
Race the Leadville Trail 100
Backcountry Ski the 10th Mountain Division Huts
Bag 54—14ers, pack into Chicago and American basins
Climb the Diamond on Longs Peak
Run the Bolder Boulder, Colorado

Florida

Kite-board the Keys
Paddle the Everglades
Swamp Tromp in Big Cypress National Preserve
Dive freshwater caves
Fly-Fish for the Florida Keys Slam
Scuba dive in John Pennekamp Park in the Keys

Georgia

Canoe the Okeefenokee

Hawaii

Kayak the Na Pali Coast
Hike the Muliwai Trail
Kiteboard Maui's North Shore
Parasailing around Diamond Head

Iowa

Bicycle RAGBRAI

Idaho

Hike the Salmon River
Snowkite Camas Valley
Raft the Owyhee River (& Oregon & Nevada)

Kentucky

Climb Red River Gorge

Maine

Kayak the Maine Island Trail
Canoe the Allagash

Michigan

Sail the Manitou's
Windsurf the Straits of Mackinaw
Bicycle the 'Mitt' of Michigan, especially in spring or fall

Minnesota

Dogsled the Boundary Waters
Wreck dive Lake Superior
Race the Arrowhead 135
Canoe the Boundary Waters
Hike the Superior Trail
Canoe the Mississippi River from Lake Itasca

Missouri

Paddle 340 Miles of the Mighty Missouri—Nonstop

Montana

Hike the Bob Marshall Trail
Climb Granite Peak
Ice Climb Hyalite Canyon
Fly-Fish the Spring Creeks of Paradise Valley
Backpack Glacier National Park
Bicycle start for the Continental Divide to Mexico

Multistate

Get fit at a Navy SEAL Immersion Camp
Bike Across America
Learn to fly a wingsuit
Backpack the Pacific Coast Trail
Bike the Continental Divide Trail
Backpack the Appalachia Trail
Run Ironman triathlons in several states

North Carolina

Paddle the Outer Banks
Learn Paddling at Nantahala Outdoor Center

North Dakota

Bike the Maah Daah Hey

New Hampshire

Ski Tuckerman Ravine
Hike the Traverse
Bicycle through the covered bridges

New Mexico

Fly-fish the Pecos
Horsepack the Gila Wilderness

Nevada

Heli-Ski the Ruby Mountains

New York

Canoe the Adirondacks
Climb the Gunks

Oregon

Kite-board the Columbia River Gorge (& Washington)
Ski the Wallowas
Bicycle tour the coast line

Tennessee

Hike the Roan Highlands
Raft the Ocoee

Texas

Float the Big Bend of the Rio Grande

Utah

Raft the Green River
Scale Red-Rock Towers
Paddle Lake Powell
Backpack the Hayduke Trail
Canyoneer Grand Staircase-Escalante
Hike the Zion Narrows
Mountain bike Slickrock in Moab
Mountain bike the Kokopelli Trail

Vermont

Ski Inn-to-Inn on the Catamount Trail

Washington

Transect the Olympic
Climb Mount Rainier
Hike Glacier Peak
Sea Kayak the San Juan Islands

Wisconsin

Ski the Birkebeiner

West Virginia

Raft the Gauley River

Wyoming

Hike the Winds
Climb the Grand Teton

Backcountry Ski Teton Pass
Kayak Lake Yellowstone
Hike Yellowstone's Wild Southwest

How to create your own bucket list:

1. John Goddard started with 127 adventures on his bucket list. Later, he added 500 adventures to his list as his awareness and interests grew. Your interests evolve as you taste different adventures in your teens, 20s, 30s and beyond. Think of your list as an evolving tapestry of your life.

2. Think beyond your own experiences. Read adventure books or magazines to get a feel and taste of what's out there. Some things will grab your mind faster than others.

3. Think about different aspects of your existence. While travel appears as the most compelling bucket list for adventuring, you may find plenty of adventure in your own town such as: learning to swing dance, ballroom or country & western. You might want to compete in dance contests all over the country. You may take up art and travel all over the country or world to paint landscapes, statues, marine life, etc. You may want to try photography in a variety of forms. Stay healthy so you can live to be 100 and try out as many avenues as possible.

4. Check out the Internet for ideas on activities that may interest you. You will find an endless stream of adventures and adventure lists on your computer screen. Use Google and the whole world opens up to you. Try www.43things.com and www.Project183.com for starters.

5. Start out small with easily accomplished adventures. Go with someone who might teach you survival skills, camping, mountain climbing or parasailing. Join clubs to get a feel for your limits. Move with your strengths, gather your confidence and grow your skills. As you progress, you may create bigger and more compelling adventures.

6. If you work a 9-to-5 job, you need to make your intentions for weekends. Then, one, two and three week vacations. If you love triathlon, you may rise at 5 a.m., swim, bike, run and weight train before you go to work. Try to avoid, "One of these days, I'm going to run a marathon." Get your butt out there, train and run it. Make time, take time and move toward your adventure intentions.

7. If you get off on blogging, take time to post your upcoming adventure.

Talk about it. Prepare for it. If you're a quiet and reserved person, write it down for yourself.

8. It's a good idea to write down your intentions for whatever adventure you anticipate. Set some timelines to anticipate the event. I write down and plan my major bicycle adventures two years in advance. That gives me time to earn money and prepare myself mentally, emotionally and physically. It also allows friends who might be going for some or all of the adventure to make their plans. I hold myself to my goals. I move toward each adventure with steadfast determination to stand on the starting line or present my ticket to the airline attendant.

9. Little adventures and big adventures. You need to work them back and forth according to your needs, your money, your time, your age and your condition. For kicks, grins and giggles, make sure you keep that list in a notebook or hanging on the wall. Each time you finish an adventure such as "The Leadville 100 Mountain Bike Race Across the Sky," you cross it off. Save your race placard from your bike as a memento on your "memory shelf." It's a heck of a rewarding feeling to know that you lived it and now, you're on to the next adventure.

10. Laugh, love and smile along the way. Beam good thoughts daily to all you meet and to every challenge. Worry? Intentions and goals come to fruition when you move them into action. Remember that failures provide you with stepping-stones to success.

KEY POINTS FROM THIS CHAPTER

1. Work with your interests to create your bucket list.
2. Talk with friends to gain their ideas for exciting adventures.
3. Read adventure books that interest you.
4. Start out with small adventures and work up to bigger ones.

Chapter 40—Will you live or die on an adventure?

"The fear of death follows from the fear of life. A man who lives fully is prepared to die at any time." Mark Twain

On my first trip to Alaska as a young adventure-seeker at 24, I woke up in my tent on the Russian River of the Kenai Peninsula hearing a "Grumph, grumph, emph" outside my tent. The Russian River enjoys fame not only for its salmon fishing, but also, its 1,000 pound grizzly bears. They visit the river to feed on millions of salmon racing for the spawning grounds.

I shot upright with a chill ripping down my spine. My brother Rex slept in his tent about 10 feet from mine. All night, I swatted no-see-ums, a tiny biting fly, but the bear posed greater danger. I opened my front flap to see an enormous grizzly looking right at me, not three feet away. As the breeze shifted, I smelled the worst case of halitosis in my life. He stunk worse than a barnyard.

He looked at me and I looked at him. My heart jumped out of my chest from beating so fast. My mouth dried up like a cotton ball in the desert. It was the strangest feeling I had ever experienced. That bear could kill me in minutes. I wouldn't stand a chance.

Within 15 seconds, he ambled around the side of my tent. As he passed by the sidewalls, he rubbed his muzzle and drooled across the bright orange nylon. The sun shone through the tent to accent the drool-line about three feet long. Seconds later, he grunted some more and started digging at the corner of my tent. I looked back to see his claws rip through the nylon and hit the blue plastic flooring.

My eyes grew wide as I stared at the four inch claws cutting through my tent. Seconds later, he withdrew them. He walked around my tent to walk right back in front of me. A moment later, he turned toward the Russian River to grab a mouthful of fresh salmon.

My brother Rex said, "Are we gonna live or die? What's the verdict, bro?"

"Could go either way if he doesn't catch any fish," I said. "I think I just stared death in the face."

Like everything in life, random chance may kill you, let you live or hurt you—depending on the circumstances. That morning, which remains vividly with me to this day, could have turned out ugly. We could have been written up in the Anchorage morning newspaper: "Two campers were mauled to death while sleeping near the Russian River yesterday. The bear grabbed one brother and then the other. He gobbled them like a can of sardines. Other campers heard the screams, but nothing could stop the bear from his morning breakfast feast. Services will be held...."

But instead, it wasn't our day to die.

Since my early 20s, through my adventures on six continents—hurricanes, tsunamis, 7.3 earthquakes, 350-pound charging seals in the Galapagos, scuba diving with sharks, mountain climbing, bicycle riding with cars coming up my rear at 70 miles per hour as their drivers text message, Australian bush fires, rip-tides, monkeys raining their feces down on me in the Amazon, moose and grizzly bears—so far, they haven't killed me.

But any of them could have killed me.

Should anyone be afraid of dying on an adventure?

Not on your life! Act like a winner. Accept danger. Agree to the unknown and life on its own terms. Go for it. Never worry about living or dying. Keep moving ahead. Think positive to bring all good to you.

"Let children walk with nature, let them see the beautiful blendings and communions of life and death, their joyous inseparable unity, as taught in woods and meadows, plains and mountains and streams of our blessed star, and they will learn that death is stingless indeed, and as beautiful as life." John Muir

On a sobering daily note, you read about someone dying in a traffic accident coming home from the big game. You hear of a kid succumbing to cancer. A buddy fell off a ladder. An average of 900 Americans annually die from falling off their bicycles because they didn't wear a helmet. They cracked their skulls. Some live a short time and others make it a long life.

It doesn't make any difference if you're rich, poor, smart, stupid, famous or average. I could name hundreds of famous people who died in their 20s, 30s, 40s, 50s or before their time. You may know some dull people living into their 90s. There is no reason or rhyme to any of it. Life happens.

I personally knew a couple that retired after 40 years at the factory. They bought a motor home to travel to Alaska and around the USA to visit 49 state capitals. The morning before their departure date, the husband walked down to the breakfast table. He grabbed the paper. His wife prepared breakfast on the stove. Suddenly, she heard a thud on the table. She looked around to see her husband slumped over—dead. Life and death happen without cause, warning or understanding.

As the saying goes, "Eat dessert first; life is uncertain."

On a logical note, you can avoid being one of the millions of humans who died but never lived. You can avoid staring into a television most of your life. One researcher reported Americans watch television for a total of 15 years of their lives. Millions of Americans suffer a mid-life crisis because they failed to live their dreams or they never discovered their life purpose.

Get your butt out there into the wind, onto the road, up that mountain, down that river, through the deep powder, under the stars and by that campfire. Live until you die and if you die while you're living, your spirit will smile all the way through eternity.

KEY POINTS FROM THIS CHAPTER

1. Answer life's calling in whatever capacity you enjoy.
2. Be smart, be prudent and enjoy a long life.
3. Do what you love and it will reward you for your entire life.

Chapter 41—Peace and harmony while traveling with friends

"Once a journey is designed, equipped, and put in process; a new factor enters and takes over. A trip, a safari, an exploration, is an entity, different from all other journeys. It has a personality, temperament, individuality and uniqueness. A journey is a person in itself; no two are alike. And all plans, safeguards, policing and coercion are fruitless. We find after years of struggle that we do not take a trip; a trip takes us. Tour masters, schedules, reservations, brass-bound and inevitable, dash themselves to wreckage on the personality of the trip. Only when this is recognized can the blown-in-the-glass traveler relax and go along with it. Only then do the frustrations fall away. A journey is like marriage. The certain way to be wrong is to think you control it. I feel better now, having said this, although only those who have experienced it will understand it." John Steinbeck, Travels with Charley

Steinbeck advises us that the journey we undertake develops its own personality. The demeanor of the group becomes the personality of the expedition. Make no mistake about that. The tenor of the group comes from the met and unmet expectations of individuals. How do they handle those gaps between what is in their mind's eye and what is the reality in which they find themselves? Not to be forgotten is how the other members of the group react. This complex mish-mash of emotions creates the personality of the journey.

All will usually start out well, but with time, like with any relationship, the journey can end up being something you can't wait to escape or something you wish would go on forever. If the individuals fail to click, a group can explode with raw emotion right before your eyes. Even the quietest individuals can find themselves erupting in anger. People may go home and end friendships. As Steinbeck warns, individuals and entire groups can dash themselves to wreckage on the personality of the trip.

However, there are things you can do before you start and while you travel via car, train, plane, boat, backpack or bicycle. No matter if you are climbing mountains, rafting, canoeing or any other mode of adventure—you can organize the best possible opportunity for a positive outcome.

When you travel alone, your personality becomes the personality of the trip. When you travel by yourself you may do what you please, when you please and how you please. You can react to your own behavior like you always do. Going it alone ensures a journey that will be easy emotionally, especially on you. But because we are social animals, a journey can be more fun when you share the experience with others.

Mountain climbing, rafting, canoeing, safari and cycle touring create high levels of sustained physical exertion. If you throw in extremes of weather and/or terrain, everyone eventually becomes tired if not worn out. Self-contained cycle touring (no sag wagon) also brings into play the very basics of daily living. Everyone must deal with shelter, clothing, meal preparation, eating, drinking, showers and bowel movements.

You will feel and react to things in ways you never let out in the public eye before. "Highs" become really high. Good situations take on a new level of enjoyment. Tailwinds and 10-mile bicycle down-hills become periods of ecstasy. Campfires fill you with moments of bliss. You'll be awestruck by the life stories of the new people you meet on the road. A hot chocolate on a cool night will become the best drink you ever savored in your life. But it also needs to be said that not everyone reacts to a 15 mile, six percent grade up to a 12,000 foot mountain pass the same way you do. How about throwing in a stiff headwind, a little rain and some cold weather? Even you may reach the end of your rope.

The challenges of adventure temporarily transform the personalities both positively and negatively. Once you're on a backpacking, rafting, climbing, surfing or any other kind of adventure, all kinds of emotions can and will arise from the members of the group. While these ideas will not eradicate all conflict within a group, they will promote better relations among the members of the party.

Therefore, when you travel with others the following guidelines apply:

- The variety and number of emotions and irritating behaviors that will need to be dealt with grows in direct relationship to the number of persons on the adventure. Two may prove optimal. Four is manageable. Six or more individuals fiddling with their gear or chores at every stop can stretch everyone's patience. You may find yourself greatly perturbed herding cats at every stop with ten or more individuals. But whatever the number in your group, you can avoid most of the pitfalls by following the ideas in this chapter.

- Before anyone spends a dime on anything connected with the adventure, the group needs to reach agreement on what the adventure means to each participant. This means the group needs to get together and share individual expectations about the trip with everyone else on the journey. That includes everyone going on the adventure.

  If you're going, this meeting or series of meetings must be mandatory. No exceptions! Where are we starting? Where are we headed? What about weather? How about the terrain? How far are we planning to ride, hike, raft or paddle in different terrain and weather conditions? What about meals? Do we have maps? Where are we going to stay: stealth camping, primitive campgrounds, pay campgrounds with modern facilities and/or motels? What about breaks along the way? What time will the group get up in the morning? How about rest days? What if we get separated? Who brings what? What is it going to cost? These meetings are best done in person but online or conference calls can work.

- Everyone on the adventure has expectations. The disparity between the expectations of the individuals needs to be dealt with before the trip begins. People need time to make changes or adjust to something they didn't expect. You've got time

209

before the group begins, not later. After these "meetings of the minds" someone in the group needs to write down what the group agreed the trip is about and send a copy out to everyone. You should expect to hand out some pre-trip task assignments at this meeting such as arrangements for getting to the jump-off spot, a consolidated contact list for emergencies, etc.

- Plan personally to be a self-contained autonomous army of one. You won't reach 100 percent of this goal, but try. Only you know your personal needs; make sure you can provide for yourself. Avoid depending on others to take care of your needs. They'll be glad to help when you need help but if you always need help you turn into a pain in the backside. Of course you need to be ready to help when asked and always ask before helping others unless it's an emergency.

- When you feel the need or when another individual within the group feels the need, the entire group should conduct a group planning session covering the next day or the next few days. This helps individuals adjust their expectations to the reality of the journey. Again, everyone needs to participate. Saying you'll go along with what everyone else decides won't cut it. Put your two cents into the discussion and live with the group decision in which you participated.

- There will be some habits and behaviors of others that come to bug you. After awhile, they will get under your skin. Some things you will have to learn to live with and some things you will be able to get changed. To find out if a change is possible, let the other member(s) know what bothers you, immediately or as soon after the incident as practicable. Remember to avoid embarrassing anyone, keep your emotions under control and remember to be polite. You will see a positive change more often than not. The corollary here: others will come to you about your irritating behaviors. React to their concerns as you would want them to react to your concerns. Avoid becoming defensive. Listen and learn.

- Avoid sticking your nose into the business of others. Your friends value your opinion and advice *only* if they ask for it. Therefore, unless someone asks, keep your opinion and advice to yourself. When someone wants to know what you think about what they eat or don't eat, how much or little they brought on the trip, why they did or didn't stop to talk to this or that person along the way—they will ask you. Until then, shut up, and expect others to do the same towards you. The one exception: when harm will be averted through your advice. The corollary of this guideline is to ask others for their opinion and advice. You'll learn a few things and they'll feel better about themselves because you asked.

- Let's talk about drama kings and queens. I don't know why, but some folks like to create emotional drama within a group. Harmony eludes them in their own lives so they attempt to bring disharmony to a group setting. They may make inane remarks, back stabbing comments and create argumentative situations. Either the group leader needs to curtail such activity by talking to that person or the whole group needs to sit around the table or campfire to discuss it. A dialogue is needed to prevent or stop it. When such people are confronted, they may not be able to change their ingrained behavior and will depart the trip. When you're dealing with emotions, it can be very touchy. You might bring up this point when you conduct your pre-trip gathering to head off such behavior before it begins. You may even create a document that members sign so they know what everyone expects and appreciates as to positive behavior in the group.

- Would you like to be the perfect traveling companion? Here are some personal habits and behaviors better left at home:

1. Tardiness
2. Making others the butt of your jokes
3. Pushing your beliefs about religion, politics or race on others
4. Belching, passing gas and/or cursing in public
5. Intentionally irritating others
6. Not picking up after yourself or others

7. Disorganization
8. Not disposing of your trash properly
9. Intentionally embarrassing others
10. Giving un-asked-for advice
11. Telling someone they can't listen to their radio
12. Telling someone they cannot talk to strangers on a trip or monitoring how long they might talk with others
13. Giving unwanted advice as to others' choice of food
14. Trying to control others or make them feel guilty for their choices
15. Taking sides in an argument
16. Complaining about the weather, people, politics
17. Talking about someone else behind their back

An adventure offers incredible moments of bliss, great physical conditioning, relaxation, goal achievement and meeting people. Additionally, it's a time for smelling the flowers nature offers along the way. By taking care of your business and allowing everyone to take care of their business, you will enjoy a fantastic adventure. Friendships will deepen and you will carry away from the experience a boatload of pictures, laughs and positive memories.

KEY POINTS FROM THIS CHAPTER

1. Conduct yourself and treat others like you would like to be treated.
2. Exhibit your integrity, character and positive attitude daily.

*C*hapter 42—*Top 99 adventure books to inspire*

"A man does not climb a mountain without bringing some of it away with him, and leaving something of himself upon it." Sir Martin Conway

These books may give you ideas, inspire you, enthrall you and educate you. At the same time, you may resonate more with men and women who jumped into life with their own particular zeal in different arenas from sailing, to mountain climbing, to scuba diving and spelunking. These men and women answered the call to a life of adventure. One or several of these books may be the inspiration you need to move into your own life of adventure that best fits you.

1. **The Worst Journey in the World** by Apsley Cherry-Garrard (1922). The author volunteered to go with Sir Robert Falcon Scott in 1910 to reach the South Pole. He met incredible challenges from 100-below temperatures, six-month-long Antarctic nights and horrific danger. I read it and I lived in Antarctica to experience the numbing cold and challenges he faced.
2. **Journals** by Meriwether Lewis and William Clark (1814). Can you think of any two American explorers more famous? Their journey took guts, cunning, courage and luck.
3. **Full Tilt** by Derla Murphy (1965). In 1963, Murphy pedaled her bicycle across Europe, Iran, Afghanistan, Pakistan and the Himalayas to reach India on her own. I have met more

than a dozen women on bicycles riding around the world on their own.

4. **Wind, Sand & Stars** by Antoine de Saint-Exupery (1940). Saint-Exupery was the greatest pilot-poet of the air. In the 1920s, he flew the mail from France to Spain across the Pyrenees in all kinds of weather. Also, with bad maps and no radio.

5. **Exploration of the Colorado River** by John Wesley Powell (1875). Powell and his men started on the Green River in wooden boats. Life, death and geology. This book hits on all eight cylinders for rafters.

6. **Arabian Sands** by Wilfred Thesiger (1959). He said, "Fail the humility test, and the desert will surely kill you."

7. **Desert Solitaire** by Edward Abbey (1968). I've read this book three times. It's a classic for all ages. Abbey is the Thoreau of the West.

8. **Miles From Nowhere** by Jessica Savage (1990). She bicycled around the world for two years. She shares great stories about her ride.

9. **Annapurna** by Maurice Herzog (1952). Herzog and Louis Lachenal reached the top. The descent proved fatal for Lachenal. Herzog lost all his fingers to frostbite and nearly died. It's a gripping icy tale of life and death.

10. **West with the Night** by Beryl Markham (1942). Ernest Hemmingway said, "It's a bloody wonderful book." Markham takes you through Africa where a lion mauls her. She said, "I have lifted my plane from the airport and have never felt her wheels glide from the earth into the air without knowing the uncertainty and exhilaration of firstborn adventure."

11. **Into Thin Air** by Jon Krakauer (1997). The author takes you on one of the most tragic moments on Mount Everest when 12 people died because of poor judgment and stupid mistakes. I've read this book and remember my time in Nepal as I gazed upon the summit of Mount Everest "The Earth Goddess" at 29,325 feet.

12. **Travels with Marco Polo** by Marco Polo (1298). Polo tells of his 27 years traveling through Asia. He will inspire you toward your own adventures.

13. **Farthest North** by Fridtjof Nansen (1897). In 1893, Nansen

purposely froze his ship into the Arctic ice. When the ship neared the North Pole, he guided his dogsled team to reach the Pole. The book proves to be an epic tale.

14. **Terra Icognita** by Sara Wheeler (1996). She writes about her year in Antarctica. I read her book twice. I wrote a companion book to hers. **An Extreme Encounter: Antarctica** by Frosty Wooldridge.

15. **The Snow Leopard** by Peter Matthiessen (1978). The author never saw the endangered snow leopard and neither did I when I trekked in the Himalayas. Nonetheless, I enjoyed peace and spiritual bliss while hiking through eternal beauty and amazing moments.

16. **Roughing It** by Mark Twain (1872). America's favorite writer traveled out west in 1860. This book records a bunch of hilarious characters and events. Twain brings the "funny" of adventure to your front door!

17. **Two Years Before the Mast** by Richard Henry Dana (1840). He describes a sailor's life out of Boston Harbor in the 1800s. This book gives you an idea of adventures on the oceans and seas around the world.

18. **South** by Sir Ernest Shackleton (1919). Shackleton's story must be the single greatest story of perseverance in the world. He and 28 men survived two years on the ice in Antarctica under mind-boggling cold future. I read it. I loved it.

19. **Endurance** by Alfred Lansing (1957). The author interviewed many of the survivors of Shackleton's attempt to walk across Antarctica. Lansing rivets readers to their seats as to the sheer guts and determination to survive minus 100 below zero Antarctic nights that lasted for six months. This is the greatest survival book I have ever read. I stepped inside Shackleton's hut near McMurdo, Antarctica.

20. **A Short Walk in the Hindu Kush** by Eric Newby (1958). He walks into Afghanistan, climbs mountains and explores the Middle East. He runs into people who said, "Here, we shoot people without permission."

21. **Kon-Tiki** by Thor Heyerdahl (1950). He sailed from Peru toward Polynesia to prove that the South Pacific was settled from the east.

22. **Travels in West Africa** by Mary Kingsley (1897). Kingsley

shows that women can adventure with gusto, drive and uncommon determination. She fought off leopards, crocs, bugs and more as she tramped through Africa.

23. **Seven Years in Tibet** by Heinrich Harrer (1953). He escaped a prisoner-of-war camp in India. This Austrian headed for Tibet and met the young Dalai Lama.

24. **The Spirit of St. Louis** by Charles Lindbergh (1953). He became the first man to fly across the Atlantic Ocean. His plane hangs in the Smithsonian in Washington, DC. He said, "Death is the last great adventure."

25. **Journals** by James Cook (1768-1779). Captain Cook sailed around the world and is known for sailing into the Southern Oceans of Antarctica. He is one of the world's greatest adventurers.

26. **Home of the Blizzard** by Douglas Mawson (1915). He marched into Antarctica in 1912 and suffered horrific misery. Heck of a read if you enjoying frost-bitten hands while you read the book.

27. **The Voyage of the Beagle** by Charles Darwin (1839). This is the voyage where Darwin cemented his book on the theory of evolution. He explored the Galapagos Islands. Since I spent two weeks in those islands, too, I saw what he saw. You will read about incredible wildlife.

28. **The Seven pillars of Wisdom** by T.E. Lawrence (1926). If you're a desert rat, this is the Lawrence of Arabia of all time. Dry, hot, camels, sand and misery.

29. **The Right Stuff** by Tom Wolfe (1979). Wolfe features Chuck Yeager and America's race to the moon.

30. **Travels in the Interior District of Africa** by Mungo Park (1799). The author traveled through Africa for two years on horseback. He shares his wild adventures in Africa.

31. **Sailing Alone Around the World** by Joshua Slocum (1900). At the age of 50, this man sailed around the world three years and 46,000 miles. He tried it again in 1909, but like Amelia Earhart, he vanished.

32. **The Mountain of My Fear** by David Roberts (1968). He said, "The deepest despair I have ever felt, as well as the most piercing happiness, has come in the mountains." He adventured in Alaska in his twenties and writes a heck of a tale.

33. **First Footsteps in East Africa** by Richard Burton (1856). He spoke Arabic and traveled in disguise around Africa.

34. **The Perfect Storm** by Sebastian Junger (1997). He writes about 50-foot waves and higher. It's a great ocean-going adventure.

35. **The Oregon Trail** by Francis Parkman (1849). This book addresses hard times and rough living on the Oregon Trail by early pioneers.

36. **Through the Dark Continent** by Henry M. Stanley (1878). He found Dr. Livingston, but the good doctor wasn't lost. Stanley runs the Congo River and lives to tell about it.

37. **A Lady's Life in the Rocky Mountains** by Isabella L. Bird (1879). This lady traveled the world and wrote about it. This book inspires women of all ages of life.

38. **In the Land of White Death** by Valerian Albanov (1917). Two dozen men suffered being frozen in the Arctic ice in 1912. Eleven frozen guys tried to walk out and only two made it. This tale freezes your eye-lids.

39. **Scrambles Amongst the Alps** by Edward Whymper (1871). He became the first to climb the Matterhorn, but his four buddies died. He's hardcore and his book remains one of the classics of climbing.

40. **Out of Africa** by Isak Dinesen (1937). Karen Blixen was her real name. She said, "The civilized people have lost the aptitude of stillness and must take lessons in silence from the wild."

41. **Scott's Last Expedition: The Journals** by Robert Falcon Scott (1913). Scott said, "Oh God, this is an awful place!" Scott and his men died after reaching the South Pole second to Amundsen the Norwegian dog musher.

42. **Everest: The West Ridge** by Thomas Hornbein (1965). Great mountain climbing adventure!

43. **Journey Without Maps** by Graham Greene (1936). Liberia in 1935. Greene dared to walk into an area of cannibals and mosquitoes that carried Yellow Fever. We're talking about an ugly, yucky and deadly adventure.

44. **Starlight and Storm** by Gaston Rebuffat (1954). Rebuffat climbed all six of the toughest north faces in the Alps. He's high energy and positive beyond measure.

45. **My First Summer in the Sierra** by John Muir (1911). In the summer of 1869, Muir traveled through the Sierra Nevada with a shepherd and his flock. Muir became the first environmentalist of the world. He was a genius of inventions and wrote compelling poetry and prose. I love the man. You will, too.

46. **My Life as an Explorer** by Sven Hedin (1925). This Swedish explorer of Central Asia set out with four men to cross 180 miles of enormous sand dunes. Temperatures drop. A camel dies. The ink freezes in his pen. It's desert adventure at its best.

47. **In Trouble Again** by Redmond O'Hanlon (1988). He is a naturalist who ventures into the northern Amazon Basin. He tells a funny story.

48. **The Man Who Walked Through Time** by Colin Fletcher (1968). The author backpacked through the Grand Canyon. Since I have backpacked and rafted it, I can tell you that he's a great writer and this is a wonderful book.

49. **The Savage Mountain** by Charles Houston and Robert Bates (1954). K2 tops Everest in climbing difficulty. People suffer, die and triumph.

50. **Gypsy Moth Circles the World** by Francis Chichester (1967). He sails around the world at the ripe old age of 64. Why? Find out.

51. **Man-Eater of Kumaon** by Jim Corbett (1944). Corbett was an Indian-born hunter who killed human-eating tigers.

52. **Alone** by Richard Byrd (1938). Spent an Antarctic winter alone in a small shed. That would drive any man insane. I think it did.

53. **Stranger in the Forest** by Eric Hansen (1988). The author walked across Borneo. Tribes, gators and jungle. Good times if you like to tempt death.

54. **Travels in Arabia Desert** by Charles M. Doughty (1888). He lived the life of Bedouin tribesmen in the desert.

55. **The Royal Road to Romance** by Richard Halliburton (1925). He bicycles, climbs, hikes, hunts and raises heck across the world.

56. **The Long Walk** by Slavomir Rawicz (1956). The author and six men escaped from a Siberian prison camp in 1941. They

walked across Mongolia, Gobi, Tibet and the Himalayas. They endured astounding hardship.

57. **Mountaineering in the Sierra Nevada** by Clarence King (1872). King was a Yale man, a lady's man and a geologist. He climbed a lot of mountains.

58. **My Journey to Lhasa** by Alexandra David-Neel (1927). At the age of 55, French woman David-Neel crossed the Himalayas in midwinter and entered Tibet.

59. **Journal of the Discovery of the Source of the Nile** by John Hanning Speke (1863). Speke located and named Lake Victoria as the source of the Nile. My friend Pasquale Scatturo became the first man to raft the Blue Nile from Ethiopia. Read his book **Mysteries of the Nile.** He also shot a movie for I-Max. Scatturo also took the first blind man to the summit of Everest. Eric Weihenmayer became the first blind man to climb all the highest peaks on seven continents.

60. **Running the Amazon** by Joe Kane (1989). He paddled from the high Andes all the way to the Atlantic. I raise a toast to his squabbling group of rowdy adventure seekers.

61. **Alive** by Piers Paul Read (1975). He and fellow rugby players crashed an airplane in the Chilean Andes in 1972. Horror, intrigue, death and survival in one big ugly and fascinating package.

62. **Principle Navigations** by Richard Hakluyt (1590). Hakluyt writes over a million words. His book is an encyclopedia of adventure.

63. **Incidents of Travel in Yucatan** by John Lloyd Stephens (1843). The author hacks his way through thick jungles. He suffered from malaria.

64. **Shipwreck of the Whale Ship Essex** by Owen Chase (1821). Herman Melville turned this tale into **Moby Dick.** A sperm whale sank the Essex by ramming it. The men escaped in row boats.

65. **Life in the Far West** by George Frederick Ruxton (1849). He traveled the American West to write this account of the mountain men. Very good reading.

66. **My Life as an Explorer** by Roald Amundsen (1927). He sailed the Northwest Passage first and he was the first to reach the South Pole. He said, "A strange ambition burned within

me to endure those same sufferings." I read the book cover to cover.

67. **New from Tartary** by Peter Fleming (1936). He set out from Beijing for India in 1930 via the forbidden Xinjiang region.

68. **Annapurna: A Woman's Place** by Arlene Blum (1980). This book, above all, inspired and inspires all women climbers. Powerful, compelling and all female.

69. **Mutiny on the Bounty** by William Bligh (1790). Rebellious sailors force Bligh and 18 loyal sailors onto four 23-foot longboats for a 4,000 mile survival trip.

70. **Adrift** by Steven Callahan (1986). Callahan's sailboat sank in the middle of the Atlantic. He spent 76 days drifting, fighting off sharks and starving before reaching land.

71. **Castaways** by Alvar Nunez Cabeza de Vaca (1555). Three hundred men land near Tampa, Florida in 1528. Only four survive to make it to Mexico. How they lived is anyone's guess.

72. **Touching the Void** by Joe Simpson (1989). He and a buddy descended a hard route through the Andes. They experienced terrible suffering.

73. **Tracks** by Robyn Davidson (1980). She traveled alone across 1,700 miles of Australian outback on a camel. One hardcore, tough lady.

74. **The Adventures of Captain Bonneville** by Washington Irving (1837). He wrote this memoir from a mountain man's notes.

75. **Cooper's Creek** by Alan Moorehead (1963). This Australian epic adventure takes you across the Outback. Since I cycled it, I know it's one miserably hot, forever desert with emus, camels, kangaroos and wombats. Two mates on the adventure starve to death. Life is tough in the Outback.

76. **The Fearful Void** by Geoffrey Moorhouse (1974). He traveled 2,000 miles across the Great Sahara Desert. Like loneliness? Follow him.

77. **Through the Brazilian Wilderness** by Theodore Roosevelt (1914). Teddy Roosevelt became a true adventurer on the River of Doubt. He takes you for a thrilling ride.

78. **The Road to Oxiana** by Robert Bryon (1937). He forges into

Afghanistan. Great read for anyone that loves the Middle East.

79. **No Picnic on Mount Kenya** by Felice Benuzzi (1953). He escaped a prison camp to climb Mount Kenya.

80. **Minus 148 Degrees** by Art Davidson (1969). Three climbers ascend Denali, Alaska, the highest mountain in North America at 20,325. As they descend, Mother Nature feeds them a blowtorch of deadly blasts.

81. **Travels** by Ibn Battuta (1354). He spent most of his life traveling throughout Asia. He was sometimes wealthy and sometimes poor. He faced danger often.

82. **Jaguars Ripped my Flesh** by Tim Cahill (1987). He tells a great yarn.

83. **Journal of a Trapper** by Osborne Russell (1914). How would you like to fight a wounded grizzly bear? Like to starve to death? This book will take you back to the mountain man days of the 1800s in America.

84. **We Die Alone** by David Howarth (1955). Norwegian commandos sailed into a Nazi trap on the northern coast of Norway in 1943.

85. **Kabloona** by Gontran de Poncins (1941). He crossed the Canadian North Country. He said, "If you see a man in a blizzard bending over a rock, you may be sure it is me and I am lost."

86. **Carry the Fire** by Michael Collins (1974). Collins piloted Apollo rockets to the moon. Want to explore space? Follow this man.

87. **The Mountains of My Life** by Walter Bonatti (1998). He writes about mountains, clouds and nature's bliss.

88. **Great Heart** by James West Davidson and John Rugge (1988). This book recounts the tale of a failed 1903 expedition to Labrador.

89. **Journal of the Voyage of the Pacific** by Alexander Mackenzie (1801). This Canadian traveled across North America ten years before Lewis and Clark.

90. **The Valley of the Assassins** by Freya Stark (1934). Stark crosses vast places in Persia as she dodges bandits and passes from "fear to the absence of fear."

91. **The Silent World** by Jacques Cousteau (1953). I read this book

in 1962. It inspired me to dive all over the world in oceans, lakes, rivers and seas. Cousteau is my environmental hero.

92. **Ultimate High: My Everest Odyssey** by Goran Kropp. He bicycled from Sweden to Nepal with a load of 170 pounds of gear. Upon reaching Nepal, he climbed unassisted to the summit of Mount Everest. He pedaled his bicycle back to Sweden.

93. **Letters and Notes on the Manners, Customs and Conditions of the North American Indians** by George Catlin (1841). He spent six years among the Plains Indians. His paintings are world famous.

94. **I Married Adventure** by Osa Johnson (1940). She married wildlife photographer Martin Johnson. He took her to Africa and the Pacific Rim for a very exciting life.

95. **The Descent of Pierre Saint-Martin** by Norbert Casteret (1954). He takes readers into the world's deepest cave explorations. It's a thrilling story for spelunkers.

96. **The Crystal Horizon** by Reinhold Messner (1982). Messner climbed Everest alone and without oxygen. He was the first to climb all seven highest peaks on seven continents.

97. **Grizzly Years** by Doug Peacock (1990). He became the model for the eco-terrorist Hayduke in Edward Abbey's novel **The Monkey Wrench Gang.** Peacock writes about grizzlies as if his head is stuck in the mouth of one of them.

98. **One Man's Mountain** by Tom Patey (1971). As John Muir said, "Climb the mountains to get their good tidings. Your troubles will fall away like autumn leaves." This book does the same thing for your spirit.

99. **Spell of the Yukon** by Robert Service (1890). This man spun poetry like a spider spins webs. Brilliant, compelling, enthralling, funny and historical. You'll love his work. He defines the wilderness. Additionally, Jack London's **Call of the Wild.**

KEY POINTS FROM THIS CHAPTER

1. These books offer you emotional, intellectual and common sense growth toward your own adventures.
2. These books give you new ideas about yourself and your potential.

Chapter 43—Top female and male books to inspire you

"Choose to use your gifts and live the adventure of this lifetime. Step into the larger scheme of following your dream. Let's deluge the world with the ultimate dancers, people who feed their souls with work and feed their work with soul." Tama Kieves

Let's say you read this book cover to cover. While you gained a great deal of knowledge, information and perhaps inspiration, you feel the need for more. It's possible that some other adventure writer, male or female, might resonate with you better. Whatever gets you to your dreams, go for it.

Many women think it is more challenging to take adventures than men. Let's not sell female adventure seekers short. You read about amazing women and their books listed in the preceding chapter. You may appreciate that prior to 1965, women took a back seat to men because of limited opportunities and a culture of being ladylike, i.e., you can't do what men do. Since 1970 and Title IX athletic programs in schools across the United States, women have gained tremendous impetus from being able to compete like never before in many athletic arenas formerly denied them by the dominant male culture.

Today women box, play soccer, football, hockey, basketball, row, ski race, mountain bike race, wrestle, climb Everest, sail around the world, row across the Atlantic and play every sport men play.

Since I am a man, I cannot know all the challenges women face. However, I have read several excellent books in which some of the finest women present new ideas, energy, enthusiasm and determination to females. These books below may unlock the door for you. They may inspire your own highly successful life as to adventure and daily living.

Books for women:

This Time I Dance by Tama J. Kieves. This lady is funny, highly metaphorical and charged with wisdom. She gives women a whole new understanding of their power, creative potential and ability to realize their dreams. You will become fearless by reading her book. I loved it and I'm a dude. I met her and she is wonderful.

Travel Tips for the Sophisticated Woman by Laura Vestanen. This woman lays it down totally and with perfect command. You will be so hungry to travel after reading her book, you will take a car trip the next weekend or backpack or bicycle—just to try out her ideas.

Gutsy Women and **Best Girlfriend Getaways** by Marybeth Bond. She takes you to where you want to go. You'll love her style and energy.

Wanderlust and Lipstick by Beth Whitman. This lady shows women how to be successful and happy travelers. Be prepared, move toward your adventure and enjoy yourself.

Bicycle Bliss by Portia H. Masterson. If you like to ride and tour on a bicycle, this lady makes it fun and fabulous—in fact, bliss.

The Girlo Travel Survival Kit by Anthea Paul. She offers more ideas to make your travels successful. She's an inspiration just because she got out there and adventured on her own.

A Woman Alone: Travel Tales from Around the Globe by Faith Conlon. She describes her travels around the world. She loved it.

Adventures in Good Company: The Complete Guide to Women's Tours and Outdoor Trips by Thalia Zepatos. This book will get your feet wet in the company of tour guides. Later, you may strike out on your own.

Eat, Pray, Love by Elizabeth Gilbert. It's an international best seller. She traveled the world to work out her troubles. She suffered self-doubt and worked through it. She found love. She's funny. She may inspire you to explore, love, eat and pray.

Unstoppable by Cynthia Kersey. This lady features dozens of women from every walk of life that chased their dreams and caught them. I cannot say enough for this book. I refer to it often. Your spirit will soar with possibilities.

The Life You Were Born to Live by Dan Millman. While he's a guy, this book offers amazing paths toward what you really love to do in life. It cuts away the mistakes and allows you to find your optimum propensities, work and life path. I've known Dan for 20 years and he provides some of the most powerful and compelling ideas for 21st century living. You might also read **Sacred Journey of the Peaceful Warrior**.

Power of Intention by Wayne Dyer. Again, another man, but his book transforms both men and women to live within a new paradigm designed to bring personal success heretofore unheard of in earlier times.

Books for men:

The Life You Were Born to Live by Dan Millman. This book will put you years of ahead of stumbling around trying to find your path and work in life. I highly recommend it for men and women.

Way of the Peaceful Warrior, Sacred Journey of the Peaceful Warrior, No Ordinary Moments, Warrior Athlete and **Four Purposes of Life** by Dan Millman. Those books will give you a leg up on successful living.

Power of Intention by Wayne Dyer. Dyer shows you how to accomplish your intentions.

Seven Habits of Highly Effective People and **First Things First** by Stephen Covey. When you engage the skills, habits and methods of successful people, your life will become highly effective, positive and thriving.

Touch the Top of the World: A Blind Man's Journey to Climb Farther Than the Eye can See by Erik Weihenmayer. I met this remarkable man who suffered blindness early in his life. He became the first blind man to climb Mount Everest.

The Adversity Advantage: Turning Everyday Struggles into Everyday Greatness by Erik Weihenmayer. If you are disabled in any way, Erik will show you the way to your own personal greatness.

Self-Reliance by Ralph Waldo Emerson. Uncommon spiritual wisdom and abundant understanding of life and all its promises.

Walden by Henry David Thoreau. One of the greats of American literature.

Travels in Alaska and **A Thousand Mile Walk to the Gulf** by John Muir.

Call of the Wild by Jack London. A man of adventure and imagination.

Some of my favorite authors for your consideration

Richard Bach wrote **Jonathan Living Seagull**. It's still a classic on the bookshelves 40 years later. In the book, a seagull named Jonathan tries to fly faster and farther than all the rest of the seagulls. They ridicule him. He suffers, but keeps flying. Day in and day out, he flies faster and faster. He crashes often, but he dusts himself off and lifts into the wild blue yonder. He learns about his weaknesses and he uses his strengths to improve.

Finally, he learns to fly really fast. He catches the attention of an elder seagull named Chiang.

"Well, Jonathan," said Chiang. "You fly pretty fast. You fly with great passion."

"What happens from here?" said Jonathan. "Where are we going? Is there no such place as heaven?"

"No, Jonathan, there is no such place as heaven," Chiang said. "Heaven is not a place, and it is not a time. Heaven is being perfect. You will begin to touch heaven, Jonathan, in the moment that you touch "perfect speed." And, that isn't flying a thousand miles an hour, or a million, or flying at the speed of light. Perfection doesn't have limits. Perfect speed, Jonathan, is being there." Richard Bach

Once I read Bach's book in my youth, it guided me toward that perfect speed that Chiang talked about. You can interpret it any way you like so long as it works for your ongoing quest to live a happy life and a life of adventure as you define it.

Author Dan Millman presents a peaceful warrior's way to turn your ideas into actions, your challenges into strengths and your life experiences into wisdom. You can live like a warrior, yet enjoy the wisdom of spiritual and mental bliss as you face daily challenges that greet you at every stage of your life.

I have seen many friends beat themselves up with such mental torture long after they left home. Those negative concepts stick in the craw of a person's mind. Millman's books will help you erase those scripts. Once erased, you may write new scripts of success, happiness, joy and drive. It's up to you and your choice.

One of the challenges many human beings struggle with arrives in the guise of negative self-concepts, insecurity and a feeling of lack. How did that happen? Usually, one or both parents instilled parent-scripts like: "You're not athletic; I wasn't good in science so you won't be either; you're awkward, just like I was…." Millman talks about it through his character named Socrates.

"But life energy must flow somewhere," said Socrates. "Where internal obstructions lie, the energy burns, and if it builds up beyond what an individual body-mind can tolerate, it explodes. Anger grows into rage, sorrow turns to despair, concern becomes obsession, and physical aches become agony. So energy can also be a curse. Like a river, it can bring life, but untamed it can unleash a raging flood of destruction."

Millman expresses what happens when so many carry their hang-ups and insecurities to the self-destructive side of life. The key is to clear the obstructions from your mind. It's better to understand them and take your energies toward a meaningful life. Choose a life of adventure or artistic expression or sports or family or whatever you choose for your time on this planet. Each day of your life offers unlimited potential and creative process. It depends on how you design it.

Choose your positive-self and avoid listening to your opposing-self. Like anything you want to accomplish, it takes practice. Delete this sentence from your mouth and mind, "I can't do this, I can't do that, I can't…."

Replace it with, "I can, I will, I am…."

KEY POINTS FROM THIS CHAPTER

1. Women from all walks of life have adventured around the world.
2. You can make your life as exciting as any of the authors in this chapter.

*C*hapter 44—*Details*

"Some people go on an adventure to see something; I go on an adventure to do something." Steve Boyka

Let's cover a variety of travel items like a potpourri in order to give you some information in various areas. Use this list of options as your starting point for total preparation. If an item applies to you, write it down and make it a part of your own customized list for "things to do before I leave."

Let your adventure desires carry you toward your dreams like Bob Wieland. Instead of lamenting what you can't do, focus on what you can do. Even if you suffer disabilities, you may find ample help at: www. disabledtravelersguide.com , www.disabilitytravel.com , www.access-able. com , www.NSCD.org

I recommend visiting Winter Park, Colorado to enjoy disabled skiing where I have been a volunteer ski instructor for 20 years. Tell them you want Frosty to take you up in a bi-ski or mono-ski for a day on the slopes. During summers, Winter Park also features wheelchair camping, horseback riding, sailing, bicycling and more for the handicapped at the National Sports Center for the Disabled. www.NSCD.org

While traveling, be sure to carry health insurance for national and international travel. Contact www.aaa.com in America and www.caa.com in Canada. Learn more from those organizations for international travel.

Tourist Bureaus and Information Centers

Be sure to carry theft insurance for your car, camera, bicycle, kayak, canoe and gear if you travel in developing countries. You might suffer theft at the hands of any number of situations. Some individuals prove cagey and resourceful to separate you from your pack, bike, camera and passport.

When traveling to exotic countries, check out alerts issued by the United States government at the U.S. Department of State. Visit www. travel.state.gov

You may find out what countries to avoid. Here's another site: www. cia.gov/cia/publications/factbook.gov , which will give you the lowdown on everything you need to know, i.e., danger, water, food, terror, etc.

If you're a woman, you need information to be safe. Try www. forwomentravelingsolo.com and www.thorntree.lonelyplanet.com

Guidebooks are a must. Get the most out of your journey with guidebooks from Lonely Planet at www.lonelyplanet.com. This publisher covers every country on the planet in books by travelers that traveled through them. You can also try www.MoonHandbooks.net for a ton of information about countries all over the planet.

If you're up for blogs telling the real deal, go to www.technorati.com

You may travel at any time of the year anywhere in the world, but you may like to enjoy certain cultural festivals around the world. Check out: www.earthcalendar.net for tons of information.

Try www.Travelingwomen.com for women that need exact information from most regions in the world they wish to travel. Also, for gay men and women try www.GayTravelNews.com

Best guidebooks: **Eyewitness Travel Guidebook** series. It's excellent.

Love great eating? Try www.roadfood.com , www.chowhound.com , www.citysearch.com , www.zagat.com

European dining guides www.viamichelin.com and www.ginkgopress. com

Don't want to get lost? Obtain a map. www.mapquest.com/mobile and www.wideworldtravels.com

Booking travel flights? Book well in advance. Try three months early for cheaper rates. Book smart and use the Internet. Not sure? Go to a travel agent.

To work the deal yourself for the cheapest fares: www.Site59.com

, www.expedia.com , www.orbitz.com , www.travelocity.com , www.
southwest.com , www.frontierairlines.com, www.jetblue.com

Be sure to check on any website if they have a lock-icon at the bottom
of your browser, usually on the right side, to make sure your information
remains confidential.

Sometimes, you can obtain cheaper flights or cheaper bookings by
waiting. You might try www.farecast.com and also, for a plethora of
information on transportation companies, try www.bts.gov

Two websites that will look for the best deals on transports are: www.
kayak.com and www.sidestep.com

Do you like globetrotting? You may enjoy e-tickets in most developed
countries, but will have to go the old-fashioned way in developing countries.
www.whichbudget.com

If you want to start early, you might procure a credit card that gives
you free flights. I carry a credit card for free flights, after purchasing
enough products to provide me flight points.

Good deals? Try www.priceline.com

My friend Brenda takes courier flights for free to carry time-sensitive
materials to foreign countries. She's traveled all over the globe on such
tickets with www.aircourier.org and www.courier.org

Always arrive at the airport two hours in advance in developing world
countries and the same two hours in advance in developed countries.
Better to be two hours early rather than one minute late. I could tell you a
few horror stories, but suffice to say, avoid making them your own.

Before you leave

1. Suspend newspaper delivery.
2. Hold mail or divert to a trusted address.
3. Make sure any bills get paid by a trusted person or automatic
   bill pay at bank.
4. Change your greeting on your home phone and place out of
   office message on email.
5. Confirm flights and shuttles.
6. Pour gasoline stabilizer in your gas tanks and run through
   carburetor.
7. Make sure someone waters the yard and mows the lawn.
8. Place luggage tags outside and inside your gear.
9. Talk to neighbors to look after your home and lawn.
10. Pets off to a friend or the vacation kennel.

CAMPING AND HOSTELS

Today, hostels offer inexpensive accommodations—at least, relative to motels and hotels. Visit www.internationalhostels.com and www.hihostels.com to obtain a registration card, directory and the keys to the front door of hostels in just about every country around the world. You must carry a sheet or satin or silk sleep sack for your sleeping bag or they will make you buy a heavy linen sheet. Beat them to the punch.

The YMCA also gives good value for travelers at www.ymca.int

Bed and breakfasts also offer friendly accommodations, but can be pretty pricy for a lean wallet.

For camping travelers, the best and cheapest way to travel is stealth camping. If you're backpacking, riding a Euro-rail, motorcycling or bicycling—slip off into the woods, a cozy corner of a hay field, behind a building, in a shaded glen, beside the still waters of a lake or anywhere you like where no one can see you. Many times, you can ask a farmer for permission to camp and he will not only allow you to camp on his land; he will invite you in for dinner and breakfast. You never know until you ask.

For those who like security try www.koa.com , www.goodsams.com

For touring cyclists, you may enjoy a free night's sleep, showers and friendly conversations from folks that like to host you for an evening at www.warmshowers.com

HOME SWAPS AND EXCHANGES

If you're retired and own a home, you can exchange with people from all over the globe. It's a great way to enjoy a country or a continent.

Find out: www.homeexchange.com , www.intervacus.com , www.seniorshomeexchange.com and www.gti-home-exchange.com

You can host world travelers at your house for amazing experiences with travelers at www.globalfreeloaders.com

If you love to see farms or travel around the world to farms try www.wwoof.org

HUT TO HUT AND RAILS TO TRAILS

In Colorado and many other states, you may use their hut systems in the summer and winter. In Colorado: www.huts.org

For hiking and biking: www.railstotrails.org all over the country.

In Europe, you will find a ton of hut to hut systems at

dolomitesport.com/2009/09/europes-mountain-hut-culture/

BICYCLES, MOTORCYCLES, RECUMBENTS

If you travel by bicycle, you can take your own by boxing it up, or you can buy or rent in different countries at www.bikefriday.com

Men and women who motorcycle may find unlimited opportunities to rent in many countries. www.globeriders.com , www.imtbike.com , www.motodiscovery.com

For motor homes in USA: www.cruiseamerica.com

For motor home rentals in Europe: www.autoeurope.com , http://www.worldwide-motorhome-hire.com/

Germany: www.motorhomerental.de

PREPARATION EQUALS NINE-TENTHS OF SUCCESS: START YOUR "TO DO" LIST

A passport and visa open most doors to most countries around the world. Make certain your passport carries an expiration date at least a year beyond your stepping into any country. If your passport is close to its expiration date, you may not be given entry into some countries.

Make sure your passport offers at least four blank pages for stamping.

You can obtain a passport at more than 7,000 post offices across the USA. Give yourself at least eight weeks before departure; better yet, obtain your new passport three months before departure. If something comes up, you still have plenty of time to correct it.

A passport remains valid for 10 years. You need two passport pictures, which can be taken at any drugstore and some U.S. post offices. You need a birth certificate, driver's license and any other forms of identification they might require. For more information try www.iafdb.travel.state.gov

In order to renew an expired passport, you may fill out a DS-82 and send it in with your old passport, recent pictures and money to cover the cost of the passport: www.travel.state.gov

If you're anxious for quick service, you can pay extra money to receive your expedited passport.

Canadian citizens may apply for a five-year passport at www.ppt.gc.ca

Follow the protocol in order to obtain your passport.

Caution: Your passport is your ticket to the world. Guard it at all times by keeping it in a waterproof pouch around your neck 24/7. You snooze and you lose. For emergencies, make five photocopies of your passport and keep two copies in different areas of your pack or belongings. Keep the others in a money belt, pouch, zippered pack, or elsewhere. If you should lose your passport or have it stolen, you may be able to show your photocopies to a U.S. Embassy for possible replacement, or at least you will possess a record of your identity with the passport photo and information.

Additionally, if a hotel requires your passport, give them a photocopy in order to guarantee that you have your original passport on you and not in someone else's hands.

VISAS

Some countries require a visa to enter their country for a specific number of days. You need to get that completed before you leave your country. Check **Lonely Planet** for such requirements. You can visit the website for countries you intend to visit. Call the consulates for information, but make sure you have your visas before you leave home. Otherwise, you will suffer some hard lessons on your dream trip.

Make sure you have all your ducks in a row before you leave town.

TRAVELING BY CAR OR MOTORHOME

If you intend to drive in a foreign country, you need to obtain an "International Driver's License" in order to be legal. Visit www.aaa.com or your local American Automobile Association office to fill out the forms for the license. If you need a motorcycle endorsement, make sure you get it stamped on the license. Be sure to carry at least 10 passport-sized pictures for emergencies. You will need one of them on the "International Driver's License."

In Canada, contact your Canadian Automobile Association for your "International Driver's License."

PHONE HOME AND CONTACTS

Make sure you carry plenty of contact numbers of loved ones or trusted friends back in your country so you have someone to call if you should suffer injury or illness or if any other emergency should arise.

Carry a little address booklet or even your notebook computer so you can write postcards to your friends.

PLANE TICKETS AND RESERVATIONS

Keep your passport, personal papers and money with you at all times. Keep reservation and confirmation numbers with you at all times.

Make photocopies of flight reservations, e-tickets, boarding passes, car-rental reservations, shuttle reservations, directions to your hostel or campground from the airport, directions to restaurants and directions to airports.

Today, with Internet cafés in just about every nook and cranny of the planet, you can scan all your important documents and email them to yourself so you can pick up anything you need by heading to the computer bank at the local café. Scan your passport, other ID, reservations, addresses, phone numbers and anything else you might need on the road.

TAKING CARE OF DENTAL WORK BEFORE YOU LEAVE

Before leaving home, make sure you undergo a thorough dental examination. If the dentist thinks anything seems "iffy," get it drilled and filled. You want to avoid a dental problem in a foreign or developing country. Let me repeat that statement with vigor: *YOU WANT TO AVOID AT ALL COSTS A DENTAL PROBLEM IN A FOREIGN COUNTRY.*

BILLS TO PAY BACK HOME WHILE YOU'RE GONE

If you're young with no property, no rent, no nothing—yahoo—take off and enjoy the ride. But, if you leave home with bills, loans or other responsibilities, take care of them or make sure your parents or someone you trust 100 percent will take care of them. If you cannot find someone, you can secure a bank that will pay your bills automatically at a specific date each month. Make sure you keep enough money in your account for your time away from home.

Make sure your car insurance or payments run on auto-pay or other means. You can suspend your car insurance for the duration of your trip.

Before leaving, let your two main credit card companies know that you will be traveling so they will be alerted that you will be charging from far-off places. Additionally, in most banks today, you can set up a debit account that will allow you to withdraw money in the local currency by using your credit card. You can use that credit-debit card for Euros or local currency with the best exchange rate. Otherwise, you will lose a lot of money with traveler's checks via cashing charges. (However, take enough traveler's checks for emergencies.) Always take $200.00 to $300.00 in $20.00 American bills with you for quick exchange.

SHOTS, MEDICAL RECORDS, PRESCRIPTIONS

Check with your medical care people about the shots you will need for whatever country you plan on visiting. Make sure you take all the proper malaria pills before you leave for the South American jungles or Africa—and keep taking them for the prescribed period. You want to avoid malaria at all costs. If you contract malaria, it's yours for life.

Additionally, get your rump ready for gamaglobulin shots to make sure you miss the hepatitis express. Bend over. Say please. The nurse will fill your wish in both cheeks.

Take skin creams for rashes, poison ivy and infections. Ask your doctor.

Get your tetanus shots and whatever else you need to make sure you don't die or come back with some nasty stuff. When you do return home, get a urine, blood and fecal check to make sure you don't have parasites or other nasties in your body. If you do, you can get them treated immediately.

If you travel to South America, be certain to take a good tent so you won't be bitten by the "Kissing Bug" that injects the Chagas parasite into your body. If you sleep in cheap hotels or other places, be prudent to protect your body from that little bug. Once inside your body, it attacks your heart and other organs. That parasite affects 14 million people in South America and kills 50,000 annually. Once you get it, there is no cure. Be smart, be safe and protect yourself from its bite.

Face it, on the road, you will suffer sickness. Be prudent, smart and cautious.

Carry your shot record and passport in a sealed plastic bag for safety. Those small sealed plastic bags will keep your important items waterproof.

Medications? Take what you need and carry prescriptions if you will be in a foreign land. Carry extras if you're traveling in remote regions. Take duplicates of everything by photocopy.

Do you have a special condition? Make sure you carry that information in your records as you trek across the planet. Check with www.medicalert. com about an instant record check for yourself.

Check for immunizations and records at Travel Health Online: www. tripprep.com

PERSONAL STUFF YOU CAN DO YOURSELF

First Aid Kit:

1. Sunscreen-30-50 SPF
2. Antihistamine
3. Decongestant
4. Pain medication
5. Mosquito repellant
6. Acetaminophen
7. Ibuprofen
8. Laxative
9. Anti-diarrheal
10. Antifungal and antibacterial ointments
11. Hydrocortisone cream
12. Band-aids, bandages
13. Tweezers—usually found in your Swiss Army knife
14. Moleskin for blisters—don't leave home without a couple of packs
15. Cotton swabs for your ears or a wound
16. Alcohol wipe pads
17. Biodegradable soap and/or hand-sanitizer.
18. To keep mosquitoes off, you might bring a nylon mesh mosquito net that drapes down over your head from a hat. Buy one that fits you for keeping the little buggers from making you miserable. That goes for Australian bush flies, which are the next best thing to the devil himself. Also, those nasty little "no-see-ems" in the higher latitudes. You may wear a nylon hooded jacket and pants in place of insect repellant. One note: always carry a pair of lightweight between-the-toes shower sandals to wear in foreign shower rooms so you avoid catching athlete's foot or any other kinds of creepy stuff that might grow on your body.

COMMON SENSE PRACTICES FOR KEEPING YOUR HEALTH WHILE TRAVELING

Keep your health by practicing good personal hygiene:

1. Wash your hands before you eat anything.

2. Stay away from cold foods from outdoor vendors, especially meats. Once you see how developing countries leave milk, cheese and meat out for the flies to feast upon—you may decide to become a temporary vegetarian while you travel.

3. When using bathrooms, wash your hands and then, use the toilet paper or a paper towel to open the door and throw the paper towel in the trash. Or use your foot or elbow to open the door. You want to avoid all the nasty stuff that others carry around on them or inside them.

4. When you're in questionable situations, like an elevator, push buttons with your elbow or even the end of your Swiss Army knife.

5. If—well, let's just say when—you suffer from "Montezuma's Revenge" or whatever they call a massive case of uncontrolled rectal evacuation in the particular country you're visiting—take Kaopectate or other anti-diarrhea medicine. At times, you'll be ejecting out of both ends and you will be miserable beyond anything you've ever experienced. But once your guts acclimate to a developing country's food, you will be fine.

6. Always use a water filter and carefully fill your water bottles to make sure you don't allow one unfiltered drop into your canteen. Just one drop can make you sick if the bad guys get into your system.

7. Take a small container of tea tree (melaleuca) oil to cover a cut or scab to keep out infection. You will be glad you did.

8. Maintain hydration by drinking water regularly. Always make certain you drink clean water. Again, take a water filter with you everywhere you travel to make certain you enjoy clean, safe water. Be prudent, be forever alert, be smart and stay healthy.

On long airplane flights, get up and move around. Keep your blood circulating so you avoid suffering cramps or other problems while on your journey. If you're older, you want to prevent deep-vein thrombosis, which is a blood clot that forms in your legs from long periods of inactivity. You can mitigate your risk by carrying compression socks that reduce the swelling. Check www.christinecolumbus.com for socks. In the end, good nutrition with a low-fat intake, water and exercise give you the best results during travel.

Some folks suffer jet lag more than others. I take melatonin upon arriving at a destination that may be eight time zones away from my normal sleep routine. You may also try chamomile at www.nojetlag.com

KEY POINTS FROM THIS CHAPTER

1. Preparation is nine-tenths of success.
2. Use these resources to be prepared.
3. Learn by doing, making mistakes and correcting those mistakes.
4. Create your preparation list and follow it.

Chapter 45—Particulars

"I see my path, but I don't know where it leads. Not knowing where I'm going is what inspires me to travel it." Rosalia de Castro

HEALTHFUL EATING ON ADVENTURE HIGHWAY

All countries and cultures offer amazing foods around the world. In developed countries, you may enjoy a plethora of culinary experiences. My mouth waters when I think about fabulous cuisine in Rome, Italy and Madrid, Spain and Bergen, Norway and Rio de Janeiro, Brazil and Seward, Alaska with sourdough pancakes. Your mouth will water and your mind will remember the great places where you dined amid the cultures and people who welcomed you.

At the same time, once you cross into countries without standards, health regulations and reasonable personal hygiene, you face disconcerting conditions. Be smart and alert.

1. Always take your Swiss Army knife to peel the skin off fruits to get to the fresh, clean inside of the fruit or any vegetable.
2. If you're not certain about silverware or glassware—use your own from your pack or your bags (don't leave without them). For extra precaution, you can take an alcohol wipe and clean your silverware and glassware yourself. If it really feels dangerous, pull out your own cook pot and utensils. Always eat hot food that has been cooked well enough and long enough to kill any germs, insect larva or worms.

3. Since I've been sickened by what I saw in some countries as to their leaving food out for all the flies to land on, I became a vegetarian early in my life. You may consider becoming a short-term vegetarian in developing countries.

4. My friend Doug did not take this advice and he suffered worms crawling up from his stomach through his throat. He spit them out of his mouth. He visited a doctor to obtain a poison to kill the little buggers in his gut.

5. Accept that you most probably will get sick from eating, but once you've gotten sick, your gut may work with the new foods it finds itself digesting and you will be fine in your new environment.

FOR WOMEN ON ADVENTURE HIGHWAY

"I have lifted my plane from the airport and have never felt her wheels glide from the earth into the air without knowing the uncertainty and exhilaration of firstborn adventure." Ms. Beryl Markham, African bush pilot

Please note that several of my long time lady friends gave their ideas for this section:

1. As a woman, you need to be prepared differently than men.

2. In developing countries, women take a backseat to men in any number of ways. Some male behavior will appall you. You must be alert and never travel alone at night, and in many cases, never travel alone.

3. If you travel in Islamic countries, you will need to cover your entire body and head. In many other countries, you may want to avoid tight jeans or short dresses. Avoid tempting your destiny with short skirts or provocative clothes.

4. Avoid responding to catcalls and whistles from local boys.

5. While on the road, through stress or food or other circumstances, you might miss your period more than once. It's not uncommon. If the situation continues, you might want to visit a doctor for advice.

You may need to carry extra tampons or sanitary napkins in many countries that do not sell such commodities. Be prepared for some rough sledding in developing countries when it comes to your menstruation. If you run out of sanitary napkins, you might check with your doctor back home so you can engage a protocol that works for you. For enterprising female travelers, you can check with Diva Cup at www.divacup.com for a soft silicone lip that collects menstrual flow.

Using the pill? Be smart as to any encounters on adventure highway. Make sure your friend wears prophylaxis and wash afterwards. Sexually transmitted diseases run wild all over the world. While the movies may be wonderfully romantic with an Italian or Brazilian lover, STDs are not.

In case you contract a yeast infection, prepare ahead by obtaining vaginal cream. You may have to see a doctor.

If you contract a bladder infection, try drinking cranberry juice, lots of water and see a doctor if needed.

Traveling while pregnant? Best time would be in the second trimester so you're not suffering from morning sickness and you're not susceptible to the discomfort of your third trimester or premature birth. See doctors about immunizations of all kinds and their effect on your fetus. Some countries demand different vaccinations, etc., so be aware that your growing child may not tolerate such things.

Further pregnancy information: if you're headed into a malaria-infested country and you're taking chemicals, or if you don't and you become infected with malaria—your unborn child can be severely affected. Choose the safe side for the life of your child.

If you get sick or suffer an injury in developing countries, seek out the best hospitals and doctors available. The International Association of Medical Assistance at www.1amat.org will guide you to English-speaking competent doctors and sanitary conditions; along with safe food.

WHAT KINDS OF SICKNESSES TO EXPECT ON ADVENTURE HIGHWAY

First of all, be gentle with yourself. Take care of the little things and the big things will take care of themselves. You may consult a number of books for many ideas and you will find some of them added to the end of this book so you may gain greater details—especially if you're a woman.

1. Be smart and avoid getting cooked in the tropical sun in southern climes. Always carry a long-sleeve shirt or blouse, brimmed hat, sunglasses and long pants to make certain you protect your skin.

2. Riding a bicycle over the years, I have caught a lot of sun radiation. Today, I keep covered in sunglasses, tights, long sleeve jerseys and gloves. I wear a bandana draped under my helmet and down over my ears and neck. I coat my face with 50 SPF sun block. It may look cool to sport a tan, but you will pay a severe price years down the road with skin cancer and premature aging of your skin.

3. Always wear broad spectrum sunglasses to protect your eyes from radiation damage.

4. Expect diarrhea because you most likely will suffer from it. Take the appropriate medications and most likely you will live through it. Oh yeah, and you will be able to tell your friends some really uncivilized stories. You can tell them how you hurled your guts out, cramped and hit a 103 degree fever. You may give an account of nausea and doing your sleeping bag. They'll laugh depending on how animated you become while telling them about your bout with diarrhea as you hiked the Inca Trail. They'll still be jealous because you hiked the Inca Trail and have pictures to prove it.

5. Ever suffered from a case of amoebic dysentery? You will wish to heaven that you never ate the wrong food or drank bad water again. How do you avoid it? Always drink filtered water, cook your food, peel your fruits, boil your water if you don't have a filter, wash your hands, keep clean with baths or showers, and avoid contact with persons in questionable areas.

6. One of the best ways to kill your adventure would be to contract giardia. It will take you down like a rock falling off a mountain. It's a parasite and it is nasty. Again, practice the highest personal hygiene that I have repeated numerous times in this book. If you do suffer from it; try drugs like Flagyl, Furoxone, Quinacrine, and/or Tinidazole. Most countries carry those drugs. If no drugs are available, eat garlic morning, noon and night. None of it is fun.

7. In jungle areas, you may run into mosquitoes that carry malaria. I've got a buddy who caught malaria in Africa. He suffers from debilitating attacks that put him down for days. Check with your doctor for the latest prophylactics. You may avoid being bitten by wearing Gore-Tex clothing from head

to toe, use a mosquito net over your head and gloves on your hands.

8. While I cycled through the Amazon jungle, I suffered horrible bites from numerous insects that made my legs bleed. I finally covered my legs with my nylon rain gear and wore a Gore-Tex jacket. I perspired more, but I didn't get bit anymore. Keep any bites clean with antibacterial cream.

9. Another nasty is hepatitis "A" which is caused by contaminated food; hepatitis "B" is transmitted by sexual activity; hepatitis "C" is transmitted through blood transfusion; hepatitis "E" is caused by bad food and water. Make sure to get vaccinations for "A" and "B."

10. Obtain booster shots for tetanus and diphtheria. They last for 10 years.

11. Why do you want to cover yourself in the tropics head to foot? Answer: Dengue Fever. It is mosquito-borne, so cover yourself. There is no treatment or prophylaxis.

12. More goodies: Yellow Fever—you will find it in Africa and South America. You may receive a vaccination to avoid this disease.

13. Finally, millions suffer from and have died from HIV, which turns into AIDS. Be certain to stay protected while engaging intimately. Better yet, avoid intimacy. But even then, it could be scary. It spreads through bodily fluids. Can you catch it from kissing someone who suffers from HIV? Beats me, but I never attempted to find out in all my worldly travels. Stay away from needles, tattoo parlors and medical facilities that may not maintain standards.

MORNING CONSTITUTIONAL IN THE WOODS AND AROUND THE WORLD

Most Americans might be amazed that somewhere around 2.5 billion of the world's humans lack a toilet and have never used toilet paper, but do use their fingers to wipe their butts. Afterwards, maybe—and that's a big, maybe—they rinse their hands. But they may not. Okay, now don't get all freaked out by this new realization. Toilet paper arrived on the scene less than 150 years ago, so you must figure that humans have practiced wiping their bums with their fingers for eons. They may have used a big maple leaf or they jumped into a stream.

In many countries, whether you squat between two bricks to hit a hole or enter a stinking outhouse full of flies and spiders or squat in a latrine in the woods with a million mosquitoes using your bum for a refueling zone—it's up to you to provide yourself with a safe and sanitary bowel-movement experience.

Always carry your TP in a gallon zip-closure plastic bag. Add a second gallon plastic bag, whose use I will explain shortly. You can also carry a lighter or matches.

While camping, carry your TP out to a quiet and secluded area. Dig a six to eight inch hole with your boot or small plastic shovel or find soft sand or whatever you can do to make sure you bury your waste.

Do your business, wipe your butt and roll the soiled TP with your roll of new TP. You need not touch the soiled TP because you're rolling it off the new roll to handle the soiled TP. Place the soiled TP into the second zip-closure plastic bag. Carry it with you to a proper refuse barrel at your earliest convenience. You can carry it to the campfire. If it's safe and you won't be starting a forest or grass fire, you can burn the soiled TP after you have buried your waste. Bury the ashes.

If you don't have TP, take your water bottle with you. Do your business and pour water into your hand and wash your bum with your hand. Wash it until it's totally clean. Bury the waste.

Wash your hands with more water and soap. Use biodegradable soap or hand-sanitizer if you carry some.

Leave no trace of yourself in the wilderness.

If you use toilets in developing countries, you will notice a box beside the toilet with used TP. Throw your TP into the box. Avoid throwing it into the toilet because developing countries' sewage systems cannot tolerate toilet paper. That's when the TP police will swarm down on you with handcuffs and send you off to clean toilets for an automatic two year sentence. Oh, the horror of it all.

WHAT TO TAKE AND HOW TO PACK IT

Depending on your particular adventure destination or mode, you will need a packing list of important gear for your journey. You will find ample packing lists for summer, fall, winter, and spring in the "Specific Adventures" sections of this book. Customize them to meet your needs. Always prepare months before you leave so you won't suffer a huge case of P-A-N-I-C! Preparation is nine-tenths of success.

Excellent companies for gear, clothes and bikes:

www.REI.com
www.EasternMountainSports.com
www.EddieBauer.com
www.EarlyWinters.com
www.LLBean.com
www.Cabelas.com
www.Travelsmith.com
www.Columbia.com
www.Coolibar.com
www.Golite.com

Just remember this: whatever you pack, you carry. Travel light, travel fast and travel lean. Travel with a smile.

If you load up on the latest fashions, you will curse yourself for every extra ounce in your backpack. "Why did I bring my electric toothbrush and my hairdryer?"

Ladies, wear black undergarments to avoid showing dirt. Also, these days, you can purchase underwear that can be washed in seconds, dries in minutes and lasts through 22 countries.

If you're hankering for an orderly backpack, be sure to use ditty-bags to separate and organize your clothes and other items. You can buy compressor bags that compact your clothes at www.eaglecreek.com

If you carry any liquids in your backpack or panniers, always use those quart or gallon freezer zip-closure bags to keep any liquids from spilling all over the pack.

FOR LADIES

You may like to keep your feminine mystique while traveling. However, when accessorizing, think lean, smart and sassy. You might carry eye-liner, lip stick, one pair of earrings, bracelet and things that make you feel special.

Carry simple jewelry that won't get ripped off your hand or neck. Head scarfs make for elegance or can be worn like a shawl. Bring your own your personal style with you.

"I've decided I'm going through this life as my best friend, as my own North Star, best life-coach extraordinaire, and Glinda the

Good Witch, complete with wand and tiara. And yes, that doesn't always mean I'll know where I'm going. But at least I know who I'm traveling with. I'm going to go through this life calling myself "beloved" and rolling out the infinite advantages that kindness offers. The voice I'll listen to inside will be loving—or I won't listen." Tama Kieves, This Time I Dance

ALONG FOR THE RIDE: MEMORIES

Make certain you bring a journal, two to three pens and reading glasses, if needed. Write every day about all that happens to you—as if you are writing to your best friend—to allow them to feel, experience, see, taste and smell the adventure as it unfolds. Make it a daily habit before you jump into your sleeping bag or bunk or hostel bed.

Next, a light-weight digital camera allows you the ability to send photos through the Internet and fill in your own website. You can take a zillion shots with 4-GB cards. Bring plenty of memory cards and batteries. Waterproof them at all times. If you have a rechargeable camera, you need to bring the conversion plugs to use it in places like Europe where the electrical current is different than the USA.

Learn how to shoot up close and far away. Learn about framing a picture, bracketing, back lighting, fill-in flash and other techniques to bring your pictures to life for friends. Additionally, you might submit your photos to your local newspaper with a travel story.

Once home, you can create a wondrous travel album of your adventure. It will bring you fantastic smiles and joy down through the years as you look back, and then, spur you toward yet another adventure.

With digital cameras, you can upload online at www.kodakgallery. com and Snapfish at www.snapfish.com to send your favorite moments back home to friends and family.

One caution about photography in foreign lands: in some cultures, people expect you to pay money to photograph them. Others feel it is an invasion of their personal beings. Find out from officials what local people feel about being photographed and respect their wishes.

While traveling, you may bring a voice recorder to document your thoughts, hopes, dreams, ideas and even frustrations. You can refer to them later. These days, you can buy a three ounce electronic voice recorder that will document all your descriptions as you go.

Another thing you can do while traveling on a bus across the Sahara Desert, Africa, or perhaps bicycling through the Atacama Desert of Chile or some stretch of lonesome road across Death Valley, you might enjoy using an MP3 player, which holds something like 10,000 songs. You can record books to listen to your favorite authors while traveling to make the greatest use of your time. Bring a Kindle eBook with all your downloaded books. Additionally, you can learn a language while traveling. Make use of great technologies to advance your brain or soothe your emotions. Recorded: www.audible.com iTunes: www.itunes.com

Language option at www.rosettastone.com

When packing any of your gear, make sure you either take out the batteries of these devices or flip them to take away their continuity or turn the switch to the lock position so they don't accidently suffer drainage.

Also, bring ear buds or headphones so you can listen to your books, music and or language lessons in the quiet of your own mind. Nothing worse than riding on a bus from Kathmandu, Nepal to Pokara with chickens pecking at your feet, babies crying and pigs squealing in the aisles of the bus. Not to mention sick babies hurling their breakfast into your lap. "Oh, the joys of world travel," you exclaim. Headphones at www.bose. com , www.radioshack.com

INTERNATIONAL AMBASSADORS FROM AMERICA

Once you step outside the United States, Canada or any country, you become a traveling ambassador. If you travel with a friend(s), you become ambassadors for your country—whether you like it or not. Your country will be graded, remembered and assessed by your actions. You represent America, Canada, United Kingdom, France, Australia, China, India, Brazil, Germany or whatever country you call home.

Everything you do will be noted by people, groups and organizations while you travel in their country. When you smile, shake their hands, offer aid or eat at a restaurant, you will be showing your best or (otherwise) to the world. Others will judge your country by your positive behavior or otherwise—for a lifetime.

That's why I make sure to learn a little of their language so I can speak in their language such phrases as: "Good morning" , "Goodbye" , "Thank you" , "Please" , "Good evening" , "Where is the bathroom please?" , "How much?" , "Miss" , " Ma'am" , "What a beautiful day." , "You are so kind."

If you get drunk and act like a fool, become argumentative, act inappropriately around women, curse or any other negative behavior—they will remember you and America for a lifetime, one way or the other.

One of the very nicest things you can do is to give a small gift from your state to those that show kindness toward you. My friend Lance, an Australian, whom I met on the way to Alaska, 30 years ago, gave me a small pendant of a kangaroo. I still keep it and I still treasure Lance as a lifelong friend. That one gift brings back marvelous memories of a stranger from a foreign land. You might carry small patches from your state or decals of a grizzly bear if you're from Montana or a sailboat patch from Florida or US flag decals or anything that will give the stranger something good to remember his or her moment with you. You will be rewarded with bright eyes, happy thoughts and incredible memories—because those small gifts will come back to you a hundred-fold.

PACKING YOUR PACK

Load your least utilized gear at the bottom of the pack. Stuff your needed gear like lip balm, lipstick, toothbrush, toothpaste, dental floss, sunscreen, eye glasses, cell-phone, business cards and other often-used gear into the side pockets for easy retrieval.

Load breakable gear into the top; anything liquid should be encased in a zip-closure plastic bag and kept upright. Note: check liquids for a tightened cap before stuffing into your pack. Also, if you unzip a pouch, you zip it immediately. Unzip, zip it back. Make it a habit or pay the price of lost items.

TRAVEL PACKS, BACKPACKS, DAY PACKS, WILDERNESS PACKS

Today, whether you backpack, take a suitcase or lug some mountain climbing gear onto the plane, train or bus—you need to think light, durable, quality and use-specific.

Ladies may go to www.REI.com for female-specific travel packs, backpacks and roll-on luggage. Additionally: www.EarlyWinters.com , www.EasternMountainSports.com , www.LLBean.com

Ask for a lady counselor and you will enjoy a wealth of information from ones who have gone before you. Additionally, you will find a list of outstanding female-oriented travel preparation books within this tome.

For guys, most top equipment stores carry specific packs for mountain climbing, walking across America, world travel, canoe travel, hut to hut, wilderness travel and more. You can add daypacks that fit your needs. Again, ask any of their representatives for specific information. They will give you first class information because all of them have hit the road themselves.

Special note: always take a specific color yarn or Velcro band to identify your pack or luggage on an airport carousel for easy pick-up from the horde of luggage that is usually all colored dark blue or black.

Not sure what you can and cannot carry onto a plane in these tense times? Check with the Transportation Security Administration, www. tsa.gov , to obtain up to the minute lists for what luggage and carry-on gear you can and cannot take onto an airplane. You can also buy a TSA-approved lock that secures your luggage against employee pilfering, but it can be opened by TSA agents. You can check with Travel Sentry at www. travelsentry.org to buy TSA locks for $20.00. These locks will cause the casual thief baggage handler to quickly jump to another pack because your zippers were locked up by those little TSA locks.

Be certain to attach an ID tag to your luggage or pack, both outside and inside. If you're staying at a hotel or hostel, you can write the name of the destination on another tag next to your name tag—so if your luggage comes in late, it can be sent to the correct destination. If you're traveling with a cell-phone, place the number on the luggage so they can call you. Are you writing this information on your to-do list? By now you know you must prepare for your trip at least three months in advance.

WHAT TO TAKE AND HOW TO PACK IT

What do you take on a weekend trip, short trip or long trip? What about your gear for backpacking, 14er climbing, canoe trip, day hike, raft trip and other adventures? We will work through exceptionally thorough pack lists in each section of the adventures that you choose.

From there, you can customize your pack lists for yourself. In your garage, keep a notebook filled with pack lists for specific adventures whether a weekend, week, month or year. Each list covers a particular sport. If you need something on a canoe trip that you forgot to pack, take note of that on the canoe trip and add it to your list.

GENERAL PACK LIST FOR MEN AND WOMEN

CLOTHES AND RAIN GEAR

1. Light bush pants with zip-off legs to create instant shorts.
2. Light slacks for women who want more of the feminine touch.
3. Shorts if you don't like the shorts created by the bush pants with zip-off legs.
4. Blouse, tank top, sweater, PJs.
5. Gore-Tex or rain jacket and pants.
6. Underwear, bra and possible other under-garments.
7. Wool socks, cotton socks, bike socks.
8. Bathing suit, swim goggles.
9. Shoes, running shoes, sandals, flip flops.
10. Bush belt made of nylon for lightness.
11. Foldable cotton brimmed hat, light gloves if needed, bandana.
12. Hiking boots.

Bathroom gear:

1. Soap
2. Deodorant
3. Cream or lotion of some kind
4. Sunscreen, hand lotion
5. Lip balm with 20 SPF or even 50 SPF, sunscreen
6. Brush and comb
7. Hair accessories
8. Medications
9. Feminine products, tampons, panty-liners, sanitary napkins
10. Makeup, lipstick, eyeliner, etc.
11. Birth control pills, condoms, etc.
12. Insect repellant
13. Moist-wipes, tissues
14. Half roll of TP
15. Razor, shaver
16. Toothbrush, toothpaste
17. Bar of soap

18. Dental floss
19. Tea tree oil
20. Anti-fungal ointment
21. Micro fiber towel that dries easily, recommended 29"X16"
22. Washcloth
23. Hand sanitizer
24. Bio degradable liquid soap to clean dishes
25. Nail clippers (must be loaded into hull of the plane)

LEGAL PAPERS, DOCUMENTS, LICENSES

1. Scuba card
2. International driver's license
3. Passport with waterproof container
4. Shot records
5. Credit cards or ATM cards
6. International phone numbers to call if you lose a credit card
7. Leave credit card company phone numbers with trusted friends
8. Twelve extra passport pictures
9. Proof of ownership of your bike or other gear

CAMERAS, ELECTRICAL EQUIPMENT AND OTHER ITEMS

1. Electrical converter devices
2. Silk or satin sleep sack for hostels
3. Watch or some timepiece
4. Cell phone, MP3, iPod
5. Maps and other direction finders like Global Positioning Device
6. Business cards
7. Book or Kindle for reading on flights
8. Language phrase book
9. Camera with chargers or spare batteries and memory cards
10. Notebook and two or three pens
11. Ear plugs (Avoid leaving home without them.)
12. Eye blinders or sunshades so you can sleep with lights on in plane
13. Binoculars (Optional)

14. Small inflatable pillow (Avoid telling the TSA inspector that it's a blow-up pillow.)
15. Small, light, electric travel alarm clock
16. Small miner's lamp flashlight with options like blinking light, red and in LED
17. Candle lantern (optional)
18. Sunglasses, reading glasses, securing cord
19. Camera tripod
20. Foreign currency
21. Plane tickets
22. Health insurance card
23. Leave a legal will in your files so that if something should happen to you, it's all cleared up in your legal papers. Let loved ones know how to find it.
24. Cable lock (Optional)
25. Photo copies of passport and shot card and health card (Recommended)
26. Legal will in your files at home
27. Swiss Army knife (must be loaded into hull of plane)

NECESSARY HEALTH GEAR DEPENDING ON DESTINATION

1. Water filter, tablets
2. Three to five spare plastic bags (5 gallon)
3. Three to five one gallon zip-closure bags
4. Melatonin sleeping tablets
5. Pair of thin rubber gloves from drug store for emergency
6. Stainless steel water container

KEY POINTS FROM THIS CHAPTER

1. Customize these pack lists and to-do lists for your own needs.
2. When you forget something, write it down and place it on your list for the next time.
3. Ask friends for their preparation list and ideas for safe travels.

*C*hapter 46—*Tidbits*

"Rush boldly and ruthlessly toward your dreams! As you rush toward them, they race toward you." Dr. Roger Teel

MAPS, LAPTOPS, GADGETS AND GOODIES FOR COMMUNICATIONS

Today, you can find an Internet café almost everywhere in the world. You can find them in Antarctica. The penguins use them to talk with their friends on Facebook.

If you carry around a lightweight laptop computer, it will enable you to communicate with anyone back home, send pictures and much more. Use those devices for your diary and remember to send your entries back to your friends so you don't lose them if the computer is lost or stolen.

Just about every place now offers Wi-Fi so you can hook up in remote areas. You can find Wi-Fi places at www.wififreespot.com and www.jiwire. com to list hook ups at airports, RV parks, malls, restaurants and hostels. Make sure your laptop carries a Wi-Fi receiver or card adaptor. Make sure to install the best virus scanners and blockers such as AVG at www.avg. com. Be sure to charge your computer before leaving and make sure you have the correct hook-up converters for all sorts of electrical outlets. You can also bring a multi-prong power plug so you can share an outlet with other travelers at an airport or bus terminal.

During checks at TSA, be sure to keep an eye on how agents treat your camera, laptop or other delicate equipment. Be methodical as you work through the security system to make sure you avoid breaking anything.

MAPS, TOURS AND THINGS

One of the coolest inventions for travel must be the Global Positioning System device. It works like magic. No matter where you are in the world, those little units, that you can hold in your hand, can tell you exactly where you are within a few meters and take you to where you want to be. They work off computers in circling satellites to engage your computer in your handheld unit.

Find out what they can do and learn all about them before buying one. They even offer language translator systems at www.garmin.com

If you want to save money, you may engage audio tours that tell you everything and talk you through a tour: www.ijourneys.com

A tour will provide highlights of your favorite places: Rome, Paris, Madrid, Rio, Beijing, Munich, Bergen, Bangkok and more. Another site for the USA, Europe and more at www.soundwalk.com

You can obtain audio travel podcasts from www.lonelyplanet.com; try www.ricksteves.com for "Europe Through the Back Door."

Today you may quickly access RSS (Really Simple Syndication) feeds for such things as travel alerts, special airfares or other worthwhile information while you travel. You can access RSS feeds through aggregator software available at Internet Explorer, Yahoo, AOL, Mozilla Fox and others. Alerts about the information that you request will be loaded to your home page. Use them and benefit. Save money on travel discounts: www.sidestep.com. Not sure how to operate this subscriber benefit? Ask a friend or a computer store. They will set you up.

Since we live in the computer age, take advantage of eBook guides instead of the published books that add weight to your pack. You can download eBooks to your laptop and/or PDA. Free eBooks can be accessed at www.gutenberg.org and www.ebooks.com

You will enjoy the low prices and versatility. Make sure to download the proper software application in order to view the books.

Want to fire up your imagination about world travel? Give yourself incentives by checking out videos that visually take you to faraway places with great audio complements. Check with www.totalvid.com and www.netflix.com

Be sure to install a media player in your computer to play all those videos.

TRAVEL AND HEALTH INSURANCE

You may find it advisable to buy medical and property insurance for your travels. Otherwise, you could be stuck for untold amounts of money from hospital stays or illness. If you become a victim of theft, you'll be amazed at what it costs to buy a new backpack and gear, or a bicycle with gear.

Check www.travel.state.gov for international and national insurance health providers. Also, www.travelguard.com will cover gobs of stuff you need to have covered. Buy your coverage a month in advance. Again, I hope you're writing a to-do list from this chapter.

In case you get hurt or deathly ill in a remote place, make sure you obtain evacuation insurance for a helicopter ride out. It could cost tens of thousands of dollars. Check out: www.wellnessconcierge.com

MONEY: SAVING IT, SPENDING IT, OUT-SMARTING IT

"I should have been born rich instead of so good looking," a friend of mine said.

"You and the rest of the whole human race," I added.

As stated in previous chapters, money makes the world go around. You need it to feed your travel passion. Whether you work two jobs for a year at 80 hours per week or three jobs at 100 hours a week with no time off or you join the Peace Corps—you need money.

The more frugally you live, the faster you save money. Let me give you an idea of the tenacity of my 18-year-old brother. He worked an entire winter at a pizza joint. He made pizzas, he delivered pizzas and he cleaned the shop. He lived in his car with two sleeping bags covering him in 20-below zero Michigan winters. He took showers at MSU's athletic center. He didn't date, he didn't spend a penny and he didn't waste a dime. His goal: to motorcycle all over Europe. After 10 months of incredible labor, his bank account showed a healthy balance. He and our other brother Rex bought plane tickets to Europe plus two motorcycles. They spent five months touring the entire continent, all its history, all of its amazing architecture and famous places from Norway to Greece.

He discovered that he loved languages. From that first trip, he has traveled to Europe 20 times plus four other continents. He attended language schools in France, Spain, Germany and Alexandria, Egypt and now speaks those languages fluently.

He later graduated from MSU. He then drove a furniture truck 70 to 90 hours a week to save enough money to travel the world extensively. Every year, he sends out Christmas cards from places he's visited. I love the one of him riding a camel with the Great Pyramids behind him. How do you top that? A few years ago, he rode a horse across America East to West and West to East—the only man in history to accomplish that feat. Heaven only knows what his next adventure will be, but you can bet it will be magnificent. Our mother livens up every conversation with her friends as she tells them where her boys traveled during the year.

Make sure that however much money you possess, you calculate a budget for your travels. Determine what your daily costs will be in food, shelter and transportation. Will you motorcycle, bicycle or rent a motor home? Will you take a bus or train? Will you hitch-hike? Will you camp out, stay in hostels or live lavishly? How will you know how to budget your money? You may find more than a dozen books in Chapter 43 that will help you.

You will go farther and longer by preparing your own food, camping out and riding public transport. Bicycling can take you to the ends of the world for the cost of your leg power and food to nourish your body. You might try vegetarian eating, which tends to be very inexpensive.

Are you careful with money? You may write an expense account to show you where your money flows. Can you write anything off if you become a travel writer? Yes! Keep receipts of all transactions in a plastic bag in your pack or panniers. Track your purchases in the back of your journal for instant access.

You may purchase the currency of the country you're visiting by visiting your bank. You can also use www.americanexpress.com for more than 50 different currencies.

Take at least two credit or debit cards in order to hit an ATM or any bank to withdraw local currency that will be charged to your cards. Carry some traveler's checks for emergencies: American Express—don't leave home without them. Always keep the numbers of your traveler's checks with you and copies at home. You will need those numbers for replacement if the checks are stolen. Make sure someone at home can answer the phone if you have to call to retrieve those check numbers and any other pertinent information. Again, scan them onto your computer for easy access when all else fails.

Unfortunately, you will get hit with a pretty steep price for exchanging traveler's checks, but that's the way of the world. Shop around for your best deal on exchanging money at the casa de cambio or bureau de change.

Black market exchange rates await every traveler. Avoid the temptation. You can be conned out of money, property and worse. When that shadowy guy asks you if you want to change money, just hurry on your way.

When you leave a country, after paying departure fees, baggage, etc., change your money back to U.S. dollars so you don't waste it once you're out of the country. In Nepal, they let you dump your spare money into a big glass box to save the children of that country. Unfortunately, it actually enriches the man in charge of the lock on the glass box and his superiors.

Bring a couple of hundred dollars in U.S. cash with you. Take clean, crisp, fresh cash with you in $1s and $20s. Keep it in a money belt and always keep it on you. Sleep with it, shower with it, swim with it and walk with it 24/7. That includes your passport.

You can find out the currency exchange rates at www.xe.com and www.megellans.com

HAGGLING OVER THE PRICE IN FOREIGN COUNTRIES

Don't want to pay the full price for a souvenir? Bargain, haggle, quibble, wrangle and barter with the shopkeeper. They expect it. It's their culture. If you fail to haggle, you failed the merchant, yourself and all creation. Avoid spending that dime until you've haggled them down to a price that meets your expectations.

If you want something, go for it. At the same time, please realize that the person you bargain with supports a family. Have fun bargaining, but also understand that just by being able to travel, you're richer than 90 percent of the rest of the world.

If you eat out, or take a cab, or ride a pedal-taxi, or hire a guide—you gotta tip baby. Find out how much from the Lonely Planet travel books, as it varies all over the world from five percent to 20 percent.

SAVING A BUCK HERE AND THERE

Trying to save a buck? Do it! Those bucks add up:

1. Camp instead of renting a motel or hostel room.
2. Check into a motel where breakfast is included.
3. Share a ride in a taxi with a fellow traveler or two or three.
4. If you never ask, you will never know. Haggle for a better price on goods and services.

5. Always check your receipts for charges so you're not overbilled.
6. Choose the train or bus over the taxi.
7. Don't buy the cheapest; don't buy the most expensive; buy in the middle for good value.
8. Carry your own bags.
9. Seek store items on sale.
10. Check ahead on the Internet for deals.
11. Try www.Craigslist.com and eBay for used, quality gear.
12. Consignment shopping from mountaineering shops can net you great bargains.
13. Many sports shops feature previously-owned gear.
14. Buy at a farmer's market for fresh bread, tomatoes, cheese and fruits.
15. Eat on the side of nature's road instead of a restaurant.

Here are more ideas for saving money. In the United Kingdom, you can sleep cheaply in dorms in London at www.westminster.ac.uk/business, www.ucl.ac.uk/residences, www.lsevacations.co.uk

In Germany, "The Tent" is where you pitch your tent inside a big tent at www.the-tent.com

In Switzerland, the Swiss Alpine Club runs more than 150 hiker huts at www.sac-cas.ch

Visit people around the world with Servas, www.usservas.org, a worldwide organization that connects travelers with host families. Some travelers swear this is the best way to see the world.

CouchSurfing is a vagabond's alternative to Servas. More than two million members in 146 countries host fellow "surfers" for free. Check them out at www.couchsurfing.com

For touring bicyclists, check out www.warmshowers.com

KEY POINTS FROM THIS CHAPTER

1. If you can't find the answers in this section, check out other books from the library.
2. Be smart, be aware, be prudent and enjoy yourself.

Chapter 47—Safety

"Somebody ought to tell us, right at the start of our lives, that we are dying. Then we might live life to the limit every minute of every day. Do it, I say, whatever you want to do, do it now." Michael Landon, "Little Joe" on Bonanza

PERSONAL SAFETY FOR MEN AND WOMEN

"You're going to get killed by drug gangs," friends warned me before I headed to South America for a year-long journey from the top to the bottom and back up to Rio de Janeiro.

Most people suffer from a fear induced by headlines from dangerous spots around the world. Okay, I admit it. I avoid war zones, drug cartel zones, mass starvation zones, HIV disease zones and other dangerous areas. You may visit plenty of other places on the planet to explore in a safer mode.

How do you know where to find safe areas? You may find travel warnings at www.travel.state.gov to find out which countries to delete from your bucket list for the time being.

Basically, most of the countries of the world enjoy reasonable safety. But, just like large cities in the United States in some areas, you can suffer unfortunate situations.

Be prudent, be smart, stick with a group, go with a friend and stay inside at night if you're not sure. Darkness provides criminals in any country with the stealth needed to commit crimes.

Women must be smarter, more cautious and cunning as to where they walk, stop and what persons they meet. One single lady traveler friend I know wears a wedding band wherever she travels and keeps a picture of her husband in her wallet. That ring deters many men. If nothing else, it may stop the catcalls, whistles and aggressive behavior of men.

Women need to be aware of their clothing in Asia and other fundamentalist countries such as the Middle East. Showing skin can get a gal in trouble. Be smart rather than fashionable.

To be wise, women need to walk with confidence and self-assurance. They must carry an attitude that lets predatory men know that they will meet an abrupt and stern rejection of unwanted advances. For more information, you will be directed to books that give more ideas for traveling women.

When in drug-infested countries and cities, beware not to accept unsolicited rides in cabs or private cars or invitations to parties. You could be set up for a drug bust. Professional criminals can and will plant drugs in your pack. The police will stop you and arrest you, and the only way you can get out of it is to bribe the cops.

Ladies, if you use crowded public transportation, you could be groped. Yell at the groper and stand your ground. Make a scene. They most likely will back off.

If you travel alone, you must maintain close contact with your pack and/or bicycle or other gear—at all times. Lock your gear to you with a small cable lock if needed. Criminals think of many ways to separate you from your pack.

Always keep everything inside your shirt or well protected—such as records, camera, notebook or personal items. The first time you set something down, you will forget and walk off. Within seconds, it will be gone.

You will meet new friends during your travels. At the same time, you must always maintain your 24/7 caution as to your safety and personal property.

CAUTIONARY TALE

While in Quito, Ecuador, I talked to a man shouldering a backpack who walked up the street alone. He said a local person stopped him to ask for directions. While he talked to the man, he felt heavy black oil being poured onto his head from behind. It totally discombobulated him and stunned him. As he turned around with oil dripping down over his face and down his neck, the first guy used a razor blade to cut his camera strap away and took off running. At that point, the other guy ran. Since the 40 pound backpack proved too much to run with, he stood there with oil dripping all over, lost his camera and learned a harsh lesson: never walk alone at night in a strange city, never show your valuable possessions to others, and never walk into large crowds where thieves can grab your gear and go. Stay alert, smart and prepared at all times for a successful experience.

While you remain alert and smart, so much more good arrives on your personal traveling doorstep than you can imagine. Always smile at everyone. Once, in a market in Porta Varas, Chile, we bought a lot of food for our bicycle journey down the Cara Terra Astral. We smiled at a couple also shopping for food items. They talked to us. After we enjoyed much laughter, they invited us to their beautiful home on their private lake. The husband, a successful businessman and his wife an artist, introduced their two college kids. Both their children showed great manners and spoke English. They lived in a one-story sprawling wood-framed home with a glorious deck that overlooked a lake. On the beach, they offered to share their ski boat, windsurfers and jet skis. Let me tell you, we enjoyed fabulous breakfasts, lunches and dinners for three days.

When we saddled up to leave three days later, they treated us like family. They cried when we pedaled out the driveway. We cried. We waved, they waved and our memories remain warm and joyful all these years later. Smile and radiate positive energy to all you meet. Much magic will flow your way.

CONTACT WITH FRIENDS WHILE ON THE ROAD

For the early years of my adventure life, I wrote postcards. Today, anyone can maintain constant communication through Internet cafés around the world.

Be aware that trying to please all your family and friends can become a huge drain on your time. However, if you like to write and you want your friends to enjoy the journey with you, by all means, create a travel blog by accessing www.travelblog.org. Try Blogger www.blogger.com and, for women traveling alone, visit www.forwomentravelingsolo.com

Set up your blog before you leave and learn how to post updates. You will receive lots of responses from your friends as you travel around the planet.

Cell phones provide instant contact with family and friends 24/7. My friend Gary called me regularly from New Zealand on his bicycle tour. His voice and the reception felt like next door. It's a fun deal to hear your friends and their delights on their adventures. To make sure your phone works in a particular country, check out Global System for Mobile Communications at www.gsmworld.com. Make certain your phone uses the technology. Also, access www.mobal.com for a prepaid mobile phone.

Another option: phone cards. Beware that phone booths around the world may become an extinct remnant of the 20th century. Technology kills them daily by the thousands. Whatever will Superman do to change clothes?

With a cell phone, you can text message to your heart's desire.

IF YOU NEED SOMETHING MAILED WHILE ON AN ADVENTURE

While in South America, I broke a granny gear crossing the Andes mountains. I called my brother to mail me a new one in Santiago, Chile. Be sure to underline your last name.

He addressed it:

F.H. <u>Wooldridge</u>
Post Restante
Santiago, Chile

You will need to show your passport to retrieve your mail. Also, if they cannot find your package or mail, ask them to look in the section with your first name instead of your last name. That usually does the trick.

HOW ABOUT TALKING THEIR LANGUAGE?

The first time my brother Howard biked through Europe at age18, he noticed that everybody spoke at least three and often, four languages. When traveling, you will make points and find folks really appreciative of your attempting to speak their language.

Before you leave home, buy a phrase book of the languages you may encounter. You can also buy Rosetta Stone CDs to learn a language while still at home. www.rosettastone.com and www.pimsleur.com

You can take language classes at a local college for a year before departing, and/or join a foreign language club in town where folks get together to speak a specific language.

No matter what, when you arrive in a foreign land, smile, laugh, use a warm handshake and realize that they want to know about you as much as you want to know about them. The more you try to speak in their language, the more they will warm to you. We all belong to one big human family.

While you will be hearing different languages, you will also be experiencing different cultures. If you've lived a sheltered life, you may be in for a culture shock when you see some things you have never seen before.

Locals may stare at you for hours. If you eat in town, they will stare at you. You will see blind kids begging for money. You will see disfigured kids with bent arms and bent legs. Their parents did it to them while they were babies to make them look more pathetic. Their disfigurement makes more money from begging. You will see things that turn your stomach, but it's their culture. You're visiting to learn and grow, but not condemn or make any judgments. Try to be sensitive to their behaviors and dress. If not, you may be breaking one of their taboos without knowing it. Please refer to these websites that give information on 75 countries and how to act: www.gacpc.com , www.cia.gov/cia/publications

The most important behaviors you can bring with you on your travels: patience, empathy, quiet acceptance and understanding. After that, more patience will keep you balanced.

KEY POINTS FROM THIS CHAPTER

1. Show your warm spirit; people from all walks of life will respond positively to you.
2. Remember to bring patience, empathy, acceptance and understanding on your travels.

SECTION V –PREPARATION IS NINE-TENTHS OF SUCCESS

This section offers you everything you need to know to enjoy successful experiences in the wilderness. It covers camping techniques, bear and mountain lion safety, water purification, personal hygiene, cooking, cleaning, human waste disposal and wilderness survival.

By following the rules of the wilderness, you may enjoy years of adventures with great health and safety.

Chapter 48—Weekend, week-long and year-long adventures

"There are many ways through the Ring of Life. All are constant spiritual movement toward self-fulfillment through growth of the mind and expansion of the senses. They are ceaseless and persistent throughout one's life." FHW

How do you begin your life of adventure? Do you purchase tickets to South America, buy a canoe and paddle down the Amazon River 4,000 miles to the Atlantic? How about buying a bicycle and riding around the perimeter of Australia? How about backpacking the Appalachian Trail? Why not sign on to climb Mount Everest? How about renting a float plane to go fly-fishing in a remote Alaskan lake? How about dropping a canoe into the headwaters of the Mississippi River for a 2,552 mile trip to New Orleans? How about rafting the Grand Canyon with its formidable rapids for a lark?

Bold, to say the least! However, how about starting out easy? You can start with tame adventures, get your feet wet, make the usual mistakes, suffer some blisters on your feet, feel like you will die of thirst and freeze your butt off on a hut to hut skiing trip in January. You can swallow some salt water on a rough scuba diving trip in the Caribbean as part of the learning curve.

It's the beginning adventures that toughen you, teach you and inculcate you into Mother Nature's inner workings. Those first weekend camping trips, hopefully with a seasoned friend, give you the tools to move toward longer trips. That first climb up a small mountain may lead to a 14er or bigger. A day raft trip on Class I, II or III rapids may whet your appetite for even bigger and more dangerous thrills on Class IV and V rivers. You may be inspired or frightened to death. You may find out that you don't like to scare the heck out of yourself. You may discover that you're cut out for poker or solitaire. You may find that you love danger and the thrill of it all. You're invited to follow your bliss.

Each of us discovers our thrill ratio during those first encounters with the wilderness. I should have been killed by a grizzly in my early twenties because I wasn't prepared. I'm lucky to have survived one of my raft trips because of my inexperience.

That's why I advise little steps that move toward bigger steps. Such fine organizations like www.MeetUp.com all over the USA will put you in touch with people who love to teach or mentor their particular passions. Go with them. You might love fly-fishing. You may love climbing mountains. On the other hand, you may dislike or even fear climbing. A camping trip with mosquitoes may shower you with an endless love of the wilderness or you may prefer a motel. The soft, quiet joy of canoe camping may fit you like a hand in a glove. For that matter, archery may be your niche. Maybe you love to paint landscapes in the wildest of places or take photographs like Ansel Adams. Get out there and find out.

KEY POINTS FROM THIS CHAPTER

1. Start out slow, start out smart and start out with friends.
2. Prepare well, be prudent and learn on each adventure.
   Utilize www.MeetUp.com to find friends that will guide you.

Chapter 49—Camping techniques, bear and mountain lion safety, safe water, personal hygiene, cooking, cleaning, human waste, leave no trace, wilderness survival

"To many Americans, the wilderness is little more than a retreat from the tensions of civilization. To others, it is a testing place—a vanishing frontier where humans can rediscover basic values. And to a few, the wilderness is nothing less than an almost holy source of self-renewal. But for every man, woman and child, the ultimate lesson that nature teaches is simply this: man's fate is inextricably linked to that of the world at large, and to all of the other creatures that live upon it." Unknown

Every time you step into the wilderness, it provides uncommon splendor and beauty. What can you do to preserve it? Answer: "Leave no trace."

By following the established protocol in this chapter—whether you ride a bicycle, backpack, climb mountains, fish, raft, canoe, hike, sail or any other wilderness activity—you will learn to take only photographs and leave only footprints.

My dad said, "Son, when you go camping, always leave the place nicer than you found it."

To this day, I have picked up a half-million pieces of trash in my life, if not more. I volunteer to pick up rivers, roadways, campgrounds, mountain paths and any place I see trash. It's frustrating that many careless people toss their cans, bottles and glass containers without a blink. I also advocate for a 10-cent bottle deposit law like Michigan's to stop the incredible littering of the landscape.

All of us enjoy a stake in our world's well-being and our own as we live this great life adventure. I hope you become one of the people that care deeply. This chapter will show you how to preserve the wilderness.

WILDERNESS CAMPING—EVERYTHING YOU NEED TO KNOW

In the United States, you can always find a campground, motel, hostel or bed and breakfast. You may find ample accommodations in every state and most of Canada. Nonetheless, you always want to be prepared by carrying a tent, sleeping bag and air mattress. Please note that I have met touring bicyclists that carry credit cards for food and motels. If that's your style, enjoy yourself.

Shelter and food take on a whole new significance during an adventure, especially in other countries. If you venture into developing countries, being unprepared may cause you great discomfort.

In developing countries, especially outside major cities, lodging may be difficult to find. That's why you must carry your own tent, sleeping bag and air mattress. For cooking meals, you need a stove, cookware, fuel, water and food supplies. When you're prepared with the basics, adventuring internationally will offer miles of smiles. Nothing beats a good night's sleep on a full stomach.

The most important gear you can carry is a quality tent. It must be big enough, light enough and waterproof. Quick "pitch time" is a nice extra. With so many tents on the market, how do you choose? You may have a friend who knows tents because he or she camps often. Since your friend learned by experience, have him or her go with you to the local camping outfitter to discuss the relative differences of tents. Buy good gear. If you go cheap, you will pay an uncomfortable price if the tent fails and you become soaked in the middle of the night.

If you're on your own, a few tips may help in your purchase. For camping, your tent should be self-standing and six pounds or less. For backpacking, you may find a 4.6 pound half-dome the most durable and dependable. It should have a waterproof floor and sidewalls. Rip-stop nylon is your best bet for durability, or if you can afford it, buy a Gore-Tex fabric tent. Make sure the tent features a loop or loft to hang clothes and candle lanterns from the ceiling. Make certain the tent is taut enough so it won't flap in the wind. Purchase shock-corded poles for easier set-up.

Make certain the rain fly covers the outside edges of the tent. Is your tent long enough? Can you sit up in it? Will you have room for two people and your gear? Is it warm enough for three seasons? A light color will be cooler in the summer and stand up under ultraviolet damaging rays better. Zippers should be YKK plastic. Make certain your tent features "no-see-em" netting. Check for good ventilation flow in the tent you buy. Most manufacturers stand solidly behind their tents with excellent guarantees. Compare for a top choice. Purchase seam sealer and apply to the rain fly and corners of the tent. Seal wherever the fabric has been sewn.

Once on the road, a few good habits will keep your tent in top condition for years of use. Purchase a nylon-backed plastic tarp for a ground cloth. Cut it to fit two inches inside the outside boundary of your tent floor. This will help stop sharp objects from cutting your floor and it will keep out moisture. Cutting it two inches less all around the tent floor will stop rainwater from pooling under your tent in the middle of the night.

Set up your tent every night as if you expect rain. Find a high spot in the land and check for sharp rocks and sticks before positioning the ground cloth. Never leave your tent out in the sun for extended periods of time. Ultraviolet rays will damage the fabric. When taking down a tent, fold the poles and put them in a safe place immediately after you pull them out of their sleeves. This will prevent them from being stepped on. Count stakes each time you put your tent into the stuff sack. If it rains, either dry out the tent in the morning or at the earliest moment. For storage, make certain your tent is bone dry before putting it away for the winter or any extended period of time.

After your tent, purchase a warm, comfortable sleeping bag. You have two choices: goose down or fiberfill. Having used both many times, it's this camper's opinion that for three seasons, a three-pound, 10-degree Fahrenheit, fiberfill mummy bag is your best bet. It dries easier and stands up to usage many years longer. Down shifts and leaves cold spots after a time and the loft breaks down. However, you may have a friend who swears by down for its compactness and lighter weight. I take a down-filled bag on my winter hut to hut skiing trips. It becomes a personal decision.

No matter what your choice, buy a quality mummy bag from a reputable company. Make certain it's long enough and features a contoured hood enclosure with a drawstring so you have a small opening for your nose and mouth. When it gets really cold, that's all you want showing so you can breathe. Make certain your bag is designed so the baffle flap drapes down over the zipper from the inside. Gravity will keep that baffle covering the entire length of the zipper and stop any cold air from entering your bag. Expect to pay more for a down bag. Keep it in a waterproof bag or stuff sack when riding, canoeing or backpacking. If you forget, you will be sliding your bare body into a cold, wet bag one night and wonder why you didn't pay attention to these suggestions.

No matter how good your tent and sleeping bag, discomfort stalks the adventurer who fails to sleep on an air mattress. The best self-inflating air mattress on the market is a three-quarter length, one inch thick Thermo-Rest mattress by Cascade Designs. It insulates against the cold ground. (You may inspect several other brands that might be to your liking.) Buy a stuff sack to go with it. It's the best investment for comfort in the world.

You need cookware while camping. A copper bottomed stainless steel set with two pots, plastic cups is light and handy. Additionally, you may like the newer and lighter aluminum and titanium cookware. Some feature no-stick surfaces for easier cleaning. Keep a scrubber and soap in the pot. A plastic fork and spoon are light. If you're traveling in a developed country, go with a propane gas stove and carry two fuel bottles. For overseas touring, carry an MSR International stove that burns any kind of fuel.

Your Swiss Army knife is a vital addition to your cooking utensils. Carry a carrot-potato peeler. Add a small plastic cutting board. Always wash cookware after dinner, especially in the wilds. You want to avoid a grizzly sniffing your toes in the middle of the night.

Depending on how loaded you are and the length of your adventure, a sleeping bag, tent and mattress will sit on your back rack or in your backpack or canoe or kayak. You may have a front bike rack with a platform perfect for a sleeping bag. Be sure to carry a waterproof stuff sack for your sleeping bag. If you travel by water, you need a dry bag. It wouldn't hurt to do the same for your tent and mattress. If you can't find water proof sacks, you may create your own with plastic bags.

The one thing you cannot count on during an adventure is a campground. Well before you begin looking, about an hour and a half before dark, have water bottles filled and an extra full gallon. If the water quality is questionable, purify with tablets, drops or filtration. Purchase your food in advance. Such things as toilet paper, matches and stove fuel should be secured.

If you find a campground with showers and you're willing to pay the price, enjoy. Try to set up away from dogs and loud music. To be assured of a shower every night, carry a "shower bag" that allows you a three minute shower anywhere you stop.

Often, you are nowhere near an organized campground, or in the case of developing countries, no such thing exists. You're on your own. That's a plus, because it offers you a chance to experience nature, animals and solitude.

The best way to find a campsite is to look for a dirt road that leads into the bush, trees, rocks and out of sight of the highway. Try to find a spot near a river, lake or stream. When you find a suitable spot away from traffic, pitch your tent.

Pitch it every time as if it were going to rain. Exceptions are the Atacama and Sahara deserts. I have broken my own rules a few times and it cost me dearly with ruined camera and miserable nights floating around in my tent on my air mattress. Pitch your tent on high ground. Check for rocks, twigs and roots before laying down the ground tarp. Set the front door away from the wind and possible rain. This will give you a wind break for cooking. Make certain all stakes are secured and the rain fly is taut. Be sure to keep the ground cloth under the tent. Once the tent is secured, take the gear off your bike or out of your backpack and put it into your tent. Cable lock your bike, canoe or kayak to a tree. A combination lock will allow everyone in your party to use the same lock without using or losing a key.

CAMPING AND COOKING IN ESTABLISHED CAMPGROUNDS

When camping in an established campground, many obstacles are overcome immediately. You enjoy a picnic table, water, washing facilities and seating area at your command. Nonetheless, you need to buy food and load up on water two to three hours before sunset in case you don't reach an established campground. Always check your map for locations.

Making Camp

After finding a spot in a campground, one to two hours before dark, you can:

- Pitch your tent on high ground.
- Roll out the air mattress and sleeping bag.
- Place all your gear into the tent. Always put your gear in the same places, so you know where to find specific items in the

dark. Always place your miner's lamp exactly in the same place so you can grab it when you need it.

- Make sure your miner's lamp is on your head and ready to work as darkness falls. Those LED headlamps can be purchased at camping outlets. You may look like a coal miner walking around in the dark, but you will find it very useful.

Remember to avoid placing food or wrappers in your tent, especially in bear country. Most established campgrounds in bear country offer a steel bear box in which to place your food items. It they don't offer bear boxes: hang food 100 yards from your tent. This applies for all critters that would love to eat your food. That means you may have to cook and eat food first then hang food in trees 100 yards from the final camping site. Don't believe me? Think you can get away with it? I did, too. But when you wake up during the night with a grizzly or black bear pummeling you inside your tent or looking at you when you open the flaps—I gave fair warning. In bear country, always carry bear spray with you from www. REI.com and other camping stores. It could save your life. I guarantee that you will be scared out of your wits, but you might live.

If you are not in bear country, you can leave food in your tent as long as you remain in the tent. If you leave or you have food odors in your tent, little critters will eat their way through the nylon and ruin your tent.

Lock your bike, canoe or kayak to a tree. If you can't find a tree, lock it to your helmet inside your tent. To do this, run the cable through the bike frame, canoe or kayak, then into your tent and lock it to your helmet strap or pack. When you zip up the tent, the cable acts like an umbilical cord between it and your property. If someone tries to make off with your bike or canoe, they won't get far before you notice half your tent being pulled away. At that point, you may need your bear spray to defend yourself.

Take out your candle lantern and light it on the table.

Always light the match before turning on your gas burner. Never turn the gas on first, unless you want to make like a Saturn rocket and blast yourself to the moon.

Set up your food and fixings, cutting board, utensils, pans, water bottles and spices.

Prepare your meal. Enjoy.

Wash, clean, dry all your pots and utensils. Replace and secure.

Secure food in a tree or bear box, or if you're looking for an exciting night of terror, leave it in your tent. You will be able to tell some hair-raising stories when you get home.

Cooking and Food Storage in established campgrounds

Before cooking your meal, make good use of the stove burner for heating water for tea or hot chocolate. If you're cooking by a campfire, let the wood burn down so you get an even heat from the coals. You will also have to tackle the problem of balancing pots on the coals.

Once you have prepared the food for cooking by chopping and cutting, place it into the cooking pot. For cooking ease in the US, Canada, Australia and Europe, you may consider rice, pasta, couscous and other packaged meals. As your dinner progresses, keep any eye on the food to keep it from burning.

After dinner, wash everything with soap and rinse with water. Leave no food out for the animals. Keep extra food in a locked food box. You will find a wooden or metal box used in some campgrounds where animals are a concern. If there are no food boxes and you're in bear or mountain lion country, avoid storing food in your tent. Hang your food in a tree 100 yards from your camp. Serious backpackers can purchase heavy duty plastic bear-proof canisters to store your food.

Leave none of your gear out in the rain. Either store it in the tent or under the tent vestibule.

CAMPING AND COOKING IN A PRIMITIVE AREA

Camping in primitive (wilderness) areas presents several challenges that must be considered. You must be more responsible to your environment, i.e., disposal of human waste, water contamination and generated food and paper waste. You are more susceptible to bears, raccoons, squirrels and wild pigs charging into your camp looking for food. If it's a big old grizzly, he might be looking for you because he perused the latest copy of the "Gourmet Bear in Search of a Bicyclist, Backpacker or Other Dinner Interests." Take precautions when camping in the wilds.

Again, make certain you have loaded up on extra water two to three hours before dusk. Always carry a filter that can purify water if there are ample places to fetch it—such as in the mountains or in lake regions.

Again, look for a campsite well off the road and hidden away from the sight of others. Not only is it a good idea to vanish into the wilderness for personal safety, you will sleep better without hearing traffic all night. Remember your earplugs and use them.

Most dirt roads or trails on public land will lead to a stealth-camping spot. Try to get behind trees, brush, hills or a mountain. You want to be concealed from sight, which includes your fire or candlelight.

Be certain to keep your tent 25-30 feet away from a fire. Keep the tent upwind of the fire. Sparks carry on the breeze and will melt nylon in seconds. Place your tent on high ground. If it rains, you won't wake up feeling like you're being swept over Niagara Falls.

After setting up your tent, place your air mattress inside and unscrew the valve so it inflates fully before you lock it. A key to camping success is having everything where you want it when you need it. That means replacing the same gear in the same pouch every time you use it. Always zip up a pouch immediately after taking out or putting something into it. Make it a habit.

Before cooking dinner, you might want to take a bath first. Do it before the sun goes down and the air cools. Soap, towel and shower shoes are all you need. If it's a swiftly moving stream, be careful with your bottle of biodegradable soap.

A special note on campfires: gather your wood before dark. Gather kindling and larger branches. Stick with dead wood. Be sure the fire pit is a safe distance (25-30 feet) from your tent. Make certain the flames won't catch adjoining grass or overhanging branches on fire. A circular rock firewall is a good safety factor. Place leaves and kindling at the bottom. Light the fire, get it going and keep adding larger and larger wood until you have a good flame. If you cook on an open fire, after cooking, keep your pot in a heavy plastic bag to keep the black soot from smudging your gear. If your campsite is in a dry zone where fire hazards are high, use common sense when building a fire. You may decide not to build one. If you're experiencing high winds, never build a fire. Always put the fire totally out with water or dirt at night and in the morning. Clean the pit and spread the rocks around. Replace twigs and leaves over the pit before you leave.

When you're ready for sleep, use your pack, panniers or ditty-bag for a pillow and/or a sweater to make a cushion. Be certain to check for mosquitoes by shining your flashlight around the tent. If you see one, squash the blood-sucking fiend. Now you're ready for sleep. Or are you? If you camp in deep wilderness where bears or other large meat-eating animals live, put your food in a plastic bag and hang it in a tree 100 yards from your tent. Be certain to brush your teeth and wash your face and hands so no food odor is left on your person. If you even consider fruit in your tent and it's touching the floor, ants will cut the nylon in a few hours. Don't give them the chance. Any time you leave camp for a hike, do not leave food in the tent. Leave it open so chipmunks can get in. If they can't, they will chew holes through your tent.

In the morning, you may need to take your daily constitutional. Just remember the rules of camping. Bury feces if possible. If not, cover it with twigs or rocks. As for toilet paper, wrap it up and carry it out to throw away or burn at an appropriate time. When burning it, use prudent judgment in high fire areas of dry grass. It's that simple. Leave the campsite cleaner than you found it. Burn or carry out the trash and put in a proper disposal. No matter how trashed a place is, you can become part of the solution. Pack it in—pack it out.

When breaking camp, pack your gear and shake out the tent. Pull your tent poles and fold immediately. Avoid laying them on the ground where they can get smashed. Pull your stakes and count them before dropping into the bag. Fold the tent along with ground cloth and place in the stuff sack. If you can't fit the ground cloth into the stuff sack, you may wrap it around the tent and secure with straps. You might try changing your folding pattern periodically so you don't cause premature deterioration on waterproofing and fabric. Strap your gear on the bike or pack or canoe. Walk the bike, canoe or kayak out of the area. Go back to look over everything to see that you have all your gear, including the food bag that you hung in a tree. Don't be surprised if you walk up on a bear scratching his head trying to figure out how to get to your food bag.

When you're satisfied that you have everything secured, it's time to pedal, paddle, hike or climb. If the camp site was beautiful, you may have taken a few photographs for memories of your latest home in the woods.

When you follow a solid routine for camping each night, you wake up refreshed and relaxed. Camping compliments great wilderness adventures.

Making Camp in Primitive Areas

- Secure food and 1.5 gallons of water two or three hours before dusk.
- Look for an abandoned road or trail and vanish into the landscape.
- Pitch your tent on high ground. The site should be safe from lightning and potential washout from a rainstorm.
- Roll out your air mattress and sleeping bag.
- Place all your gear in the exact same place every night.
- Place your miner's lamp near your headrest. Once your tent

and gear are secured inside, either lock your bike, canoe or kayak to a tree or run the cable into your tent and attach to your helmet or shoes. Zip up your tent.

- If you build a campfire, make sure it is 25-30 feet away from your tent. If that is not possible, use your stove for cooking. Camp away from rocky ledges or where rocks may fall upon you in the night.
- Spread your tablecloth on the ground outside your tent. Tablecloth can be a square yard of plastic.
- Secure your candle lantern where you can use it.
- Organize all your cooking gear and food in front of you.
- If you are using a stove, make sure it's stable. You want to avoid a scalding injury while away from medical help.
- If you drink coffee, hot chocolate or tea, boil your water first.
- Prepare your food. Eat like a ravenous T-Rex.
- Wash dishes and clean up all traces of food.
- Always leave the bottom zipper of your tent open if you leave camp to take a bath or for any other reason. Whether you have food in the tent or not, curious squirrels or chipmunks may bite their way through the nylon to see what's inside.

Building Campfires Safely in the Wilderness

If you enjoy ashes in your soup and burning embers in your potatoes, make yourself happy—cook on an open fire. It's primordial. Humans enjoyed campfires before they invented the wheel.

You need to remember a few points about making a fire to keep it safe and under control:

- Always check for and obey no-burn rules. Use common sense when camping in a dry area. Avoid building a fire in high wind conditions.
- Build a protective rock ring around the fire. You can wet the ground around the fire ring if you have ample water.
- Keep the fire away from tents and other fabrics. Watch out for your Lycra or Gore-Tex. One flying ember will burn a hole in it.
- Keep your eyes on the fire at all times.

- Build the fire away from overhanging tree branches or dry brush. If you build under some low-hanging branches, you might turn the tree into a bonfire. Explain that to the local fire department chief. Finally, avoid building a fire against a large rock or cliff because it will leave unsightly smoke scars.
- Keep a water supply handy in case you need to douse the flames.
- Let the fire burn down before you place your pots in the embers. You want an even heat on your food.
- If it's windy, eat pork and beans out of a can or a sandwich or energy bars. Avoid the chance of a runaway fire.
- Before hitting the sack, be certain to put the fire completely out by smothering it with water or dirt. If you fail to put it out completely, you could cost people their lives and homes. Repeat with emphasis: put that fire out completely.
- When finished with the campfire, spread the rocks out and return the fire area to its natural appearance. Spread the ashes and place leaves and brush over the fire pit. Really give nature a chance by keeping the wild beautiful. Leave no trace.

No Fire in Your Tent

On those rainy or windy days, your first inclination might be to cook in your tent. Ignore that thought. Okay, you're starving to death and you hunger for hot soup. Again, avoid cooking in your tent.

There are so many little things that can and will go wrong when you burn an open flame inside your tent. I'm as careful as a person can be, but once, I nearly turned my tent into a bonfire. Avoid learning this lesson the hard way.

Candle Lantern

The only flame that can be used in a tent, and I haven't done it in a long time because of miner's lamps with LEDs, is a glass and aluminum-encased candle lantern. Even then, never leave it in the tent unattended. Make sure it's hanging from the roof on a string. You can also set it on a flat surface such as a notepad or book. Please use utmost care if you burn a candle lantern in your tent.

Sanitation and Human Waste in the Wilderness

It's very important to follow a few rules when camping in primitive wilderness situations.

When washing dishes, heat the water and use biodegradable soap. If you're washing in a lake or stream, make sure you discard the soapy water onto the soil at least 15 feet away from the lake or stream water so it drains into the soil. Rinse your cooking gear thoroughly.

Pack out what you pack in. I pick up trash left by careless campers. I honor Mother Nature by leaving a place cleaner than I found it. In the immortal words of the great philosopher Goethe, "Do not think that you can do so little, that you do nothing at all." Avoid burning plastic in the wilderness. Carry it in a bag to a proper trash can in the next town or wherever it's responsible.

Since no toilets are available in primitive campsites, please follow strict wilderness rules:

- Find a spot 25 to 30 yards away from your campsite and away from a water source. Carry your TP in a one gallon zip-closure plastic bag and another one gallon zip-closure bag inside it.
- Dig a hole four to six inches deep. Do your business. Cover your waste with soil. If that is not possible, cover with a rock or leaves. Roll your soiled TP into a ball with new TP and place it into the second zip-closure bag. No, you don't have to touch the soiled TP. Again, leave no trace.
- You may burn your used toilet paper in the campfire. If dry conditions exist or combustibles are present, just carry the used TP in the zip-closure bag and toss used TP at the next proper disposal.
- In Chile, my friend Doug nearly burned an entire wheat field because the flame he used to burn his toilet paper ignited the dry stalks. The next thing I knew, Doug waddled toward me with his shorts around his knees, screaming, "I just crapped in the wrong place." We grabbed six water bottles and ran back to the fire. We squirted it with our tiny water guns. A passing motorist and an old lady stopped to help us. You can imagine her shock and confusion when she saw Doug with his shorts at his ankles and me screaming and squirting at the flames. She didn't know whether to help us or faint. Moral of this episode:

be careful where you strike a match to your toilet paper—and pull up your pants before you light it.

- Also, clean your hands with hand sanitizer or soap and water, or at least rinse your hands.

Cleaning and Hygiene

While on tour or any adventure, you're living at a basic level. You're closer to being an animal than you have ever been. Bugs will try to invade your tent and mosquitoes will buzz around your head. Spiders will spin webs across your tent at night and they will be eating their catch when you step out the next day. You may find slugs crawling up your tent in the morning. You'll go to sleep under moonlight and wake up with the sun. The morning alarm clock might be the laughing cry of an Australian kookaburra or a Norwegian cuckoo bird. It's natural, but it's dirty out there cycling or backpacking or mountain climbing or any extended outdoor activity.

That's why you must maintain good sanitation and hygiene practices.

Wash your hands with biodegradable soap in the wilderness. If you don't have any, use any biodegradable soap or hand cleaner, but make sure you use it. Avoid throwing soapy water into a stream or lake.

After any use of pots and pans, make certain to wash and rinse them. Use your camp towel to wipe them or let them dry in the sun. Please honor Mother Nature and she will bless you with wonders around the next bend in the road or turn of the river.

Bear and Lion Country

"Bears are made of the same dust as we, and breathe the same winds and drink of the same waters. A bear's days are warmed by the same sun, his dwellings are overdomed by the same blue sky, and his life turns and ebbs with the heart pulsing like ours. He was poured from the same fountain. And whether he at last goes to our stingy heaven or not, he has terrestrial immortality. His life, not long, not short, knows no beginning, no ending. To him life unstinted, unplanned, is above accidents of time, and his years, markless and boundless, equal eternity." John Muir, hiking in Yosemite Valley, California, 1839

Camping in Grizzly, Black Bear and Mountain Lion Country

The North American grizzly bear symbolizes the wilderness. His domain reaches from Yellowstone National Park in Wyoming to Alaska. To catch a glimpse of this great animal is to fill your eyes with wonder. His wildness defines the wilderness. In his domain, he is king.

Nothing will scare the daylights out of you faster than coming face to face with a bear. Few animals will kill you faster than a grizzly if he or she is so inclined. If she comes in the night, you will feel terror like never before because you have the added uncertainty of darkness. The sound of her grunting will drive your heart into a pumping frenzy and your blood will race around your body like a Formula One race car at the Indy 500.

I shivered in my sleeping bag while a grizzly dragged his muzzle across the side of my tent one morning in Alaska. His saliva left a mark on the nylon for a few weeks while he left a mark on my mind for a lifetime. I'll never forget the three-and-a-half-inch claws that tore through the back of my tent that day. He let me live so I lucked out.

Bears prove capricious, unpredictable and dangerous. They search for food 24/7. Anything that looks edible to them makes for fair game. They eat berries, salmon, moose, deer, mice and humans without discrimination.

That's why this section deals with camping in grizzly bear, black bear and mountain lion country.

If you travel, hike and camp in remote regions of North America or other areas of the world, sooner or later, you will camp in bear country. It's not something to be feared, but it is something you must respect since you enter his dining room.

The key to your safety and survival in Mr. Grizzly's domain is respect. You must honor the rules of the wilderness. You must follow those rules each and every time you camp, hike or otherwise make your way into his territory. You may not get a second chance.

Imagine looking into a grizzly's eyes, backed by his 800 to 1,500 pounds of teeth and claws. You might plead, "Gee, Mr. Bear, could you give me a break this time…I'm really sorry I left my chocolate chip cookies inside my tent…can we make a deal, like, I'll give you my extra box of bon-bons…please, pretty please…."

Never assume a bear won't walk into your life.

At the same time, you cannot camp in fear. During my many journeys to Alaska, I enjoyed extraordinary moments watching rogue grizzlies fishing for salmon and mother grizzlies playing with their cubs. I enjoyed great wonder and breathtaking moments.

I also had the living daylights scared out of me because of my own carelessness.

By using common sense and following the rules, you can minimize the chances of a bear confrontation. But your safety cannot be guaranteed. You could do everything right and still run into a bear—especially if he's trying to find food for his evening dinner.

However, since I've alarmed you, let me put this in proper perspective. Former Alaska Governor Sarah Palin lives in Alaska. She alleges to have outrun a few grizzly bears. Therefore, if you're camping near Sarah, the only thing you have to do is run faster than her.

If you follow nature's rules, your chances of a bear confrontation are less than a lightning strike. Therefore, go ahead and enjoy yourself. If you do encounter a bear, you will return home with great bear stories that will keep your friends glued to your every word.

Remember: food and food odors attract bears, which makes them overcome their fear of humans. Be smart and keep food odor off your body and tent, and away from your camping site.

Bringing the bear danger home

On July 6, 2011, a couple hiked a popular trail in Yellowstone National Park. They came upon a grizzly mother and her cubs. The mother bear immediately attacked and killed the man and nearly killed the woman before grabbing her cubs and vanishing into the wilderness. Neither hiker carried bear spray nor did they know any defensive techniques for dealing with a bear.

"If a grizzly bear actually makes contact, surrender," advises the US Forest Service. "Fall to the ground and play dead. Lie flat on your stomach or curl up in a ball with your hands behind your neck. Typically, a bear will break off its attack once it feels the threat has been eliminated. Remain motionless for as long as possible. If you move, and the bear sees or hears you, it may return and renew its attack. In rare instances, particularly with black bears, an attacking bear may perceive a person as food. If the bear continues biting you long after you assume a defensive posture, it likely is a predatory attack. Fight back vigorously. Carry bear spray in the wilderness at all times."

Always carry bear spray with you in the wilderness. Have it ready at a moment's notice. Most backpackers carry it in a pouch secured to their chest. They can pull it out faster than a gun slinger. Remember that you cannot out run a bear. You must stand your ground. Read the directions on how to pull the pin and how to spray the bear. If you're not certain, set up a large cardboard box about 30 feet away from you in your own backyard. Practice by pulling the pin and engaging the lever to the spray can. Make sure you know the nozzle is facing the bear. You must aim at the bear's face. You can watch the stream of spray while you guide it to the bear's face. Most bear spray will continue the stream for 10 seconds. You may waste a bottle of spray, but you will become a seasoned veteran in case a live bear attacks you.

If you're not sure of yourself, go to REI or any outdoor store that carries bear spray and engage one of the seasoned employees. They will help you or guide you to an instructional video.

Rules for Camping in Bear Country

Camp in an area least likely to be visited by bears. Stay away from animal trails, large droppings, diggings, berry bushes, beehives and watering holes. Don't swim in streams where salmon run. If you do, you may end up running for your own life.

Make absolutely certain your tent has no food odor in or on it. If you have spilled jam or peanut butter—grizzlies especially like crunchy style—wash your tent clean.

Cook 100 yards away from your tent. Wash your gear thoroughly. Avoid sleeping in the same clothes that you wore while eating and cooking dinner.

Avoid keeping perfume, deodorant or toothpaste in your tent. Keep anything that has an odor in your food bag and hang it away from your camp.

Hang your food in a strong 1.5 millimeter thick plastic bag at least 100 yards feet from your tent. That means your camp, cooking and food hanging areas are in a triangle 100 yards apart. If a bear does amble into your sector, he will go after your food bag, and more than likely, he won't bother you. Hang it on a line between two trees and 15 feet high with parachute cord.

Bear-proof canisters that can carry several days of food supplies cost about $100 and can be purchased at most camping outlets mentioned in this book. Carry the canister in your pack.

After you have hung your food, take out a wet cloth and wipe your face and hands to ensure you have no food odor on them.

Finally, brush and floss your teeth. You wouldn't want a tiny piece of food between your molars to be the reason you inadvertently invited Mr. Grizzly to feast upon your tender body at night. Can you imagine the coroner's report in Whitehorse, Yukon, "Gourmet camper was mauled last night because he left one little piece of fried chicken between his teeth."

Also, remember to employ the same sanitation rules you learned in the primitive camping section.

Hanging food: attach one end of a parachute cord to a rock or carabineer and throw it over a tree limb. Use the other end of the cord to tie your food bag. Pull the bag into the air at least 12 to 15 feet above the ground, at least five feet from the tree trunk and at least five feet from the limb where the cord is hanging. Secure the parachute cord by tying it to a limb at the base of the tree or some other tree.

A second method for hanging food: loop two bags over a limb so they balance each other and let them dangle with no tie-off cord. Some bears have figured out to follow the tie-off cord and release it by batting or pawing it—mostly in Yellowstone National Park where so many careless campers visit. This second method should discourage a bear's efforts. Again, keep it 12 to 15 feet off the ground and at least five feet away from the tree trunk.

A third method: throw a line over the branches of two trees about ten feet apart. Throw the same parachute cord over the line and hang your food bag between the trees on the line. Do what works best for you.

Grizzlies do not intentionally prey on humans. A grizzly will attack if you accidently disturb a mother with cubs. As long as they are not drawn to any food odor, you should enjoy a good night's sleep.

If a Bear or Mountain Lion should Confront You

Okay, you've followed the rules, but you wake up to the sounds of a bear outside your tent or something else that's breathing and prowling through the night mist. Your nostrils fill with the stench of something that's got a really bad case of body odor.

You don't carry a gun, but you do have your Swiss Army knife. Yeah, great! The bear would snatch it out of your hands and use it as a toothpick afterwards. If you did carry a gun, it would only upset him. But you kept your bear repellant spray right next to your sleeping bag, so you pull it out. Yes, bear spray will stop a grizzly better than a gun.

At that moment, you wish you could sprint like an NFL halfback or fly like an eagle.

What to do: stay calm. Remember that bears and mountain lions don't like humans. It could be a deer, moose or elk. Unless you're in bear country in early spring, when a bear is just out of his den and hungry, he may only be curious and sniffing around.

I have been told that a good strategy is to play dead inside your sleeping bag if you're attacked by a grizzly. If you're with another person, you may opt to run in different directions. At least one of you would live. Keep that bear spray in your hand. No hard and fast rules exist that guarantee anything in this situation.

During the day, be alert. If you come in contact with a grizzly, try to move out of his area without running. Make a lot of noise by blowing on a whistle if you're hiking. If a bear sees you and charges, turn sideways and do not look at him directly, but do point your bear spray at his face. He may still attack you, but then again, if you are not threatening, he may not. If he continues charging to within 30 feet, spray a stream of bear spray at his nose, and follow the stream with your own eyes until you hit him right on the nose and continue the stream. It should stop him.

Make sure your friend carries a second can of spray to continue the point-blank spraying if needed. If you don't have bear spray and the attack continues, drop to the ground and assume the cannonball position with your hands over your head to protect your head and stomach.

If you run, he most likely will chase you down. At this juncture, you may want to cry, pray, scream or faint. It may not do any good, but it may make you feel better. If you die, you died while living a great adventure, which makes it a bit heroic. It's better to die this way than suffering a heart attack while eating chocolate bon-bons on a couch in front of an NFL game with the remote glued to your hand.

When confronting black bears, you have a much better chance of survival. Stand your ground. Do not drop to the ground or play dead. Don't look into his eyes; stay on your feet and keep that bear spray pointed right at his nose. Don't look scared, even if you're wetting your pants with fear. Maintain your composure until the black bear leaves your area. In any bear situation, you have to "buck up" your mind with a sense of fearless power. In other words, you must overcome your fear in order to think straight and take positive action.

If confronted with a mountain lion or puma, stand your ground and make yourself appear larger if possible by spreading out your hands and/ or hopping up on a log or rock. Move away slowly and keep the bear spray aimed at the lion. If you have a child with you, pick him or her up and hold the child close to you. With a cat, you can fight back and it may run away. It also may run if you throw rocks at it. Avoid running away. Again, it's between you and lady luck.

Adventure is not always comfortable, but it is still adventure. I am a firm believer that neither bliss nor adventure is ever obtained by staying home in your rocking chair.

As a final note, be confident that you will make your way through bear country safely when you follow Mother Nature's rules. When you respect her, she will respect you right back.

I can see you sitting around the table with your friends after your adventure in Alaska.

In your journal, "Yeah, I woke up one morning on the Kenai River when I heard a blood-curdling growl...I thought the sun was shining through my mosquito netting, but it was the pearly whites of a thousand pound grizzly...well sir, I didn't have much time to think, so I pulled out my big knife—like Daniel Boone—and stared back into that grizzly's eyes. That's when I gave him a toothy growl of my own. It scared him so badly, he scrambled up a tree where we used him for an umbrella to keep the 24-hour sun from burning down on us while we ate fresh salmon steaks on the campfire."

You made Jack London proud.

KEY POINTS FROM THIS CHAPTER

1. Follow the rules of the wilderness for maximum safety.
2. Develop your own camping and wilderness style based on basic rules.

SECTION VI –MAJOR VENUES FOR WORLD ADVENTURE

This section offers you a few of the top sports you may pursue in your lifetime. Because I am a bicyclist, I brought a great deal of knowledge from a life of pedaling around the planet. You may use some or all of it in different venues that you pursue.

Many of these websites will help you in pursuing a dozen other sports. Many other sports exist that you will be able to discover on the Internet for your own exploration.

Chapter 50—Pick your adventures from an endlessly growing list

"I'd rather wake up in the middle of nowhere than a city any time!"
Steve McQueen

In this amazing 21st century, you enjoy endless opportunities to experience this planet in the air, on the land, in the mountains, underground, on seven continents, at the North and South Poles, and under all of its lakes, oceans and seas. You may be one of the lucky ones to fly to the moon and Mars before this century ends.

You may become a mountain climber who climbs all of the highest peaks on seven continents. You may scuba dive in all the seas and oceans. You might fly a plane to every country. You may enjoy multiple pursuits as an adventure dilettante who enjoys everything or changes pursuits as you add birthday candles. The list grows beyond imagination.

While you may pick from hundreds of adventures, move toward the ones that turn your crank. The following chapters give you a taste of different modes of adventure. Most likely, you will meet others on adventures that turn you on to sailing around the world or climbing Mount Kilimanjaro in Africa.

Be open, be excited, be enthusiastic and jump into life.

KEY POINTS FROM THIS CHAPTER

1. It's all good.
2. Go for it.

Chapter 51—Bicycle touring the United States and the world

"When I go biking, I repeat a mantra of the day's sensations: bright sun, blue sky, warm breeze, blue jay's call, ice melting and so on. This helps me transcend the traffic, ignore the clamorings of work, leave all the mind theaters behind and focus on nature instead. I still must abide by the rules of the road, of biking, of gravity. But I am mentally far away from civilization. The world is breaking someone else's heart." Diane Ackerman

WHAT IT'S LIKE BEING A LONG- DISTANCE BICYCLE RIDER?

What is it like being a long-distance touring rider? Is it exciting? Does it make traveling special? Why do I ride? I am asked those questions often while on tour.

On an emotional level, it's a sensory involvement with natural forces surrounding me. It's a tasting of the wind, a feeling of the coolness and the warmth. I see swirling clouds above me and grasses bending in soft breezes. Touring puts me into intimate contact with sunrises and sunsets.

Along seacoasts, I watch waves charge their white fury against sandy beaches. Touring, in its elegant silence, allows me to see an eagle swoop out of the blue, and with its talons extended, grab a mouse and lift into the sky headed toward its nest. Touring allows me to see a kangaroo hop across the road in Australia. I may ride into the teeth of an approaching storm.

I witness quiet and wild moments depending on nature. I get caught up in the forces that swirl around me and I feel at peace with them. Why? Because I place myself in a wilderness orbit that synchronizes with the natural world.

My journey carries me through deserts, mountains, forests and plains. As I ride along, three aspects of living become important with every turn of the pedals. Whether I ride through a country or across a continent, I meet people and see the sights. The most important thing is my connectedness with the natural world, and therefore, myself—and that is—keeping my body, mind and spirit in balance.

I feel that life provides a moving drama. A friend of mine, Duncan Littlefair said that when you walk forward, it's not that you walk forward, you fall forward, you're falling forward into the unknown, and the only thing that prevents you from falling down face first is that you put your other foot out and stop your fall, yet you continue to fall into the unknown with each step.

I think bicycling replicates that metaphor. I ride into each day having no idea what's going to happen. I ride with a positive attitude. Invariably, good things happen. It's rare that I ever ride into a negative situation— because life is generally positive. Some people may complain that it's raining out today, so that's a negative. I see it another way. Rain makes flowers bloom. A mountain rises ahead. I have to drop into lower gears. My legs must power the pedals—yet that's a positive because it's a part of the process of moving into the unknown and experiencing it. It's a lot like anyone's life as they grow toward their own fulfillment.

Starting with the body, a long distance touring rider is concerned with health. That translates into taking care of it. My nutritional approach is an emphasis on raw natural foods—vegetables, fruits, nuts and grains. I complement them with whole breads and pastas. This nutritional stance gives my body maximum clean burning fuel to push the pedals throughout the day.

The five senses play an important part of the day on a bicycle tour. I taste, touch, hear, smell and feel nature. I taste the rain on my tongue and touch the bark on a tree. I hear an owl hooting and smell a skunk. My senses soar because I am involved with the swirling energies of nature. I sweat in the desert and get chilled in the mountains.

Touring fills my mind with expectation. Something new lies around the bend in the road ahead. Nature creates inexplicable beauty. I love seeing it for the first time on my bicycle and my mind swallows it in big gulps.

GETTING STARTED WITH LONG DISTANCE TOURING

THE RIGHT BIKE

Everyone has a bias about something dear to his or her heart. When it comes to bicycle touring, I've tried various approaches to equipment. Many of my lessons have been learned the hard way. Experience is a stern taskmaster. I have stood in rainstorms with a breakdown while wondered why I hadn't listened to a friend who had been through it. Even with miles and years behind my wheels, new ideas pop up daily. I'm willing to learn from other riders. Each one has a different style that incorporates something better into their bicycle touring operation.

Ben Franklin said it best: "Penny wise, pound foolish."

That wisdom holds true to this day. It is unwavering with the bike you buy and your gear.

More than once, I've been asked for advice on what kind of bike to ride. Am I biased? Yes, I am. My inclination for bikes and equipment comes from a long trail of mistakes. You may obtain a bucket full of experts' opinions. They are valid relative to each person's needs and aspirations in touring.

Light touring machine or heavier mountain bike?

Hands down—a mountain bike makes the best touring machine. It's the greatest thing to happen to touring either nationally or internationally. Cost? If your touring plans mean two weeks per year in the USA, buy a bike in the $600.00 range. For international tours of six months duration, spend $1,000.00 or more and save money in the long run. For those who want the best, a custom built mountain bike will cost $2,000.00 to $3,000.00. It's a lot of money and it's a lot of bicycle. I ride a www.franklinframe.com. Check out all touring bikes at: www.bicycle-touring-guide.com

Some will tell you that a mountain bike is too heavy. Balderdash! We're talking five pounds more at the most. That goes for women or men. You won't feel the weight. They say it handles harder. Your body adapts to any load. That bike will become as comfortable as your favorite easy chair.

Why a mountain bike? First of all, comfort levels increase because of the fat tires. I recommend 1.75 X 26 tires for a smooth ride. (Top touring tires at www.schwalbe.com, recommended are Marathon Tour Plus and Dureme.) A mountain bike rides better. You avoid front end shimmy from being overloaded in the panniers or handlebar bag. Another big plus is the rarity of flat tires on a mountain bike. I've gone five months without a flat.

Few conventional touring bicycles can boast that. Those 1 1/4 inch tires get cut or worn out much too often. I love the security of knowing my tires are sturdy, especially on high-speed descents. Additionally, you can load a mountain bike up with lots of weight and not worry about spokes breaking or wheels warping out of true.

Customize that mountain bike for touring. Install drop bars. That will give you three-hand holding positions. Buy an Aero bar that will give you a place to rest your forearms and take you over the front of the bike for hours of comfortable riding. That means your shifting levers can be relocated on the down tube or bar-end shifters are available. You may check for the Long Haul Trucker as one of the best mountain bike touring cycles at a very good price at www.surly.com. Two of my best friends own them and love them. Also, REI offers Novara Safari mountain touring bikes and Surly Long Haul Trucker bikes at www.REI.com. My sister and brother own them and love them. Install a 40-spoke rear wheel, (although a 36 spoke rim will work fine in the United States), for added endurance, especially for international touring. A 40-spoke wheel will remain true much better. Buy the heaviest gauge, highest quality spokes for that back wheel and make certain the person who builds your wheel knows what he or she is doing. For international tours, try Sun tandem rims for beefed up strength. Check around and obtain several opinions. By investigating, you will discover the best bike person in your town. Ask them how much and where they have toured. Do they know how to fit a bike to your body? Make sure they do it. Learn how to do it yourself in this chapter. It's important to get a perfect fit. Your comfort and enjoyment depend on it.

Two items in the drive-train stand out as very important. I install a front Granny gear 24-tooth chain ring with a 34-tooth low end freewheel gear. Use the same gearing with a cassette on the rear wheel. No sense killing yourself on climbs. Best rear derailleur? Recommended: Deore XT. That derailleur outlasts anything on the market.

You will develop your own style given a few miles, but it's nice to feel confidence in your bicycle when you start out with a quality machine that fits your needs.

PREPARING FOR INTERNATIONAL BICYCLE TOURING

Are you going on a bicycle tour to some exotic country? Whether you're going three weeks or six months, you must take care of dozens of things before boarding the airplane, boat or train. Preparing for an international tour is like battling a four-alarm fire. When you think one blaze is under control, another one needs immediate attention.

Begin preparing three to six months in advance. If you work forty or fifty hours a week, solid preparation will keep you from going crazy a week before departure. In my own world tours, I've found that each continent needs special consideration. For example: in America, you can expect a bicycle shop in the next town if you need a spare part. In Africa, forget it. Whether you crank your bicycle across the Arctic Circle in Norway, push through the Andes Mountains in Peru, or sweat your way across the Nullarbor Plains of Australia—the success of your journey depends on what you do before you depart.

The key to that success is completion of your to-do and to-buy lists months before you leave. When you make your target date seven days to a month in advance of departure, you can relax at the bon voyage party without suffering an ulcer. Additionally, your health during the ride may depend on your advance preparation.

To make things easier on you, major and minor areas of concern will be covered. You may refer to "What to take and how to pack it" in this chapter. As you begin to acquaint yourself with the enormity of international touring preparation, get out a pen and a paper. Start a list.

BICYCLE AND EQUIPMENT

Two-week guided tours usually offer a sag wagon and mechanics to repair and maintain your bicycle. With those tours, your bike, whether you rent or bring your own, is not as critical a factor in the success of your tour. However, buy a bike and gear that will serve you well so you may ride in confidence. Before going on tour, a basic tune-up is a must. If you buy a new bike, be sure to ride it 300 miles and have the wheels trued. Be certain to have the bike fitted to your body.

For persons riding into developing countries, a mountain bike is highly recommended. You must convert it for touring by adding drop bars, 40 spoke wheels, extra bottle racks, anatomical touring seat, Aero bar, lower gearing and fenders added. It not only offers a superior ride on gravel roads, the tires last longer with far fewer flats. Make sure the quality of the bike and components match the length of your ride. Insist on sealed bearings, but if you can't buy them, make sure your hubs have been overhauled. Carry tools that work with every part of your bike. Take a course in bicycle repair. Be able to repair a flat tire.

TENT, SLEEPING BAG, AIR MATTRESS AND COOKING GEAR

If you take a guided tour, these items may not be important because lodging and food will be provided. For those on individual tours, this equipment is extremely important. A quality, self-standing tent in the $250.00 to$350.00 range is a good bet. If you want to scrimp, you can buy some pretty good tents in the $150.00 range. Be sure to seal the seams, carry extra seam sealer and carry a waterproof ground mat.

A three season sleeping bag at three pounds (down or fiberfill) and good to 10 degrees Fahrenheit will keep you warm in most conditions. If you get caught at high altitude, you may need to wear your tights, mittens, sweater and cap to bed for extra warmth. The best air mattress is a three-quarter length self-inflating Thermo-Rest by Cascade Designs. I buy my gear at:

www.REI.com
www.LLBean.com
www.EarlyWinters.com
www.EasternMountainSports.com
www.NorthFace.com
www.bicycle-touring-guide.com
www.performance.com
www.nashbar.com
www.golite.com

They offer top notch equipment and give excellent guarantees on their products.

Cooking gear includes a large pot, secondary pan, utensils, cups and a stove. Buy a stove that will burn many kinds of fuel for international destinations. An MSR International is one of the most popular and costs around a hundred bucks. Talk with a veteran employee about your specific needs.

DAYPACK OR SMALL BACKPACK

On top of your back rack, you may want to carry a 2,000 to 3,000 cubic inch capacity pack with three external pockets. On top of the main pack you can carry a utility pack for easy access to your camera, film, valuables and food. Carry your most often used gear in it. When stopping at a restaurant or whenever leaving the bike unattended for a few moments, you can release the bungee cords and sling the utility pack over your shoulders.

RAIN-PROOFING YOUR GEAR

No doubt about it, you're at the mercy of the elements on a bicycle tour. Your equipment must be kept dry. Protect everything in plastic bags. Keep your rain suit easily available. Make certain your papers, passports, film, digital cards and camera gear are securely rain-proofed. Do the same for your sleeping bag and tent.

INTERNATIONAL TOURS

When riding in a foreign country, you're subject to different conditions. You may be vulnerable to infectious diseases, spoiled food and contaminated water. You need extra precautions with eating, drinking and medicine. Boil, add purification tablets or filter your water. Eat only cooked foods. I use an MSR or First Need water filter. They are inexpensive and effective. Always peel fruits and vegetables. Wash your hands and keep your eating utensils clean. Drink only water you have filtered.

In a developing country, you can expect a case of food poisoning at some point in your tour. Once you feel it coming on, induce yourself to vomit until your stomach is empty. Drink plenty of water to rinse out your system. This procedure may save you from prolonged suffering. If not food poisoning, you may pick up a new bacterium that doesn't agree with your intestines. In that case, you must tolerate the unknown bugs until your system settles down to normal again.

Because you will not be able to bathe every day, carry anti-fungal ointment. Take a washcloth and wipe yourself down nightly with water. Carry a shower bag. This will help prevent fungal growth on your skin. For poison ivy or skin rashes, carry appropriate creams. See your doctor for counsel.

Your passport is vulnerable to theft. Always keep it on your person or at arm's length.

IMMUNIZATION AND INOCULATIONS

Don't you love this category? It's a real pain in the rump, but necessary. Tell the doctor which countries you will be visiting and get your inoculation card completed with each shot or series. Take no chances with yellow fever, tetanus, typhoid, diphtheria or cholera. Insist on a Gamma Globulin shot for the best, but not perfect, prevention available for hepatitis. Tell them how long you intend to tour, so they can adjust the dosage accordingly. Seek out all information you need in this area and act upon it. Call or write the Center for Disease Control, U.S. Department of Health and Human Services. The number is in your local phone book under U.S. Government. Look it up on line. For shots, call your local hospital immunization department. If you demand answers, you will receive them. In this area, preparation and prevention are keys to your health.

Upon returning to the USA from a developing country, have a blood, urine and fecal check to make sure you haven't picked up any liver flukes or other parasites. If tests are positive, begin treatment immediately.

In countries where malaria is present, you must start taking pills two weeks before leaving. With two or more people on the tour, take them on the same day, so everyone can remind each other during the ride. Follow instructions as your doctor tells you.

PASSPORT

Pick up the application at the post office. Fill it out and provide all documentation exactly as required. One mistake and they will write you a letter listing needed items for completion of your passport.

Make certain you send them recent (within six months) official passport pictures and sign them on the back. Use those same pictures for visa applications. When applying for visas to different countries, use a travel agency's courier services. If you have any problems in processing, call your congressional representative. For peace of mind, make a list of the locations of American embassies in the countries you plan to visit.

Keep a dozen extra pictures for an international driver's license, hostel card and other needs that will pop up on an extended tour. Color or black and white pictures are acceptable.

For extra precaution, take a photocopy of your passport, driver's license and birth certificate. Put them in a separate compartment. Scan them onto your computer for easy access.

CAMERA EQUIPMENT

When the adventure ends, the pictures you snapped will be your most prized possessions. Avoid running your film through an airport x-ray machine or soaking the camera in a rainstorm. Be certain to bring plenty of batteries. Today, most of us use digital cameras. Keep your memory cards in a safe place and zipped up for safety.

Camera gear needs special attention whether you carry an expensive single lens reflex or a pocket automatic. Keep your film in a waterproof bag and insist that airport security people hand inspect it. Always ride with your camera in a plastic bag and out of the sun. Carry a small tripod.

CUSTOMS

Before leaving the states, have customs officers document U.S. ownership of your bike, camera equipment, expensive jewelry and any other gear you consider worth claiming as previously purchased property. Otherwise, you could be liable for import taxes upon your return. You could be charged more than $100.00 for an import tax in a developing country.

NUTS AND BOLTS INFORMATION

Carry theft insurance for all your valuables overseas. Check with your insurance agent to make certain your bike and gear are covered. (Review Chapter 44—Details, with its websites and addresses for help in preparing.)

Money matters are very important. Purchase American Express traveler's checks because that company has the most offices throughout the world. Carry credit cards that are honored internationally. Pay advance money into your credit card company, so you will have that to draw on if you're not back in time to pay a bill. You may need it in a pinch. Make certain that credit card expiration dates are good until after your return. Always keep them in your money belt. I keep my passport and valuables on my person 24 hours a day and within reach when taking a shower.

When sleeping in a hostel, stuff your valuables into the bottom of your sleeping bag. Camera gear can go into the closed end of your pillow case. Never assume your gear is safe from theft. It will be gone in seconds if left unattended.

For additional financial preparation, you can order foreign currency from your own bank. If you arrive in a country during a festival or other holiday, you will have at least $50.00 worth of their money for your immediate expenses.

If there is any question as to safety, write the embassy of the country you want to visit. I avoided Colombia completely on my tour through

South America. Hostile guerrilla action broke out on the routes I had to take to get to Ecuador. My body is allergic to bullets, so I never take any chances. For complete information from USA sources, call the Citizen's Adviser Center in Washington, D.C. at (202) 647-5225. Consider their suggestions seriously in your travel decisions. (Refer to the websites in other chapters of this book.)

Carry a booklet with addresses and phone numbers of embassies in a foreign country. Check in with the USA embassy staff and out when you leave a country.

Drugs: anyone who carries or consumes drugs in a foreign country is absolutely out of his or her mind. Jails in developing countries are loaded with Americans who thought they wouldn't get caught. I can't stress this enough. Stay away from drugs or anything that looks, feels or sounds suspicious. If someone traveling with you carries drugs, insist he or she gets rid of the contraband. If they refuse, separate yourself from them. You may be considered an accomplice. Police in developing countries lock you up and throw away the key. I have visited guys in foreign jails that spent 13 years in confinement for smoking a joint. Got the picture?

Purchase your plane tickets two or three months in advance for possible discount prices and assurance that you have a plane seat. Shop for an airline that charges the lowest price for a bicycle. It is considered extra baggage. Some airlines charge $150.00 for your bicycle one-way.

If you won't get back before April 15th, you need to fill out a Federal Income tax extension form. By proving you were out of the country, you have an automatic 90-day extension (you can show a copy of your airline ticket). However, you must have enough paid into the IRS in advance in order to avoid penalties.

If someone is taking care of your house or you are renting it out, you need to fill out a Power of Attorney form giving someone you trust the legal right to handle your personal affairs, such as eviction of destructive renters or those who bounce rent checks. Leave that person with extra funds to pay for emergency or unexpected bills. You may also employ a real-estate firm that rents out private houses and takes care of everything while you're gone.

Fill out a will and register it in probate court. Notify your benefactor. It costs less than $10.00 to register.

Make sure your insurance payments are in order. Car, house, bike and any other insured items must have up-to-date premiums paid.

Carry a travel handbook that gives you the ins and outs of each country and major cities. Carry a Youth Hostel book with locations and phone numbers. Carry a foreign language phrase book to help you along. People will warm up when you make an effort to speak their language.

Leave a travel itinerary with loved ones of post office addresses in major cities. They can write you letters. Tell them to address the envelope with your name and underline your last name, c/o Poste Restante, Central Post Office, City and Country. Poste Restante is the international phrase for general delivery. You can pick up your mail at a post office by showing your passport. Tell your friends to write to each address three weeks in advance of the tentative dates you have written down on your itinerary. If you're not sure where you will be and don't want to write all your friends each time with a possible new address, you can have your friends write to one address in the states at your best friend's or parent's house and have your mail forwarded from there. It's easier that way. Letters are like Christmas gifts and mean so much when you are a long way from home.

You can pick up your Internet email virtually anywhere around the world today.

Carry the international dialing phone number of your local bicycle shop or its website. If you suffer a major breakdown, they can express mail you a replacement. By keeping stocked with parts from the pack list, you should be covered.

When traveling through multiple countries, you must have a plane ticket home and enough money to show you are financially responsible while touring that country. Otherwise, authorities may not let you enter.

Check with your travel agent to see if you need a visa for a particular country or whether they give an automatic 30-day visa. Once you arrive in a country that has granted you an automatic visa, but you didn't obtain one for the next country you will visit—you can apply at the embassy in the capital of the country you are now touring. Remember to take extra pictures for the visa.

Always be cordial and smile. Arrive well dressed and groomed. Act respectfully toward authorities.

For anyone going on a long distance tour, buy a special padded anatomically-correct seat with the latest in silicone cushioning. It will save your rear end. For double insurance, seats now offer this material and you can add the cover for ultimate comfort. I ride a Serfas Hybrid. It gives fabulous comfort. Each night before going to bed, take a zip-closure plastic bag and cover your seat to protect it from the rain.

PHYSICAL CONDITIONING

Your physical preparation is one of the most important keys to enjoyment while on tour. Ride your bike three to four hours every day for a month before departure. If you're headed into the mountains, find some steep grades where you live and ride them with your loaded panniers. If none exist, ride a high resistance stationary bike at the local health club.

If you fail to prepare your legs, a slight strain or ligament pull will finish you abruptly on a bicycle adventure because it will get worse with every added mile. Make sure you avoid that. Get your butt into seat shape and get into pedaling shape.

BIKE SECURITY

Maintain your bike security at night or while visiting a monument. Either check into a safe hostel where you can keep the bike in your room (You may cable it to a pipe or anything secure.), or have someone in your party stay with the cycles and gear. When camping, lock the bikes to something solid and keep equipment in your tent at night.

ATTITUDE

In developing countries, during any situation, remain calm, patient and respectful. Learn to accept their ways even though they may be frustrating and different from your own.

One last point on international bicycle touring. You are pedaling into strange lands, meeting new people and experiencing different cultures. You will enjoy the time of your life. Leave excess baggage like prejudice, discrimination and discourtesy at home. Stretch your emotional, mental and spiritual wings to learn about the world. Ride as a personal ambassador from your country. The impressions you make on people will remain with them forever. Share a smile and kind words. Good things will come your way.

Enjoy a grand bicycle adventure in good health and high spirits.

WHAT TO TAKE AND HOW TO PACK IT

One of the most frustrating feelings on a bicycle tour is when you dig into your pack for something and can't find it. Even worse is realizing you didn't bring it. It can be as small as a pair of tweezers or as important as a spoke wrench. The best way to prevent such a calamity is to keep a pack list that you can check off before leaving for your adventure.

Special precautions must be taken each time you load your gear into your panniers. When you need an item, you want it easily available. That goes double for your first aid kit.

International tours require extra attention to details.

EQUIPMENT ORGANIZATION

Organizing your equipment is the best way to have it ready for your use. If it's small, light and you use it often, the best storage place is a zipper pouch on the rear panniers or your daypack. Depending on how you park your bike, items used often need to be on the free side of the bike when you lean it against a railing or tree. For efficiency, group common items like a toothbrush and soap in the same nylon ditty bags. Those drawstring pouches are handy. You can use clear plastic bags to separate clothes into organized compartments. You can do the same for tire repair tools.

When your gear is packed, especially on your first trip, it takes a few days of rearranging everything to place it where you like. Once that's accomplished, draw a schematic of where everything is placed. Use it for quick reference when packing for future rides.

WEIGHT DISTRIBUTION

The first rule in bicycle touring is: if you don't use it, leave it. Why? Weight adds up quickly. Every excess pound you pack will cost you in miles covered daily. When riding with four panniers, you need to pack the heaviest equipment, like stove and cooking gear, into the lowest sections of your rear panniers. That will keep your lean-weight closer to the ground. Lean-weight means the amount of weight you have on the bike and where it is located. If you pack heavy items higher up in the panniers, the bike will become top heavy. If you ride with a trailer, you will not suffer such problems because all the weight rides in the middle of the trailer and not on your bike.

When loading your bicycle, you need to balance weight from side to side. More weight should be in the rear panniers than in the front. If you experience a shimmy in your handlebars, it means you have too much in your handlebar bag. Keep less than four pounds in it. If a shimmy persists, lighten your front panniers and check the side-to-side balance. Traditional touring bikes with light frames and skinny tires have a shimmy problem more than touring mountain bikes. That's why a mountain bike makes a better touring machine.

CAMERA EQUIPMENT CARE

Keep your camera equipment in zip-closure freezer bags at all times. While on tour, dust swirls around you from cars and the wind. Also, you must be concerned about rain. Keep camera gear in the daypack cushioned over your sleeping bag and air mattress rolls.

DAYPACK AND INTERNAL FRAME BACK PACK

A small daypack will keep many of your valuables safe and ready for use. That pack is as handy as the one you used back in school. It'll carry your camera and valuable gear that you want with you at a moment's notice.

A 2,000 cubic inch internal frame pack offers versatility while on tour. You can store your air mattress, gear, along with extra film, valuables and food. Make it the easy access pack to your most often used gear. If you happen to find yourself in a backpacking situation, you're ready to go.

CYCLING SHOES, GLOVES, GLASSES, SHORTS AND HELMET

Buy the best, most comfortable cycling shoes you can afford. Avoid riding with tennis shoes. You need the plastic or steel shank on the bottom of the shoes to give you protection from the pedals. Without that shank, you will suffer pain.

Buy a good pair of real leather cycling gloves to protect you from stressing your hands. The first week of a cycling trip, keep shaking your hands at regular intervals so you won't crush the ulnar nerve in the palm of the hand. If you have Aero bars, you will be able to give your hands a rest. That Aero bar will take the pressure off your hands.

With the ozone vanishing, you need to buy 100 percent UV glasses to stop damage to your eyes. Wear the very best eye protection you can afford. Buy the sunglasses with leather side blocks to protect you from the wind and they have a cord to keep them around your neck.

Buy two pairs of cycling shorts, either regular touring shorts or Lycra. Make sure you buy the suede-padded shorts instead of leather because suede is easier to wash and wear. If you are riding in extremely sunny weather, you might want to wear a thin jersey that covers your arms and neck. If it's blistering sunshine, wear thin tights to protect your legs from hours of radiation from the sun. A tan looks nice, but the damage to your skin accumulates into wrinkles and potential skin cancers. Your body does not need all that sun. Protect your face daily with maximum sun block.

Please wear a helmet. An average of 2.5 persons die daily in the USA while riding a bicycle. (900 deaths annually) When they crash without a helmet, their heads imitate an egg yolk in a frying pan when they hit the pavement. Over 50,000 persons visit hospitals with broken bones and cuts severe enough to require medical attention after bike crashes each year. They can stitch you up and they can set your broken bones, but they can't pour your brains back into your head the right way. If the helmet doesn't have a visor, you can buy one at any number of utility shops. Drill new holes and fit it on yourself.

You may also wear a bandana draped over your head and under your helmet to cover your ears and neck from intense sun while you ride in the saddle all day.

PACKING LIST *(You can add or subtract these items as needed for your requirements.)*

TOP OF FRONT PANNIER RACK

1. Sleeping bag and silk cocoon in water proof stuff sack
2. Handlebar Bag
    a. Front of bike light (3 AAA batteries)
    b. Rear of bike LED red warning light (2 AAA batteries)
    c. Chamois cream
    d. Tire pressure gauge
    e. Riding carb fuel
    f. Eyeglass cleaning liquid & cloth
    g. Sunglass case w/reg. glasses
    h. SPF 50 sun block
    i. SPF 50 lip balm
    j. Hand sanitizer
    k. Swiss Army knife
    l. Mobile Phone
    m. Camera, extra digital cards
    n. Travel wallet
    o. Temperature gauge

    p.   Small bell on handlebars to alert pedestrians of your approach

    q.   Small North, East, West, South bubble device to show direction; you can usually buy one with a small bell on it

    r.   Maps

    s.   Small tripod for camera

LEFT FRONT PANNIERS

1. Instant oatmeal
2. Hot drink mixes (tea, coffee, hot chocolate)
3. Peanut butter
4. Bread or tortillas
5. Three one-gallon freezer bags
6. Three one-quart freezer bags
7. Three one-pint freezer bags
8. Riding carb fuel (dried fruit, apples, bananas, oranges)
9. Stuff sack with energy bars
10. Sports drink mix

RIGHT FRONT PANNIER

1. Spice shaker
2. Vegetable broth cubes
3. Dinner staples (pasta, lentils, couscous, quinoa, etc)
4. Dehydrated evening meals
5. Salad fixings
6. Extra riding carb fuel (dried fruit, apples, bananas, oranges)
7. Thin plastic vegetable-fruit cutting board at 6"X8"

RIGHT REAR PANNIER

1. Outside pocket
    a.   First aid kit
    a.   Folding water container
1. Fuel bottle in freezer bag
2. 325ML Fuel bottle w/pump
3. MSR 2.0 L pot w/strainer lid
    a.   Cook stove
    b.   Dish towel

      c.   Matches

      d.   Pot gripper

      e.   Fork

      f.   Liquid soap

      g.   Scouring pad

4.   Individual cook set, MSR cook set, you decide for your needs

      a.   Cooking pot

      b.   Lid

      c.   10 oz. cup

5.   Gallon freezer bag

      a.   Plate

      b.   Long handled spoon

      c.   Long handled knife

      d.   Stove/ wind shield

6.   Repair kit

      a.   Assorted bandages

      b.   Three metal reinforced tire irons

      c.   Open end wrenches, 7-10 mm

      d.   Allen wrenches, all sizes to fit bike

      e.   Leatherman pliers

      f.   6" adjustable wrench

      g.   Chain tool

      h.   Three grease rags

      i.   Nuts, bolts (assorted)

      j.   Chain links

      k.   One tire patch kit (6-8 Patches)

      l.   Brake cable

      m.   Gear cable

      n.   Brake blocks

      o.   4 – 6" plastic tie straps

      p.   Short length of electrical tape

      q.   26 X 1.5 – 1.75 Presta or Schrader valve tube

      r.   Tent seam sealer

      s.   Ink marker to "X" a puncture in the tube for spotting for repair

      t.   Five spare spokes

      u.   Spare tube(s)

      v.   Spare tire(s)

LEFT REAR PANNIER

1. Outside pocket
   a. Clothes drying net bag
   b. Insect repellent
   c. Cable and combination lock
   d. Chain lube, grease rag & small tube of grease remover hand cleaner in plastic bag
2. Street clothes stuff sack
   a. 1 – Light weight long pants w/zippered Legs
   b. 1 – Light weight long sleeve shirt w/roll up sleeves
   c. 1 – Light weight underwear
   d. 1 – T-shirt
   e. 1 – Speedo swim suit
3. Bike wear stuff sack
   a. 1 – Pair biking socks
   b. 1 - Thermax long sleeve jersey
   c. 1 - Thin sun protection long sleeve jersey
   d. 1 – Pair riding shorts
   e. 1 – Pair biking tights
4. Cold weather stuff sack
   a. 1 - Under armor top
   b. 1 - Under armor bottom
   c. 1- Stocking cap
5. Shower sandals in net bag
6. Toiletry kit
   a. 30 days aspirin
   b. 30 days vitamins
   c. Sewing kit
   d. 1 disposable razor
   e. Tooth paste
   f. Toothbrush
   g. Dental floss
   h. Fingernail clippers
   i. Comb
   j. Travel wallet contents list
   k. Toilet paper and two plastic bags
7. Small net bag
   a. Microfiber towel

      b.   Deodorant bar soap in plastic bag

TOP OF REAR PANNIER RACK

1. Nylon duffle bag, preferably oblong and squared off
   a. Rain protection plastic bag with closure device
   b. Tent in stuff sack
   c. Poles in stuff sack
   d. Ground cloth & rain fly in stuff sack
   e. Fourteen tent stakes in bag (1 extra)
   f. Air mattress in stuff sack
   g. Lightweight camping chair at 1.6 pounds
   h. Plastic bag for bicycle seat rain cover
   i. Thirty feet of nylon parachute cord
   j. Mini clothes pins
   k. Shower bag for short showers
   l. Very large nylon duffel bag to pack all your gear to and from your adventure
2. Daypack
   a. Rain cover plastic bag with Velcro strap closure
   b. Rain jacket
   c. Rain gear stuff sack
      i. Rain pants
      ii. Rain booties
      iii. Helmet cover
      iv. Gloves
   d. Gallon Plastic Freezer Bag
      i. Gear location schematic
      ii. Maps
      iii. Bike specs.
   e. Zippered Pocket
      i. Night LED head light (3-AAA batteries)
      ii. Ear plugs
      iii. SPF 50 Lip balm, Sun block SPF 50
      iv. Nighttime eye cover
      v. Spare batteries, 3-AAA, camera
   f. One roll camper toilet paper in plastic bag
   g. Small net bag
      i. Phone charger
      ii. Camera battery charger

     h.   Quart freezer bag
- i.   Postcard stamps
- ii. Journal
- iii. Address list

     i.   Two pens
     j.   Two carabineers on outside of pack
     k. Water purification tablets
     l.   Tri-pod for camera shots when you ride solo

REMOVABLE BIKE ACCESSORIES

1. Frame mounted air pump and air gauge
2. Three water bottles
3. Handlebar mount warning bell
4. Rear view mirror
5. Two 14" bungee cords
6. Four 18" bungee cords
7. One 11" bungee cord
8. One short 36" safety flag
9. One long 7' safety flag
10. Two parking brake 11" Velcro straps
11. Bike computer(1 Cr 2032 + 1 12v)
12. Three spokes with nipples mounted on left chain stay
13. Two extra halo sweat bands on aero bars
14. One cotton shopping bag to save on paper or plastic bags
15. Grease cloth with four ounces of hand cleaner in plastic bottle
16. Skull rag (2 of them) or sweat band for your head

For women:

Bras, tampons, panty liners, leg warmers, arm warmers, blouse, skirt, rain booties, bathing suit, cosmetics, hair dryer (Opps, just kidding!), bracelet, ear rings, (Check main list for female backpackers for more ideas as to what to bring.)

International extras (also check this list for touring in USA and Canada, some items optional)

You may choose to take the following items on international tours: extra front derailleur, extra front Granny gear chain ring, extra chain, two extra tires and two extra tubes, extra toe clip, 10 extra spokes, extra nuts and bolts, extra emergency derailleur hanger, mini-cassette lock, spare reading glasses, extra brake cable, extra brake pads, extra gear shifting cable. Extra tire irons. Carry plenty of duct tape and rim tape. Bring a tool to break loose your freewheel or cassette. Two spare pulleys. Folding gallon container, spare spokes, spare reading glasses, chain oil, freewheel cog remover, spare ball bearings, bottom bracket puller, pocket vice, crank remover, crazy glue, valve stem remover. Be sure to bring a shower bag to give you short quick showers at the end of the day. Gimp emergency derailleur hanger. GPS system. Frisbee. Hacky sack. Rod, reel and fishing lures. Scuba card. International driver's license. Compass. Bird book. Bandana(s). Thirty feet of parachute cord. Snake bite kit. First aid kit. Butterfly closure suture. Rain booties. Swimming goggles. Tennis shoes. Shower sandals. Two extra bungee cords. Malaria pills. Passport and shot record. Metric conversion card. Small binoculars. Copies of passport and all other documents. One dozen color photos of you. Spare batteries. Money belt. Helmet. Headphones. Water filter. Crazy glue. Correct converter plug-ins for different current for your electrical gear such as cameras and laptop. Sewing kit. Tent repair kit. First aid kit. Extra pair of riding gloves. Small roll of electrical tape. Frisbee and hacky sack. Ink marker for tube puncture repair. Temperature gauge. Small handlebar bell with North, East, South and West floating compass. Cotton bag for groceries to save from using paper or plastic when you shop for food. Very large nylon duffel bag for carrying all your gear to and from your adventure. It's light and can be carried with you to pack your gear for the trip home. For bad hair days, bring a baseball cap. Maps to guide you on your journey. Gore-Tex repair kit. Spare tire(s) and tube(s). Yoke cable for center pull brakes. Extra ball bearings. Roll of rim tape. Extra pedal strap. Snake bite and bee bite kit.

Tool Bag

Your tool bag must hold every tool you need to break down your bike while on tour. You must be able to dissemble the head tube, bottom bracket and hubs. You must be able to crack the freewheel loose from the rear wheel. Carry a "Multi-19 tool" for economy of weight and variety of tools. You need a chain repair tool, Allen wrenches, needle nose pliers, pliers, and open ended wrenches to take of your pedals. Before leaving, make sure you carry a tool that will work on every nut, bolt and screw on your bike. Carry tools to disassemble your head tube, bottom bracket and hubs. Make sure you carry metal tire repair irons, glues, instant patches, air gauge and a spoke wrench. Tube patches and glue. Instant patches for quick repair. Also, carry a purple or orange ink marker to "X" the exact spot of the puncture in your tube for easy spotting.

WEARING TO RIDE

1. Helmet
2. Halo sweat band
3. Sunglasses
4. Short sleeve bike jersey
5. Bike shorts
6. Bike socks
7. Bike shoes
8. Bike gloves
9. Food in jersey pockets
10. Hydration pack

NEEDED (These are examples; make yourself a need-to-buy list)

1. Long handled peanut butter spreading knife
2. Adjustable nylon webbing straps instead of bungee cords
3. Velcro straps to attach grey handlebar bag to sleeping bag and front pannier rack
4. Ink marker for tire tube to mark leak
5. Hacky sack or Frisbee
6. Rear view mirror mounted on handlebars or on helmet

On departure day pack added

1. Lip balm
2. Bike repair book
3. Camera instructions
4. Destination tour book
5. Blanket & pillow
6. Toiletry kit
7. Sunglass case with sunglasses
8. Eye cover for sleeping
9. Riding clothes
10. Riding shoes
11. Bike computer
12. Radio or I-pod with earphones

13. Prescription glasses

On Departure Day Pack Deleted (again, use as backup)

1. One roll toilet paper
2. Trowel
3. Packable broad brim hat or baseball cap

Travel Clothing

1. Long pants
2. Long sleeve shirt
3. Light travel sneakers
4. Normal socks
5. Poly underwear

Ship Back – UPS (You may want to ship gear back to lighten your load, examples)

1. Shoes
2. Regular socks
3. Two duffel bags (optional)
4. Blanket and pillow
5. Eye cover for sleeping
6. Radio with earphone
7. Tool kit stuff

MAIL BACK ON LEAVING DESTINATION CITY OR COUNTRY

1. Tour book
2. Bike repair book
3. Camera instructions

First Aid Kit (optional ideas or suggestions for your needs)

1. 6 -10 4x4" pads for cleaning wound
2. 6 4x4" Non-stick pads for covering wound
3. 1 – 2" Stretch wrap
4. 1 Triangular arm sling
5. 4-8 Large safety pins
6. 4-6 Bandage strips with 2 to 3 inch square pads
7. Tape, 1 Inch wide, surgical tape (3-6 yards or meters).

8. 6-10 Packets or 1 small 2-3 oz. bottle of wound sanitizer/cleaner, Betadine, Hibiclens,
9. Peroxide, baby wipes or soap and water
10. 1 Small tube triple antibiotic salve for dressing cuts and abrasions
11. 1 Small Tube, Hydrocortisone, 1% or 2.5%, topical usage only. Reduces inflammation, rashes, saddle sores and allergic reactions.
12. 10-20 Tablets/capsules Tylenol, *Acetaminophen*: For muscle and body pain, joint pain, headaches, fever, allergies, cough, cold and flu
13. 10-20 Tablets/capsules Motrin or Advil, *Ibuprofen*: Anti-inflammatory, pain killer, 5-10 Tablets/capsules Benadryl, *Diphenhydramine Hydrochloride*: general anesthetic, antihistamine, anti-swelling, melatonin for sleep, sedative, anti bleeding - called: Nuprin, Medipren, Brufen, anti-vomiting/nausea, motion sickness.
14. 3-4 Band aids one-half wide (1.5 Cm & 2.5 Cm Wide), keep in small plastic bag, Solarcaine-sunburn relief, Imodium Ad-anti-diarrheal, Visine for eye irritation, moisturizing lotion, Anti-acid, Lotrimin AF-anti-fungal, Calamine-sting relief

Safety and extras for national and international travel

1. Take a seven foot, fiberglass orange/lime green flag pole, vertical position on back rack.
2. Take a three foot, fiberglass orange/lime green traffic side flag pole, bungee into traffic side.
3. Two extra tires, two extra tubes, 20 patches. (International)
4. One extra chain. (International)
5. Extra rear derailleur. (International)
6. Extra freewheel or rear cassette. (International)
7. When traveling on a train, boat or plane, make sure you buy a new fuel bottle and mark it a water bottle with duct tape. If the TSA people try to confiscate it, and they will, put some water in it and drink it to show them it's a water bottle. Otherwise, they will take it away from you and you will be without a fuel bottle when you reach South America or Africa or some other destination.
8. Spare brake cable, spare gear cable, spare brake pads, spare

pulley, photocopies of passport, driver's license, sewing kit, MSR stove cleaner and repair kit, birth certificate copy, water purification tablets, suture and thread, folding gallon water container, spare spokes front and rear, spare reading glasses, chain oil, chain breaker, freewheel cog remover, spare ball bearings, bottom bracket puller, pocket vice, crank remover, crazy glue, valve stem remover, swimsuit, cable and combination lock. Bear spray, shower bag, rear view mirror on handlebar or on helmet, spare screws for the bottom of your shoes if you ride with clip-less pedals.

9. Passport, shot records, international driver's license, scuba diving card, extra passport-sized pictures, hostel card, silk sheet for sleeping bag, bird book, Frisbee, Hacky sack, snake bite kit, 30 feet of nylon cord, spare toe clip, washers, nuts and bolts, toe clip strap, swimmer's goggles, malaria pills, small binoculars, metric conversion card.

INTERNATIONAL TOURING RECOMMENDATIONS

When riding outside the grocery-store-and-fast-food borders of the United States, you open yourself up to new culinary challenges and concerns. In America, you can count on clean water. The U.S. Department of Agriculture inspects meats. Most people speak English. You enjoy smooth roads and easy living.

You're sick of it, right? You've seen too many motor home mentalities for your taste. You have had it with cable TV hookups in campsites. Every town in America looks like every other town with the same fast food joints and motel chains. Whatever happened to regional flavor, small town diners, personal dress and style? Does anyone remember what an old-time hardware store smells like? Do they know the wooden floors creak? Not a chance!

Sounds like you're ready to see how the other 90 percent of humanity lives. Hold onto your handlebars and pull up your Lycra shorts because you're in for one heck of a surprise. You face astounding sights and experiences around the world.

Always be aware of your potential circumstances on tour in developing countries. Be smart and be prepared. Your life may depend on your thoughtful and measured actions. You cannot hope someone will rescue you like they do in the movies.

Riding Outside the United States

While on tour in any one of more than 193 countries, give or take a revolution, you will notice many differences. The freedoms you take for granted at home may be turned upside down in other countries. The way people dress on the altiplano, treeless land above 12,000 feet in Bolivia, is different from the natives in Bali. People in the Middle East bow to Allah five times a day and the women are covered except for their eyes. Australia's kangaroos may enthrall you with their 40 foot leaps. Europe's architecture and history will seduce you. The cultures, languages, animals and people you visit will change dramatically from country to country. Your patience and understanding will be challenged in foreign lands.

Please appreciate that people around the world offer smiles and friendships. They laugh, cry and struggle through different parts of their lives just like you do. You travel through the village of humanity.

Along the way, you need to adapt. Adaptation is the key to your success. When it comes to eating, you face challenges and fabulous experiences.

First, you face a 70 percent chance of suffering from food poisoning or bacterial disruption of your stomach and colon. Whether it's giardia cysts, worms, dysentery, hepatitis or food poisoning—you're headed for the bathroom. The key: accept it, treat it, endure it and get on with your journey. Carry medicine for diarrhea and pills to kill parasites. Obtain those medications in your doctor's office.

Water on International Tours

Water constitutes the primary concern on international tours. The rule remains simple: always filter your water. Use purification tablets to ensure safety. Make certain when you're filtering water to avoid mixing droplets of unfiltered water with filtered water. Just one unfiltered or untreated droplet can cause you sickness. That's why a purification tablet gives you a second line of defense in making your water safe. No matter how much time it takes to filter water, do it meticulously. It can mean the difference between miles of smiles or days of lying on your back with giardia making your colon feel like it's an arena for a bumper-car rally.

Diseases

Several diseases await you while on tour in developing countries. Be prudent and you will save yourself from most of them. Take every preventative shot in the book to protect yourself. Your physician can provide immunizations for you.

Hepatitis causes one heck of a lot of misery in developing countries. To combat it, take gamma-globulin shots that last up to six months. So far, so good. Make sure you take the shots several weeks before the trip. Avoid taking gamma-globulin shots with any live virus vaccines. Your doctor will know about that.

If you contract hepatitis, you will feel like someone used your body as a practice target for a dart board. You will become weak, your eyes will turn yellow and your urine will darken.

You can contract hepatitis from food or water. If you come down with it, see a doctor as quickly as possible.

Montezuma's Revenge gives you an idea of bowel-affliction called diarrhea in the United States. You will spend entire days on the toilet and your face in the lavatory. If you discover blood in your feces, along with cramps in your stomach, it could be dysentery. You may need to take tetracycline. See a doctor.

Food Transport Over Long Distances

One of your biggest challenges will be transporting food and water across long stretches of desert or uninhabited mountains. Be sure to look at a map and find out how far it is to the next food and water. We carried seven days of food with us when we rode from La Paz, Bolivia to Arica, Chile. Our bikes looked more like pack mules than touring bicycles.

Our supplies included seven days of oatmeal, dried beans and rice, dried breads and rolls, tuna, dried fruit, potatoes, carrots, onions, and other sturdy, non-perishable foods. With rice and beans, and oatmeal, you can enjoy protein and carbs to power you anywhere. Canned tuna gives you safe access to protein.

In desert situations, like the Atacama Desert of Chile or the Sahara in Africa, you're looking at hundreds of miles of sand. You won't see a fly or mosquito. You will need to bring three to four gallons of water with you to ensure making it to the next road house. That's especially important on the treeless Nullarbor Plains in the Outback of Australia where temperatures exceed 115 degrees Fahrenheit. The sun sucks water out of your skin like a vacuum. I have toured 100 miles through Death Valley at 116 degrees Fahrenheit and 190 degrees at ground level. I downed five gallons in one day and never hit the bathroom.

Preventative maintenance and health on tour

Because you will not be able to bathe every day, carry antifungal ointment. You can carry a 1.5 gallon shower bag with you to keep clean after a day of sweating. It's available at most camping stores. You can rinse down, soap up and rinse off within three minutes. Just hang the bag on a tree branch and you're clean for sleeping. Still carry the anti-fungal ointment. Also carry cortisone cream for poison ivy.

During a tour anywhere, preventative maintenance is very important. Check your spokes and screws daily to make sure they are tight.

There's a reason you're traveling along adventure highway. As John Muir wrote, "Camp out among the grass and gentians of glacier meadows, in craggy garden nooks full of Nature's darlings. Climb the mountains and get their good tidings. Nature's peace will flow into you as sunshine flows into trees. The winds will blow their freshness into you, and the storms their energy, while cares will drop off like autumn leaves."

Be smart. Stay prepared. Enjoy the peace and silence. It's all good.

Touring Suggestions

You will develop dozens of personal habits while touring. Your gear will be placed where you want it and you will evolve an almost ritualistic style of doing things.

Bike Fit

The most important thing you can do is buy a good bike and have a touring veteran fit it to your body. Have the bike fitted at four junctures.

- Buy and fit the right-sized bike for your height and leg length. Most good touring bikes utilize a top tube that is parallel to the ground. You should be able to straddle the top tube with 1 to 1.5 inches from your crotch to the tube. To check, you can raise the front wheel off the ground with your hands pulling up on the handlebars. If your front tire shows only 1 to 1.5 inches off the ground, you are pretty certain to have the right sized bike for your leg length and body height. With newer model bikes with backward slanting top tubes, you will need to ask a competent specialist at the store. There are several formulas for fitting a bicycle frame to your body so check them all out with a professional. Many bike shops feature a fitting machine to give you an exact fit.

- Fit your seat to pedal height. You want to avoid your hips rocking back and forth while you pedal which means your seat is too high. Your hips should remain still as you pedal. Put your left shoe heel on the left pedal at the six o'clock position while sitting in the seat and have someone keep you vertical. You need to have a 10 percent bend in the knee at the six o'clock position with your heel on the pedal. Adjust the seat up or down to acquire that 10 percent bend in your knee. This will give you maximum pedal, muscle and power coordination.

- Fit your knee to your pedal axle. Place your left pedal to the nine o'clock position as you are looking at the pedal from the left side of the bike. You should be able to drop a plumb line (you can use dental floss with a nut attached) straight from the back of your patella (knee cap) to the axle of the pedal. Adjust your seat forward or backward to make sure your patella is vertical over the pedal axle for a perfect fit and comfort. This part of the fit will make sure you avoid pushing against bone and muscle. You want your body to work in unison with the crank on your bicycle.

- Fit the length from your seat to your handlebars. A general rule of thumb is to hold your elbow from the tip of the seat and your middle finger will touch the handlebars for a perfect riding angle and fit. The ideal for a rider is to comfortably reach the handlebars from his or her position on the seat while leaning at a 45-degree angle. The seat should be level with the ground. Your arms should be comfortable to hold the handlebars for long periods of time. The saddle should be about the same height with your handlebars for your best riding comfort. Go to a professional bike shop to get it done for you if you are unsure.

Buy a bike from a good bicycle store where you will enjoy competent service after the sale. If you buy mail order, be sure you know what you're doing or have a friend who knows what he or she is doing to help you select the best bike.

Riding tips:

- Buy the best sunglasses you can afford to protect your eyes. Protect yourself from radiation from constant sun burning down on your face and body.

- Learn how to maintain and repair your bicycle. Take a bicycle repair class with hands-on instruction. You must be able to disassemble your head tube, hubs, bottom bracket and freewheel or cassette assembly. If you're on a world tour, you must be able to true your wheels and possibly rebuild a rim. You must know how to repair a tube or save a tire with duct tape to the side walls to get more mileage when you're in a remote village in South America. Take the tools you need and know how to use them.

- Your nutrition on a bike trip is important. Stay as close to complex carbohydrates and simple proteins as possible for maximum efficiency. You will gain more stamina, power and endurance from pasta, grains, fruits, cereals, vegetables and breads. For carnivores, canned tuna, salmon and meats provide you with plenty of animal protein. You may want to take multiple vitamins on an extended tour for added micro-nutrient nutrition. Your body experiences considerable depletion of resources while pedaling for weeks.

- Drink liquids constantly. Water provides the best hydration on tour.

- While touring in high mountains, allow your body to acclimate itself to the altitude. If not, you could suffer from altitude sickness. If you push too hard and too fast, you could suffer from pulmonary edema. If you feel weak, short of breath and start coughing, drop below 10,000 feet and stay there for a few days until you feel well enough to climb again. Cerebral edema is a more serious sickness because it affects your brain. You will suffer a pounding headache and possible double vision. If you do not take action, death could result. Descend to below 10,000 feet and get medical attention.

- You will attract lots of attention while touring and many people will invite you into their homes. I have never encountered a problem, but you need to be cautious, especially if you are a woman. You might accept lodging only if you meet a family or couple. I would shy away from single men asking you to stay the night. Also, many men enjoy a faster cadence and move ahead of their women partners. This is important: if you're on tour with your wife or a female companion, ride behind her so you stay together. If you pedal too far ahead, she will feel alone and vulnerable. She will become agitated given enough time, and your relationship will suffer—along with your tour. Trust me on this one, guys.

- Dogs can be the bane of your bicycling tour. They will frighten the daylights out of you and worse, bite you. You could be sent to the hospital for stitches or rabies shots. If a dog or dogs attack, they usually bark first so you know they are coming. It's worth your best efforts to deal with their attacks quickly. Always be alert for dogs by keeping an eye on a house or any areas where dogs might dwell. If you can outrun dogs by pedaling past their territory, go for it. You can carry a dog repellant spray, or better yet, pull your traffic side three foot long fiberglass safety pole out from under your bungee cords and show it to them by waving it back and forth. That "whip" will calm them down quickly and they will leave you alone. As a last resort, dismount your bike and walk behind it as you move out of their territory.

- Always be prepared for survival situations by carrying ample water, food and shelter. Carry minimum amounts of food that will keep you fed for up to seven days in remote regions. Make sure you can stay warm in a summer blizzard at high altitude. Bring those waterproof glove protectors and rain booties to keep hands and feet protected.

- Leave the road and find camp one to two hours before dusk. If you happen to get caught in the dark, attach a front LED headlight and rear blinking LED red light. You can carry a blinking strobe light to let traffic know your presence.

- Always cross railroad tracks slowly and at a perpendicular angle. If they are really nasty, get off and walk across.

- When riding in town, stay a doors length away from parked cars. You want to watch for anyone getting out of their car so you don't get hit by their door.

- Always get off your bike and carefully roll your wheels softly down from a curb so as to not abuse your rims by allowing them to drop off the curb.

- Take an electronic recorder to take notes and describe your journey. It's very light and portable. Describe your journey and record new ideas as they flow into your mind.

- When stopping for a break, create your own stretching routine to give your muscles a different range of motion. Move your head side to side, forward and backward, left and right. Flex your arms and legs as you stretch them out and keep them limber.

- If you ride with clip-less pedals on tour, be certain to carry two spare screws in case you lose one of them. Check the bottom of your shoes frequently.

- Watch out for rocks, holes and glass in the breakdown lane as you travel along a highway. Drop your hand down as you point to the glass or dangerous object so the cyclist following you is alerted.

- If you ride in a pace line on tour, stay at least 18 to 24 inches off the lead person's rear tire. If you accidently hit his or her back wheel, you're going down. Avoid that problem by keeping a safe distance away.

- Keep applying sunscreen to your lips and face throughout the day to protect yourself as much as possible.

- For those who want to protect themselves from burning their neck and ears, drop a bandana over your head before you put on your helmet and have the bandana cover your neck and ears.

- If a vehicle is directly behind you (at the six o'clock position), you may call out to your partners, "Bogie 6!" If it's a big truck in front (at the twelve o'clock position), you may call out to your partners, "Bogie 12!" If both vehicles may pass each other at your location, you might call out, "Bogie 6 and 12, exit!" That means you and your partners may choose to ride off to the side of the road for your own safety on a two lane highway. Some riders call out "Car back!" when a vehicle approaches from the rear. Either way, keep your friends alerted to traffic.

- If it's a dark day or rainy, be sure to turn on your front headlight in blinking mode and your rear red light in blinking mode.

- Always keep your water bottles filled. If you have a long stretch between towns, fill up your extra one or two gallon container to cover yourself.

- If you do run over glass, quickly take your leather riding glove and place it on the front and back tires to clear any glass from the rubber. If you have fenders, get off and run your glove over the tire as you rotate it to clear the glass from the rubber. You could save yourself from having to repair a flat tire.

- Check your tires every two to three days for tire pressure and your spokes for tightness. Also check the screws that secure your racks, brakes, fenders and everything else.

- If you open a zipper in your pack, close it immediately.

- Be sure to keep your chain rollers wet with oil to reduce wear.

Also, keep the pitches wet so they remain lubricated as they run around freewheel and chain rings.

- No matter how comfortable a seat you buy, your body cannot tolerate too much weight bearing down on your butt. Try to remain as lean a cyclist as you can through proper nutrition and exercise.

- A lot of touring riders find a water pack on their backs with a mouth feed right to their mouths is a very handy way to keep hydrated. It's about two pounds and gives you easier access to your water. Try it to see if it agrees with you.

- At the top of a hill, immediately shift into your highest gear in order to maintain pedal control at high speed as you descend.

- At regular intervals, take a rag or piece of paper towel and hold it to your wheel rims to clean them of oil and dirt buildup. As you apply the paper towel, run your bike forward and backward until you clean the entire rim. Do the same for both sides of the rim and front and back rims. Your brakes and rims will last longer and provide you with more efficient braking power.

- Utilize a handlebar mirror or helmet mirror to keep you aware of the traffic behind you.

- If you run off the pavement into sand or gravel, avoid trying to pull back on to the pavement to save yourself. Your best bet is to ride into the gravel or sand. When you regain control, you can pull back onto the pavement at your convenience. If you try to pull back onto the pavement too quickly, you may crash when the front wheel catches the solid pavement at a bad angle.

- While riding on a gravel road, watch for flying stones and avoid smiling at oncoming traffic or you might suffer a stone colliding with your front teeth or glasses.

- When you stop for a drink or food, you want to keep your front wheel from spinning sideways on you. It may cause you to lose control of your bike. You can buy a nylon string attached to a rubber grommet and place it between your brake and brake handle to make a brake block. If you can't find anything to fit, you can buy a Velcro strip with a "D" ring and have it attached to your handlebars. When you need it, you can wrap it around the brake handle and the handlebars to secure your front brake. That way, you won't have your front wheel going squirrely on you.

- When shifting gears, always back off on the pedal to allow the chain to slip to the next gear gently. That will save your chain and teeth from wearing out sooner.

- Maintain your brake adjustments at all times as if your life depended on it.

- While on tour with a group, make certain everyone yells out when they are stopping and everyone must give hand signals for turning right or left. Always obey traffic laws as if you are driving a car.

Breaking down and packing your bike for travel

Secure a correctly-sized bike box at your local bicycle shop. You can also find boxes at the local grocery store and tape them together. You can buy a plastic box at bike shops if you plan to have a safe place at your destination to store it. If not, a cardboard box will work fine.

Break down your bike by taking off the handlebars, front wheel, pedals, seat and pulling off the rear derailleur. Take the rear derailleur off the hanger, tape it to the chain and encase it in cloth with tape. Do not forget this procedure or you may suffer a bent hanger and possibly a broken rear derailleur. Lock the front forks with a plastic axle and secure it with tape. That will stabilize the forks from breakage. Pack the bike with paper so it won't move inside the box. Place the front rack under the forks. The front wheel will fit beside the frame opposite the chain drive side. Tape the pedals to the frame so as not to lose them along with the bike seat and shaft. Slip a piece of cardboard between the wheel and your bike so it won't suffer scratches. Everything you can do to keep the bike stable in the box is important. Toss in your seven foot fiberglass safety flag and three foot fiberglass traffic-side safety flag along with empty water bottles. Secure all nuts and bolts by replacing them where they belong or place in a sock and tape to the top tube. Tape the box up with plastic tape. Tape all the four corners and all seams for extra strength on international journeys where they throw your gear around without regard to damage to your precious bike.

Be sure to place your name and address all over the box. Draw big arrows pointing up with a magic marker and ask handlers to keep the bike vertical in transit. If they fail to keep it upright and it is placed under heavy luggage, you could suffer a bent chain ring or rear derailleur.

Best safety gear on the planet for cyclists

Let's cover the most important safety device on your bike: be sure to strap that seven-foot long fiberglass pole with orange-lime green and even white safety flag to your rear rack. A second three-foot fiberglass safety pole with orange-lime green flag will fit under your bungee cords that secure your rear pack to the rack—and it extends about 18 inches into traffic. In town, you can shove it closer to the bike so you won't be such a wide profile trying to maneuver around cars in heavy traffic.

The total affect is two orange flapping flags that can be seen a half-mile away. They command the attention of approaching drivers both front and rear. When you command their attention, you are less likely to suffer consequences. You must remember that you are sharing the road with 2,000 pound vehicles traveling at 65 miles per hour. Just one yawn or sneeze, a glance back at the kids or someone texting could have a car running up the back of your panniers. Those flags are your lifeline to safety. Engage them as if your life depended on them. Buy them at bike shops or department stores.

Always wear clothing that is white, orange, yellow and/or lime green for maximum visual impact. Also, wear a white helmet to maintain optimum visual attention. It's cooler in the summer, too.

Bicycle gear and clothing shops include www.REI.com , www. Performance.com , www.BikeNashbar.com

For those just starting out on touring bicycles, you might try one or two nighters. You may visit www.bikeovernights.org for details on accommodations for short tours.

*C*hapter 52—Mountain climbing

"In a sense, everything that is, exists to climb. All evolution is a climbing towards a higher form. Climbing for life as it reaches towards the consciousness, towards the spirit. We have always honored the high places because we sense them to be the homes of gods. In the mountains there is the promise of...something unexplainable. A higher place of awareness, a spirit that soars. So we climb...and in climbing there is more than a metaphor; there is a means of discovery." Rob Parker

Climbing mountains allows a sense of freedom, energy, danger and triumph far beyond normal living. Over my lifetime, I ratcheted my body up high peaks in the Andes, Himalaya, Swiss Alps, Alaska Range, Rocky Mountains and even in Antarctica. Each mountain, no matter how big, tall or small—offers challenges, joy and danger.

Some of the most famous mountain climbers who conquered Everest and K-2, died by falling off 30-foot rock walls. You never know what will happen on a mountain climb.

How do you start? Again, begin with a climbing club or buddy who climbs.

You may love rock-climbing vertical walls. You may like 14er climbing that takes endurance, but not a lot of gear. Colorado offers 54—14er peaks. Once you finish all 54, you can tackle 1,100—13ers in Colorado. Some men and women have climbed them all. You might enjoy ice climbing.

You might like climbing all of the highest peaks on all seven continents. You can grab all the danger or delight you desire.

Mountain climbing web sites to get you started

1. www.rockclimbing.com
2. www.abc-of-rockclimbing.com
3. www.abcsofrockclimbing.com
4. www.indoorclimbing.com
5. www.climbingatabout.com
6. www.howrockclimbingworks.com
7. www.spadout.com
8. www.newenglandbouldering.com
9. www.climbingaustralia.com
10. www.alanarnette.com/alan/climbinglinks.php
11. www.allwebhunt.com/dir-wiki.cfm/Top/Recreation/Climbing
12. www.elephantjournal.com/2010/01/top-ten-climbing-web-sites-jamie-emerson/
13. www.top20sites.com/Top-Mountain-Climbing-Sites

For 14er climbing gear list:

1. Tent
2. Ground mat
3. Sleeping bag
4. Pillow
5. Camp chair
6. Moleskin
7. Five gallon water container
8. Mess kit
9. Small towel
10. Miner's lamp, flash light
11. Paper towels
12. 50 feet of parachute cord
13. Small ax and saw
14. Gore-Tex jacket
15. Wool sweater
16. Boots/socks/liners
17. Underwear, pants and T

18. Travel kit
19. Rain pants
20. Swiss Army knife
21. Anti-bear spray
22. Compass
23. Sunglasses
24. Adventure hat
25. Gloves/mittens
26. Day pack
27. Sun block/lip balm
28. Notebook and pen
29. Camera/tripod/film/digital cards
30. Plastic trash bags
31. Binoculars
32. Ice axe
33. Books for reading
34. Bandana
35. Food, drinks, fruits, energy bars, dinners, oatmeal, trail mix
36. Plastic box with food, stove, water filter, soap, shower bag
37. Toilet paper and two one gallon zip-closure plastic bags, small shovel
38. Firewood
39. Spare keys to vehicle, one for each person
40. Add to this list as you see fit from your experiences.
41. First aid kit
42. Two aluminum telescope walking poles
43. Helmet

*C*hapter 53—*River rafting*

"Something will have gone out of us as a people if we ever let the remaining wilderness be destroyed, if we permit the last virgin forests to be turned into comic books and plastic cigarette cases; if we drive the few remaining members of the wild species into zoos or to extinction; if we pollute the last clear air and dirty the last clean streams and push our paved roads through the last of the silence."
Wallace Stegner

For anyone who loves the eternal wilderness at the perfect speed, you can raft a river, fish a river, dive into a river, swim a river—and come away with serene ecstasy.

After having rafted rivers on six continents, I feel that few activities beat a river trip for tranquility of the spirit. Nothing beats living by the slow, quiet and peaceful river-time.

Whatever you do in your river rafting life, be sure to take the 17-day Grand Canyon raft trip from Lee's Ferry to Diamond Creek takeout, some 225 miles and 1.7 billion years of geological magic. Few other raft trips offer such dramatic scenery and ecological magic.

Top ten river rafting destinations in the USA:

1. Grand Canyon, AZ
2. Salmon River, ID
3. Arkansas River, CO

4. Colorado River, UT
5. American River, CA
6. Rogue River, OR
7. Glacier National Park, MT
8. New River, WV
9. Chattooga River, GA/SC
10. Snake River, ID/WY
11. Deerfield River, MA

How do you get started?

1. America's Top 10 River Outfitters: http://www.class-vi.com/
2. Rafting America and Canada: http://www.raftingamerica.com/
3. Adventure Connection in California: http://www.raftcalifornia.com/
4. Rafting, canoeing, floating: http://www.wareagleresort.com/
5. Jim Thorpe River Ad ventures in Pennsylvania: http://www.jtraft.com/
6. Blue Sky Outfitters Washington State: http://www.blueskyoutfitters.com/

*C*hapter 54—*Backpacking*

"How hard to realize that every camp of men or beast has this glorious starry firmament for a roof! In such places standing alone on the mountain-top it is easy to realize that whatever special nests we make - leaves and moss like the marmots and birds, or tents or piled stone - we all dwell in a house of one room - the world with the firmament for its roof - and are sailing the celestial spaces without leaving any track." John Muir

It's been said that backpacking becomes Mother Nature's way of feeding mosquitoes. You must love it. Millions do love backpacking, whether for a day hike or weekend or for the hard core, a whole summer—such as backpacking the Continental Divide.

Nothing in the world beats a trek into the wilderness, whether mountains or woods or rolling hills. Peace, serenity, campfires, stories and friendships.

How to get started:

1. Information and gear reviews: www.BackpackerMagazine.com
2. Keep yourself abreast of gear and classes: www.TheBackpacker.com
3. Recreation Equipment Incorporated: www.REI.com
4. Trails and maps for your treks at: www.slackpacker.com

5. Ins and outs of light weight backpacking: http://www.backpacking.net
6. Yosemite: www.nps.gov
7. New Zealand: www.backpackerboard.co.nz/directory/worldwide-backpacking.html
8. General info: www.wilderness-backpacking.com/index.html
9. Europe: www.bakpakguide.com/europe/europe101/highlights/index.shtml
10. Australia: www.backpackersinaustralia.com
11. Canada: www.outdooradventurecanada.com

Chapter 55—Sailing around the world or just a weekend

"The pessimist complains about the wind; the optimist expects it to change; the realist adjusts the sails." William Arthur Ward

It's been my pleasure to sail and scuba dive in the Caribbean, Indian Ocean and on mountain lakes at 9,000 feet. There's nothing like filling the sails with a brisk wind. It fills your mind, body and spirit at the same time.

Humanity has sailed the oceans of the world from the beginning of recorded history. Whether you sail around the world or sail around the bay—what a glorious way to spend your life for however long you allow the winds to fill your sails.

How to get started:

1. Sailing info: www.sailnet.com/forums/cmps_index.php
2. More sailing: www.sailinglinks.com/
3. Canada: www.sailingforyou.ca/
4. Sailing needs: www.home.ussailing.org/
5. Sailing magazine: www.sailingworld.com
6. World sailing: www.internationalsailingfederation.com
7. Sailing: www.48degreesnorth.com
8. Solo sailing: www.singlehandedsailingsociety.com
9. Sailing: www.latitude.com

*C*hapter 56—*Canoeing*

"The first thing you must learn about canoeing is that the canoe is not a lifeless, inanimate object: it feels very much alive, alive with the life of the river. Life is transmitted to the canoe by currents of air and the water upon which it rides. The behavior and temperament of a canoe is dependent upon the elements: from the slightest breeze to a raging storm, from the smallest ripple to a towering wave, or from a meandering stream to a thundering rapid. Anyone can handle a canoe in a quiet millpond, but in rapids a canoe is like a wild stallion. It must be kept on a tight rein. The canoeist must take the canoe where he or she wants it to go, not where it wants to go. Given the chance, the canoe will dump you overboard and continue on down the river by itself." Bill Mason

For the power of a paddle, give me a chance to power my own canoe. I love the peace, quiet and serenity of canoeing, canoe camping and canoe adventure. As Henry David Thoreau said, "Canoeing is pure nature."

You may enjoy turtles sunning themselves, swans flapping their wings, cormorants spreading their feathers to dry them in the sun, diving ducks and a chance to see loons playing their circle games—all in the quiet of the canoe.

Whether you paddle a lake, the Boundary Waters or the Mississippi River, a canoe gives you special magic.

How to get started:

1. Minnesota: www.redrockstore.com
2. Guide to canoes and products: www.canoeing.com
3. Top canoes: www.oldtowncanoe.com
4. Canoe Australia: www.canoe.org.au/?page=20186&format=
5. North American rivers: www.nationalrivers.org

Chapter 57—Scuba diving

"Scuba diving is sensual. To breathe underwater is one of the most fascinating and peculiar sensations imaginable. Breathing becomes a rhythmic melody of inhalations and exhalations. The cracks and pops of fish and crustaceans harmonize with the rhythmic chiming of the bubbles as you exhale. Soon, lungs act as bellows, controlling your buoyancy as you achieve weightlessness. And, as in your dreams, you are flying. Combine these otherworldly stimuli and you surrender completely to the sanctuary of the underwater world." Tec Clark

My dad got me into scuba diving at age 15. After a lifetime of diving in exotic places around the world, including the Great Barrier Reef, Galapagos Islands, Caribbean, Hawaii and Australia's east and west coast—I am ready to jump into any lake, river, sea or ocean to see the magic beneath the surface.

Whether you like wreck driving, a slow drift on the Crystal River in Florida or John Pennekamp Park in the Florida Keys or a sink hole—scuba diving allows magic and freedom of flight, fancy and beauty.

How to get started:

1. Scuba directory: www.wv-travel-directory.com/scubadiving/view.html
2. Scuba vacations: www.scubasuperpower.com/
3. Scuba products: www.odysseydiving.com/links.html
4. Scuba gear: www.diversdirect.com/

*C*hapter 58—*Skydiving*

""When the people look like ants-PULL! When the ants look like people-PRAY.""

This kid has never jumped out of an airplane with a parachute in his life. But the people who do it love it. If skydiving turns your crank, it may be the sparkplug that lights your fire. Go for it.

How to get started:

1. Learning to skydive: www.skydiving.com
2. Wing suit: www.dropzone.com/
3. Skydiving: video.search.yahoo.com/search/ video?p=sky+diving+websites
4. New Zealand: www.skydivingnz.co.nz/
5. Canada: www.vancouver-skydiving.bc.ca/
6. Australia: www.sydneyskydivers.com.au/

Chapter 59—Surfing and windsurfing

"When talking with co-windsurfers and trying to get your shoulders out of your wetsuit, be careful not to also grab your bathing suit strap as you forcefully pull down on the wetsuit. It tends to interrupt the flow of the conversation." Marcy Kennedy

As a kid, I surfed in Hawaii off Diamond Head. I couldn't get enough of riding those waves. Years later, as a landlubber, some bright guy stuck a sail on a surfboard and called it windsurfing. It's also known as boardsailing. Either sport, what a rush.

Wild winds may drive your soul. Whether surfing the big ones in Australia, Hawaii or anywhere in the world, you may enjoy surfing and windsurfing as you choose.

How to get started:

1. Surfer Magazine to get started: www.surfermagazine.com
2. California: www.surfingcal.com/surf-links.html
3. Australia: www.sasurfschools.com.au/
4. United Kingdom: www.magicseaweed.com/UK-Ireland-Surf-Tools/1/
5. Hawaii: www.surfline.com/home/index.cfm
6. Windsurfing: www.windsurfingmag.com/
7. Gear: www.windsurfing-direct.com/

*C*hapter 60—*Hot air ballooning and parasailing*

"The winds have welcomed you with softness, the sun has greeted you with its warm hands, you have flown so high and so well, that God has joined you in laughter, and set you back gently into the loving arms of Mother Earth." Known as The Balloonists' Prayer

You can't help but sense the wonder of rising into the biosphere inside a basket carried aloft by a hot air balloon. Peaceful, joyful and serene. If it's your cup of tea, rise in the morning in a hot air balloon.

If you're into hang-gliding or parasailing, go for it. To soar like an eagle may give you great joy and spiritual bliss.

How to get started:

1. Getting started: www.hotairballooning.com/
2. Director for sites: www.eballoon.org/directory/balloon-sites. html
3. World ballooning: www.hot-air-ballooning.org/
4. Parasailing: www.hot-air-ballooning.org/

Chapter 61—Snow skiing, snowboarding, cross country skiing, snowshoeing, water skiing, wake boarding, knee boarding, disabled skiing

"The sensual caress of waist deep snow...glory in skiing virgin fluff, in being the first to mark the powder with the signature of their run." Tim Cahill

As one who lived the ski bum dream, it's worth it. You will enjoy fantastic powder runs all your own. First tracks! Busting the bumps! Screaming at the top of your lungs from so much excitement! For two years, I skied 110 times a winter, bartended, danced and played in the powder at Winter Park, Colorado. I enjoyed a fantastic time in my life. Do it while you're young or do it while you're old, but live the life of a ski bum for one winter and you will have made it to heaven before you died.

Also, if snowboarding chimes your bells, go for it. You may like snowshoeing, skiing, hut to hut mountaineering skiing and water skiing. Life awaits you in the mountains anywhere on the planet. You're in for the time of your life wherever you strap on a board, skis or any other gear to move you across snow or summer warm water.

How to get started:

1. Ski Magazine: www.skinet.com/
2. Hut to hut: www.huts.org/
3. Ski Utah: www.skiutah.com/winter/index.html
4. Ski California: www.snowsummit.com/ski/

5. Ski Vermont: www.skivermont.com/
6. Ski Europe: www.ski-europe.com/
7. Snowboarding: www.lovetoknow.com/top10/snowboarding.html
8. Snowshoeing: www.snowshoemtn.com/jobs/faq.htm
9. Water skiing: www.usawaterski.org/
10. Disabled skiing: www.NSCD.org

*C*hapter 62—Many other ways to travel around the world

"There must be 50 ways to leave your lover…hop off the bus Gus, we don't need to discuss much, drop off the key Lee, set yourself free…get out the back Jack; make a new plan Stan; don't try to be coy Roy, just listen to me…." Neil Simon

After presenting components of this book along with a slide show at a sports store in Denver, Colorado, an older lady stepped up to me at the end. She said, "You didn't talk about the wonders of RV'ing around the United States. We RV'd for two years and had the time of our lives. Please talk about that travel mode in the future."

Another guy came up, "I liked your show, but what about motorcycle adventures?"

"I'm with you," I said. "Whatever travel mode turns you on is the best way to go."

"Thanks man," he said.

As you can see, this book already stretches beyond 350 pages. I could not cover everything or it would resemble an encyclopedia.

You may like to travel by RV (camper van), motorcycle, plane, sailboat, canoe, scooter, unicycle, Penny Farthing, bicycle, paraglider, horseback and a dozen other travel modes. You may choose to make yourself happy along your path. You may apply the concepts and practices in this book to make your dreams come true.

*C*hapter 63—*Gear, adventure companies and more*

"You've ridden so long in the rain, you feel like a dish rag. But despite the misery of your soaked body, you look around to see verdant leaves dripping with water. The air enters your nostrils vibrantly clean. To experience adventure, you must be willing to be uncomfortable at times and enjoy loneliness by being happy with your own singing. A song pops out of your mouth...It rained all night the day I left, the weather it was fine...." The Gourmet Bicyclist in the Washington State rain forest

Adventure seekers, a special breed of individuals, require muscles and guts to pedal, pack, paddle, ski, sail, run and climb into nature's inner sanctum. Mountains test your gumption and deserts test your will. Life offers you challenges. Nature tests your character daily. Hardships impact your inner being. At the same time, you experience joys and bliss during sunsets or after a rainstorm when a double rainbow arcs across the sky.

Your quest creates something special in your life and draws magical moments that cannot be generated any other way. You hike, bike, climb, paddle and move forward between personal power and exhaustion. Life mingles with death. Enchanting moments happen. You can't look for them nor can you expect them. You interlock with the forces of nature.

In order to enjoy that charm, equip yourself with the best gear you can afford. The following organizations base their research and development on making camping and outdoor adventuring optimum for you. They guarantee their products. I have utilized gear from all of them and I have never been disappointed.

By contacting their 800 numbers or websites, you will receive a catalog with all their equipment that you may need.

QUALITY OUTDOOR OUTFITTERS

Recreation Equipment Incorporated: This company is popularly known as **REI** and offers top quality as well as environmentally responsible merchandise. They offer a money back guarantee on all their products. Additionally, over 100 REI stores across the nation sponsor top adventure experts that educate, inspire, guide and mentor audiences throughout the year. *REI* offers backpacks, bikes, canoes, skis, GPS, safety gear, rafting, sunglasses, mountaineering gear, sailing, camping, food, winter gear, snowshoes and more than can be listed in this short paragraph. Additionally, you may become a member and enjoy bonus dividends annually. Call 1-800-426-4840. www.REI.com

The North Face: Top quality gear for every kind of adventure. Excellent guarantees. Camping, skiing, rafting and mountaineering. For a catalog call 1-800-447-2333. www.thenorthface.com

Eastern Mountain Sports: Excellent outdoor gear all around. Guarantees on all products. www.ems.com

L.L. Bean: Excellent selection of clothing, boots and more for the great outdoors. Full guarantees. Call 1-800-341-4341. www.llbean.com

Early Winters Outfitting: High quality, lightweight camping and outdoor equipment. Great service and excellent guarantee. www.earlywintersoutfitting.com

Campmor: Excellent camping store. Latest equipment and fair prices. www.campmor.com

Marmot Mountain Works: Excellent sleeping bags, running gear, camping gear and more. Excellent guarantee. www.marmotmountainworks.com

Go Lite: Exceptionally light backpacks and outdoor gear. Excellent guarantee. www.golite.com

Army-Navy Surplus stores: You can find one in any big city. They feature surplus outdoor gear and reasonable prices. They will stand by their products with a money back guarantee. Look them up in your local phone book. Full guarantee.

Performance: Primarily bicycles, parts, tires, clothing, gloves, helmets, tents, shoes, panniers, rain gear. Excellent quality and full guarantee. www.performancebike.com

Bicycle Village: Primarily bicycles, tires, repair, fitting, shoes and jerseys. Full guarantee. www.bicyclevillage.com

Bike Nashbar: Bicycles, parts, jerseys, shoes, jackets and pretty much everything you need for your bicycle adventures. Full guarantee. www. BikeNashbar.com

Foothills Ski and Bike: Located in the Rocky Mountain foothills west of Denver, Colorado. If you are ever bicycle touring east or west on Route 40 alongside I-70 in Genesee, Colorado, (about 15 miles west of Denver city limits) be sure to stop by Foothills Ski and Bike just off Exit 254. It is the buffalo viewing exit and it also leads to Buffalo Bill's Grave. After exiting, go south 50 yards to hit a T, take a left, travel another 50 yards and take a right. Go up the hill to the first right into the Foothills Ski and Bike sign. John Rathbone, the proprietor, will give you the finest in bicycle sales, equipment, fitting and repair. He also features unlimited ski equipment with expert boot fitting. All work guaranteed. Open seven days a week. Call him: 303-526-2036. www.FootHillsSkiandBike.com

Accommodations

American Youth Hostels: If you enjoy meeting travelers on a budget, you will meet the best in hostels around the planet. You will find 5,500 hostels worldwide. You need a hostel sheet, your membership card and a smile. www.AmericanYouthHostels.com and www.YHA.com

Magazines

Adventure Cycling Magazine: For long distance bicycle touring riders, this magazine excels. You will find ideas, innovations, bike reviews and stories from around the world. www.adventurecycling.org

Bicycle Times: This magazine gives you an excellent overall view of touring, commuting and many other great stories about bicycling. www.bicycletimes.com

Bicycling Magazine: This magazine carries a great deal of information about bicycles, clothing, travel, food and fashion. www.bicycling.com

Tandem: This is a great magazine about folks that like to ride two up. www.tandem.com

Mountain Bike Magazine: This magazine gives you everything you need to know about competitions and more. www.mountainbike.com

Outside Magazine: This magazine will take you to adventures around the world. Amazing photographs and compelling stories. www.outsidemagazine.com

Canoe and Kayak Magazine: This magazine will take you into the calmness of canoeing and the wildness of kayaking. www.canoeandkayak.com

Cruising World Magazine: This magazine is for sailing around the world. www.cruisingworld.com

Backpacker Magazine: This magazine gives you the best in trips, tips and stories. www.backpackermagazine.com

Campground Sources

Rand McNally Campground and Trailer Park Guide: Enjoy information about campgrounds in every section of the USA. Also, www.goodsamsclub. com , www.koa.com

National Bicycling Touring Companies and Gear

Austin-Lehman Adventures: First class, inn to inn cycling adventures. Offers a guarantee. Bike all over the country and more. Experienced group leaders. www.austin-lehmanadventures.com

Backroads: Class act and a ton of fun. Quality tours and cuisine. For all abilities and all levels. Get your feet wet in style. Cycling, backpacking and many other outdoor adventures. They really offer first class adventures. www.backroads.com

Bicycle Touring Gear: Expedition panniers, racks and bicycle touring gear. Call 1-800-747-0588. Email: wayne@TheTouringStore.com , www. thetouringstore.com

Recumbents, tandems, trikes: Everything you need for bicycling in a variety of styles. www.jayspedalpower.com

Custom Franklin Frame bikes: For incredible workmanship of a custom bicycle, try www.franklinframes.com. I have owned a Franklin Frame custom mountain expedition touring bike for 21 years.

Hubbub Custom Bicycles: They fit, design and build a bike for you. www. hubbubcustom.com

Classic Adventures: Bicycle tours in USA and around the world since 1979. www.classicadventures.com

Pedal and Sea Adventures: You name it, they will take you there. Austria, France, Germany, Lake Constance at the foot of the Alps, Quebec, Vermont and more. www.classicadventures.com

Women Only Bike Tours: Fully supported, all ages, all abilities, quaint inns, cross country, national parks, Europe and more. Wine tasting. www. womantours.com

America by Bicycle, Inc: Choose 38 tours from five to 52 days. Coast to coast. Highly recommended. www.abbike.com

Alaska Bicycle Tours: Ride Alaska and the Yukon. www.cyclealaska.com

Wandering Wheels: They will guide you coast to coast inexpensively. www.wanderingwheels.org

Historical Trails Cycling: Lewis and Clark Trail, Oregon Trail, the Wilderness Road and more. www.historicaltrailcycling.org

Bike Flights: Bicycle shopping, airline tickets, travel insurance. www.bikeflights.com

Easy Rider Tours: Bicycle Europe and America. They will take you first class. Since 1987, Jim and his wife have been taking folks on great tours. You'll love your time with them. I know them personally and give them a five star rating. Call 1-800-488-8332. www.easyridertours.com

Australian Adventures: Top quality touring company. Thirteen individual tours in the land down under. Call 1-800-889-1464. www.AustralianTours.com

New Zealand Pedal Tours: Local guides, inns, quiet roads, incredible scenery. Twenty years in the business. www.newzealandpedaltours.com

Backpacking trips with "Just roughin it": Top quality backpack trips into the Grand Canyon and beyond. www.justroughinit.com

Backpacking for women with Adventure Chick: These ladies will take you to wild places to enjoy great fun. USA and around the world. www.adventurechick.net

Backpacking in Yellowstone: Play in the wilderness of geysers and waterfalls. www.bigwildadventures.com

Backpacking in Alaska: Huge, wild and amazing. www.trekalaska.com

Backpacking and hostelling worldwide: Around the world. www.abouthostels.com

Backpacking South America: Inca Trail, Amazon jungle, waterfalls. They take you to the best in Central and South America. www.bambaexperience.com

Backpacking and how to get into it: They give you information from A to Z. www.easybackpackingtips.com

Backpacking in Utah: Profound beauty and sunsets. www.excursionsescalante.com

Caribbean backpacking: Water, islands, exotic. www.adventurefinder.com

Backpacking in the USA: They take you into the inner sanctum of nature's playground. www.outwardbound.org

Backpacking Canada: Try a trip in the Yukon. www.yukoneh.com

Backpacking for teens: Hit the Appalachian Trail. www.outdoors.org

Sea kayaking in Alaska: Sea kayak Prince William Sound with whales and glaciers. www.alaskasummer.com

Backpacking in Thailand: Exotic, stunning, beautiful. www.backpackersthailand.com

Luxury backpacking: For those that enjoy comfort. www.luxurybackpackers.com

Backpacking in Australia: Travel down under. www.backpackingaround.com

Backpacking in New Zealand: Packing the Milford Trek or Rootburn Trek. Expect an amazing time in that country. Raft the Shotover River. Bungee jump. Stand on the four billion year old Meroki Boulders. www.NewZealand.com

Backpacking in Switzerland: Whether you bicycle or backpack, Switzerland offers incredible sights and beautiful villages filled with flower boxes. www.backpackeurope.com

Finding partners

For backpacking, camping, hiking, climbing, rafting, cycling, windsurfing, para-sailing, scuba diving, horseback riding and a hundred other sports, you may sign up to enjoy new friends at: www.MeetUp.com

For companions wanted in cycling. You may sign up on line for free. www.adventurecycling.org

Chapter 64—Unlimited sports activities worldwide

"There are so many things to do in this world that you need twenty lifetimes to pursue them all." FHW

The more you travel the world, the more you realize that you cannot do it all in one lifetime. However, you can accomplish as much as possible by sticking your nose into everything along the way.

In the final reality, you captain your life, you choose and you live it to your satisfaction.

You may participate in different sports and activities at various stages of your life. When one activity grabs you more than another, pursue it. You might battle on the racquetball court with unending passion. You may climb mountain peaks with a sense of high adventure. You may crash the gates snow skiing. Windsurfing may have you raging on the water with the wind. You might pursue triathlons with swimming, bicycling and running. Mountain bike racing may hook into your soul. You may turn into a swing dancer and compete all over the country. You may become an artist, screen writer, sculptor or chef. This life allows you unlimited opportunities to express yourself.

In the end, this book presents you with useful information and techniques that will allow you to adventure around the country or around the world for your entire life. If a Michigan farm boy can chase after his dreams and live them one by one, so can you. May you enjoy your life journey with persistence, passion and action.

Whatever your interest, go for it, love it and live it.

Remember: steadfast conviction, relentless enthusiasm and a sense of purpose will take you anywhere you want to go in this world.

As my dad said, "You can do it!"

As you can now say, "I can do it!"

The End

About the Author

Frosty Wooldridge is an environmentalist, mountain climber, scuba diver, dancer, skier, writer, speaker and photographer. He graduated from Michigan State University. He has taught at the elementary, high school and college levels. He has rafted, canoed, backpacked, sailed, windsurfed, snowboarded and more all over the planet. He has bicycled 100,000 miles on six continents and seven times across the United States. His feature articles have appeared in national and international magazines for 30 years. He has interviewed on NBC, CBS, ABC, CNN, FOX and 100 radio shows. You may enjoy a one hour DVD video of this book as Wooldridge presents it in front of a live audience. If you have ideas to improve the book in the next printing, please suggest them through his websites. His new website will contain more information for anyone aspiring toward a life of adventure:

www.HowtoLiveaLifeofAdventure.com

Other books by the author

Handbook for Touring Bicyclists—Bicycling touring is growing in popularity each year. Men and women around the world are taking to the highways and the "open air" is their kitchen. On the pages of this book, you'll discover how to buy, carry, prepare and store food while on tour. Discover the ins and outs with a "Baker's Dozen" of touring tips that are essential for successful bicycle adventuring. Whether you're going on a weekend ride, a week-long tour or two years around the world, this handbook will help you learn the artistry of bicycling and cooking.

353

Strike Three! Take Your Base—The Brookfield Reader, Sterling, VA. To order this hardcover book, send $19.95 to Frosty Wooldridge, POB 207, Louisville, CO 80027. This poignant story is important reading for every teen who has ever experienced the loss of a parent from either death or divorce. This is the story of a boy losing his father and growing through his sense of pain and loss. It is the story of baseball, a game that was shared by both the boy and his father, and how baseball is much like life.

An Extreme Encounter: Antarctica—"This book transports readers into the bowels of million year old glaciers, katabatic winds, to the tops of smoking volcanoes, scuba diving under the ice, intriguing people, death, outlaw activities and rare moments where the author meets penguins, whales, seals and Skua birds. Hang on to your seat belts. You're in for a wild ride where the bolt goes into the bottom of the world." Sandy Colhoun, editor-in-chief, The Antarctic Sun

Bicycling Around the World: Tire Tracks for your Imagination—This book mesmerizes readers with animal stories that bring a smile to your face. It chills you with a once-in-a-lifetime ride in Antarctica where you'll meet a family of Emperor penguins. Along the way, you'll find out that you have to go without a mirror, sometimes, in order to see yourself. The greatest aspect of this book comes from—expectation. Not since *Miles from Nowhere* has a writer captured the Zen and Art of Bicycle Adventure as well as Wooldridge. Not only that, you may enjoy a final section:"Everything you need to know about long distance touring." He shows you "How to live the dream." You will possess the right bike, equipment, money and tools to ride into your own long distance touring adventures. If you like bicycling, you'll go wild reading this book. If you don't like bicycling, you'll still go wild reading this book.

Motorcycle Adventure to Alaska: Into the Wind—"Seldom does a book capture the fantasy and reality of an epic journey the magnitude of this book. Trevor and Dan resemble another duo rich in America's history of youthful explorers who get into all kinds of trouble—Tom Sawyer and Huckleberry Finn. They plied the Mississippi River, but Dan and his brother push their machines into a wild and savage land—Alaska. My boys loved it." John Mathews, father of two boys and a daughter.

Bicycling the Continental Divide: Slice of Heaven, Taste of Hell— "This bicycle dream ride carries a bit of mountain man adventure. The author mixes hope with frustration, pain with courage and bicycling over the mountains. John Brown, a friend left behind to battle cancer, provides guts and heart for his two friends who ride into the teeth of nature's fury. Along the way, you'll laugh, cry and gain new appreciations while pondering the meaning of life." Paul Jackson

Losing Your Best Friend: Vacancies of the Heart— "This is one heck of a powerful book. It's a must read for anyone that has lost a friend or parent. It will give you answers that you may not have thought about. It will touch your heart and you will learn from their experiences. It also shows you what you can do if you suffer conflict with your friend's wife or girlfriend." Jonathan Runy

Rafting the Rolling Thunder— "Fasten your raft-belts folks. You're in for the white water rafting ride of your life. Wooldridge keeps readers on the edge of their seats on a wild excursion through the Grand Canyon. Along the way, he offers you an outlaw-run by intrepid legend "Highwater Harry," a man who makes a bet with the devil and nearly loses his life. The raft bucks beneath you as Harry crashes through Class V rapids. And the Grand Canyon Dish Fairies, well, they take you on separate rides of laughter and miles of smiles. Enjoy this untamed excursion on a river through time." Jason Rogers

Misty's Long Ride: Across America on Horseback— by Howard Wooldridge (Frosty Wooldridge's brother). "As good as Howard was, sometimes there was nothing he could do about our situation in the burning inferno of Utah. In that agonizing desert, a man's mouth became so dry, he couldn't spit. I felt the heat cook my hooves at ground level where it felt like walking alone in the middle of a farrier's furnace. Above us, vultures soared in the skies searching for road-kill. Yet, Howard pulled down the brim of his hat and pushed forward. I followed this cowboy because he was a Long Rider and I was his horse." For anyone who loves horses and high adventure, Howard's horse Misty tells one of the great adventure tales in the 21ˢᵗ century by galloping across America. You'll enjoy horse sense, horse humor, unique characters and gallop across America.

All books available at: 1 888 280 7715, www.amazon.com, www.barnesandnoble.com, also on Kindle.

"Frosty Wooldridge is one remarkably passionate individual. I'm glad he's a friend that allows me to participate in some of his tamer adventures. In *How to Live a Life of Adventure,* he raises the lid on a treasure trove of fascinating and challenging experiences. You will be inspired by the retelling of his adventures and guided by his bountiful advice. He shares what he's learned after undertaking a cornucopia of challenges around the world. If you choose to follow the advice contained in his book, you'll never look back and be disappointed by the things you never tried. You will have transformed the course of your own life." Bob Johannes, Chrysler Corporation executive

"Frosty Wooldridge physically and emotionally came into my life and changed it. He inspired me with his positive passion. He got it into my mind to ride a bicycle across America and I did. It was a dream fulfilled because of him. This book will give you the same chance to change your life and live your dreams. You can go from as small a dream to as big a dream as you want. You can live a truly adventurous life. Frosty has no desire for you to just read his book and then sit back. He says, "Let's get out there and do it." So get him in your mind as you read this amazing book. He has written this book for you, to you, to help you fulfill the passions and dreams you have bottled up inside." Dr. Scott W. Poindexter

"Half way through the concepts and practices in this profound book, I realized that the author may have meant to show readers how to live a life of adventure, but it occurred to me that this book shows anyone how to lead a very happy and successful life on a day to day basis. His concepts support mental, emotional, educational and spiritual health. Every kid and adult in America would benefit greatly by reading this book. It's that good." Arthur Daniels, teacher

"This book is extraordinary. The information is so valuable that it should be read daily for inspiration and guidance. I feel like the author is right beside me all the way, guiding me to a successful and happy life. You can tell that Mr. Wooldridge is real and genuine and it comes across clearly in his book. It's great to read a book by someone who actually puts his own advice into practice. For me, this validates the information. I had to stop myself from underlining every sentence in the book. The author makes it clear that one does not have to enjoy the same adventures as he does. He makes the great point that whatever it is we desire, is *our own* valid adventure. No matter what it is, this book will give us the instructions, the reasoning, and the encouragement to lead a life of fulfilling adventure. I love how he summarizes each chapter with the key points for easy reference, making it easy to run out the door in the morning with some great one-liners to practice throughout the day. The hardest thing I found about expressing my opinion on the book was narrowing down the multitude of good things I wanted to say about it. I love that the author actually tells the reader *specific* things to do instead of leaving us with ambiguous ideas that may leave us in limbo. Mr. Wooldridge brings the world to us with phenomenal quotes from famous people, and then expects us to go out into the world, and experience our own life-changing quotes. I want to buy this life-changing book as a gift for everyone I know, *especially* my kids. This book is just what I needed. It defeats the "aging process," opening the door to a successful, active, positive life and retirement. I love how the author gives relatable examples. I wish I'd read this book forty years ago. But you know what? It doesn't matter because after reading it now, I realize that everything is still available to me. It's mine for the taking. Even though my kids are grown and I am older, they see a youthfulness in me that enlightens them and encourages them to never give up on an attainable, rich life. I look back at all the great ideas I once had, never believing I could bring them to fruition. Loving parents, who thought it better to prepare me for disappointment rather than success, stifled an untapped potential. This book makes me realize that those dreams were all possible if only I had believed in myself. Today, I do and I am 100 percent convinced that my new dreams will come true." Susan Scollozi, traveler and aspiring writer

"After reading the first 20 chapters, I was ready to go out and tackle a grizzly bear, wrestle a sea lion and climb Mount Everest. Wooldridge takes you where you want to go. Not only does he inspire you to take adventures, he shows you how to do it. He wraps you around his little finger with some of the most amazing tales on the planet. While I loved the educational aspects of the book, I couldn't stop reading the adventures between every chapter. If I could live a tenth of his life, I'm signing up today. I loved how thorough he was with references, key points and guides." Roger Hamilton, teacher

"If you endeavor to live like you mean it, to aspire to show up with passion and purpose, and take your being to maximum heart rate in mind and body—please allow Frosty to coach, inspire and guide you. *How to Live a Life of Adventure* will rock your body and soul, and enliven within you your belief and practice of living like you mean it—with passion and purpose." Dr. James Rouse, world traveler, Founder of Optimum Wellness Media.

"It's nice to know that a farm boy can dream big dreams and live them. I loved his references to average people living amazing lives. I've always thought that only rich people can live extraordinary lives. Mr. Wooldridge shows how the "little guy" can step into his dreams. He gave easily understood concepts and practices to make our dreams come true. My wife read the book from cover to cover because it addresses women's issues, too. We will use his concepts for our kids." Keith and Linda Bruett

"Very, very, very instructional as well as inspirational. I could tell the author knew exactly what he was talking about. He knows his stuff. I've traveled around the world myself. I wish I had this book to guide me in the first place to save me money, time, frustration and heartache. Wooldridge brings the "extreme" down to "do-able" by anyone. He gives intelligent methods and choices for people to follow. I loved the adventure stories." Jack Modell, businessman

"Listen up ladies! I am a tomboy and I like traveling and playing sports. I'm also sassy and bold. The author of this book addresses women who love to try everything once, twice and more. He covers everything women need to know about traveling, mountain climbing, rafting, windsurfing, para-sailing and much more. He gave me countless ideas. I'm going to use them." Sarah Gingrich, rodeo cowgirl

"*How to Live a Life of Adventure* is about living an exciting and adventuresome life. Few books embrace the innermost nature of their author like this work. A book can only speak a message that has first been imbued by its author. In a sense, a book is a look into a writer's soul. This work is more than an instructional manual or a mere recounting of a process; much more. It is personal, intimate and relevant. In that regard, Wooldridge gives us that unique and rare gift–permission to do. In the words of Yoda in Star Wars, "Try not! Do! Or do not! There is no try." Ken Hampshire, president of Advanced Health Group

"Hands down! This is one of the best adventure books I have ever read with stories from all over the world. But wait! Wooldridge shows you "how" to go adventuring so you can make your own stories and fill your own scrapbook with memories. It's excellent in every way." Paul Margeletta

"How could anyone pack so much living into one life time? Funny thing is you can do it yourself. This author shares his secrets on making money, finding adventure mates, planning and preparation. He dots every "i" and crosses every "t" for you. He presents excellent information for women adventurers. Nice balance!" Sandra Hopkins, housewife

"Life is meant to live and not waste. Wooldridge nails it in this "can't put it down" book just as he does every time I book him for a radio show. His insight to the passions of living make this a must read. Just as Columbus maneuvered across the Atlantic Ocean, Wooldridge maneuvers readers to an understanding of living life to the fullest and creating their own adventurous lives." Tom Danheiser, producer, Coast to Coast AM

"Wooldridge is one of a small number of people who understands the vast forces that are now acting upon our planet and the changes they will bring to all our lives. Much of his knowledge has been gained from his extraordinary treks by foot and bicycle across six continents. In this book he offers the reader both the knowledge and wisdom of living adventurously. He shows you how to live a remarkable life." Bromwell Ault, 80 year old traveler

"As a lifelong aging adventurer, I see far too many of my friends and family reaching the "winter of their lives" and once again repeating that practiced mantra, "Maybe next year." But of course, "next year" will never come. Far too many Americans fall into the life-consuming conventional false promise of the illusive American Dream. Frosty Wooldridge cuts through all the junk in his latest book and demonstrates through *real experiences*, that an affordable fulfilling life of wonderment and adventure is waiting just outside all of our doorsteps. Take this easy two-step plan, read the book and then go do it. It's your life; live it." Mike Folkerth, Alaskan bush pilot and world traveler

"Can it be true that this man was born in the land of the couch potato? Can one man live the lives of ten ordinary people? Wooldridge is that man.

He shares multiple lifetimes of experience to inspire others to break the mold to find their own way. Ride, walk, pause, gaze, consider, enjoy and start again with Wooldridge. You cannot live through this book without inhaling extra oxygen. Give the book to your kids and hear them thank the man who wrote it!" Eric Rimmer, United Kingdom

"Wooldridge is a man who lets nothing stand between him and his vision. This book so invigorates the soul and heart that it is hard to write a review good enough for it. Take a good look at the staggeringly beautiful cover. Let Wooldridge pluck you right out of the turbulence and turmoil of today's work weary world. Travel with him along the length and breadth of human experience and prepare to be transported to areas of your mind that you probably never dreamed were even there. His marvelous book will tantalize and challenge you to get up and get going. This utterly unique American has lived his dreams and unquestionably embodies and reflects the timeless values and passions of our Founding Fathers. It's their spirit which drove this great nation to the legendary and inspirational heights. See what you've been missing in life and learn how easy it is to acquire it. Let him show you how to embrace your passion and let it lead you to magnificent experiences which are so brilliantly reflected in the breathtaking grandeur of this book's unforgettable cover. It is never too late to discover more of what LIFE is supposed to be about...and thanks to Wooldridge, here is your guide, your personal handbook to achieving just that." Jeff Rense

"Wooldridge loves adventure. From Antarctica to Death Valley and from the Bolivian jungles to Norway's Arctic Circle and from Australia's Outback to climbing the Himalayas. Frosty is peerless in his relentless pursuit of life itself. In this book, he shows you step by step how to create your own life of adventure. Step up and take a sip from Frosty's wisdom and common sense concepts. You are sure to write your own book from your own experiences as you become a painter, musician or world traveler. This book will get you on your way." Sandy Colhoun, photographer, editor, globe trotter

"*How to Live a Life of Adventure* is filled with inspirational tales of average people who have lived without allowing anything or anyone to hold them back. There is great storytelling with a sense of humor and more importantly a sense of perspective about what is really possible if we just get off the couch and go do something. Not sure what adventures are out there? There is page after page of adventures organized by state in case you need a little help. There are six practices to help you re-frame your life. Most of us have myths that guide our lives. We can change them. This book will help you do this by following the guidance provided. You will also find 99 of the top adventure books of all time. Not sure what kind of sport/adventure to stretch yourself with? You will find eleven listed. Last and not least at the end of each chapter there is a section which I especially love. The key points are summarized in an easily digestible form. It is likely that I will have to buy another copy. One to use after I wear out the first one." Reg Gupton, life-long fly fisherman

"This book with its many different stories held my attention from beginning to end. I never realized there were so many adventures awaiting us in this world and all we have to do is choose. I appreciated all the useful information and techniques Wooldridge gave me that will allow me to follow my dreams. I especially liked the section for women and the recommended books. I'm ready for my first 14er. He's got a sense of humor." Linda Humphrey

"This book is literally flowing, moving and pure fun to read. We're on the journey with Wooldridge every moment and he creates an out-of-body experience for the reader." David and Deb Martin, long distance touring rider and supportive wife

"I would go on an adventure with Frosty any time. It's bound to be fun. His secrets to adventure will inspire young and old alike. If you climb to the top of a mountain in winter or summer, you had better be in shape to make the summit with him. Reading Frosty makes me smile as I fondly recall my winter accents with friends and re-appreciate the richness in my life." Dr. Jack Alpert

CPSIA information can be obtained at www.ICGtesting.com
Printed in the USA
BVOW021459261111

276830BV00002B/26/P